Jesus and the Trojan War

Jesus and the Trojan War

Myth and meaning for today

Michael Horan

imprint-academic.com

Published in the UK by
Imprint Academic, PO Box 200, Exeter EX5 5YX, UK

Published in the USA by
Imprint Academic, Philosophy Documentation Center
PO Box 7147, Charlottesville, VA 22906-7147, USA

ISBN 978 184540 0811

A CIP catalogue record for this book is available from the
British Library and US Library of Congress

Contents

Introduction

To Begin at the Beginning

This book is about ways in which the past has been crafted by storytellers. More specifically, it looks at ways in which stories are presented and understood; and how storytellers — and their listeners or readers — may wittingly or unwittingly confuse fact with fiction.

The book began life as a brief enquiry into aspects of historicity, asking what grounds there may be for believing that events in what we call the past actually took place, and how we can know that the people who are said to have taken part in those events did in fact live. In its early stages, the discussion was in an even simpler form than the one it has finally taken.

Initially, the scope was a relatively narrow one, using Homer's *Iliad* and *Odyssey* as a model — which is not to imply, let it be added, that Homer is anything less than a lifetime's study. However, from a perusal of the texts and the social context of the Homeric epics, a number of parallels, or at least comparisons and contrasts, began to emerge, between Homer's poems and the biblical narrative of the Israelites' exodus from Egypt.

At the time, I was blissfully or naïvely unaware of centuries of scholarly debate about parallels between Greek literature and the Bible. Like others before me, I had been studying Homer and the Bible in separate water-tight compartments, with no inkling of how much the two have in common.

As my compare-and-contrast project progressed, two apparently unrelated incidents raised new questions, broadening the enquiry and ultimately (so it seemed to me) turning the discussion from an interesting, academic one into a challenge with wider implications. It may be helpful to summarise those two incidents here, as they influenced the direction that my thinking was to take, and began the metamorphosis through which the enquiry was to go.

In quite different parts of the country, I heard two ordained men — an Anglican vicar preaching an Easter sermon, and a Baptist minister speaking to a study group — use identical words: 'the historical evidence for the resurrection of Jesus'. Neither indicated to his listeners what that 'historical evidence' might be, but left the undefined statement hanging in the air. Unable to question the first man on his sources for this evidence, I was able to ask the second for his. Disappointingly, but possibly predictably, his references were the already familiar quotations from the first-century writers Pliny, Tacitus, Suetonius and Josephus, all of whom wrote almost in passing about the early Christians.

Now, it seems reasonable to accept these references to Christians within the Roman empire as reliable historical evidence that *something* extraordinarily dramatic happened after the death of Jesus. His followers, doubtless demoralized initially, were somehow inspired to renewed faith, and became zealous in their efforts to convert others to their beliefs, against all the odds. But it does seem to be quite another matter, to claim that these few brief Roman fragments provide historical, reliable evidence for a dead man's return to life.

The second influence on my broadening enquiry was an article in a local church magazine, under the title 'Can we rely on the Bible?'. The article's author proposed that one proof of the Bible's truth and reliability, in the sense that it records events that actually happened, is the existence of biblical sites in the Middle East which it is possible to visit and see for oneself. In his view, the existence of these ancient sites *in itself* provides tangible evidence for the historicity of the biblical patriarchs, the judges, the kings, and the prophets, since the biblical stories about these people are full of references to those places.

That argument seemed less than convincing. To use another example: when visiting Mycenae in Greece, one is aware of being in an extremely ancient place, one which is named in Homer's *Iliad* and *Odyssey*. But the existence of this citadel does not *in itself* provide tangible evidence for the historicity of the Trojan war. Mycenae is certainly a place that features in legends, and is doubtless the original for the home of the legendary king Agamemnon, but its existence does not itself provide historical proof of the people and events in Homer's epics.

So now yet another element seemed to have invited itself into my enquiry. It had begun with a study of Homer's epic poems. That study had extended into an examination of parallels between the Greek Homeric texts and the Hebrew exodus narrative, comparing (for example) their oral origins and structure, but most significantly noting their common central theme of divine intervention and the dealings of gods with men. In considering the extent to which these ancient, heroic traditions could be seen to form the basis of what we call history, there arose the question, What grounds might there be for believing the content of the biblical narrative to be more reliably historical than the Greek ones?

In addition to thinking about how we might discover historical truth within ancient epic narrative and what, if any, historical fact lay behind legend or myth, I had now been surprised by two attempts to use dubious history as a technique of persuasion. The first attempt was the claim that passing references to Christians by first century Roman writers provide historical evidence for an actual event early in the present era, one which is without question a most fundamental tenet of the Christian faith – that is, the literal resurrection of Jesus from the dead. The second attempt was the suggestion that ruined ancient Middle Eastern cities and sites with names dating from biblical times afford _in themselves_ an historical basis for religious belief.

What had taken my interest was this: conservative evangelical Christians appeared to be appealing to history to add authenticity to their beliefs. The conservative evangelical position is quite different from that taken by Christians of a liberal persuasion, who would say that whereas some biblical narratives may indeed be historical, others are much less reliably so, and may need to be read and understood as myth or metaphor. By contrast, the conservative position centres on a belief in the Bible's inerrant nature as holy writ, on its infallibility in matters of doctrine, and, significantly, its reliability as an historical record of God's dealings with mankind. And the more ardent the conservative standpoint, the further back in the Bible's pages is to be found what is claimed to be the historical truth of, for example, a world-wide flood and Noah's ark, the tower of Babel as the origin of linguistic and racial diversity, and at the very beginning, the six-day creation itself.

The conservative evangelical strand of Christian belief maintains that the Bible contains its own unquestioned and unquestionable truth, a kind of self-checking validation. Accordingly, faith requires no external, independent evidence. Religious faith is based on a belief in the supernatural and has no need for historical back-up. As the ancient writer of a letter included in the Christian Bible's New Testament expressed it, 'Faith gives substance to our hopes and convinces us of realities we do not see' [_A Letter to Hebrews_ 11:1].

I was surprised by this paradox: that those who hold the Bible to be the unique and infallible word of God, containing literal and factually true accounts of God's dealings with mankind throughout history, felt a need to authenticate their faith by reference to secular historical evidence. It was this that finally altered the direction that my thinking was to take and substantially shifted the book's centre of gravity. It seemed valid that within my original enquiry into historicity there should be included questions con-

cerning the continuing and widespread modern-day presentation and acceptance of biblical narrative as though it
is historical fact.

All in good time, we shall give thought to what we mean
by history. So far, the word has been used very loosely to
signify little more than the past. We shall also come to
what may be an obvious fact, that 'what seems unquestionably true to one age or civilization differs from
what seems unquestionably true to others'. That,
E.L. Fackenheim continues, is the result of 'an ever-
increasing historical self-consciousness [which] has not
been without grave spiritual effects. In earlier ages, most
men could simply accept religious beliefs as unquestionably true' [Fackenheim 1996]. Just how grave any spiritual
effects brought about by 'historical self-consciousness'
have been is a point for discussion.

In *The Bible in History*, Thomas L. Thompson has asked,
'Why is an understanding of the Bible as fictive considered
to undermine its truth and integrity? ... To learn that what
we once believed is not what we should have believed, is
the ordinary intellectual process by which understanding
grows' [Thompson 1999]. That important question and
observation underlie the argument in this book.

* * *

What, then, is my purpose here? Before summarising what
it is that this book sets out to do, there is perhaps a need
first to state what it does NOT set out to do.

It is not the aim to make what would in practice be a
futile attempt, trying to prove that the events in the narratives which we shall be discussing did not take place or
that the *dramatis personae* encountered did not exist. They
may have done. Hopefully, it will be clear from the outset
that to ask the question 'How can we know?' is not the
same as saying 'This is not true'. Emphatically, there is no
intention of attacking religious belief in itself: quite the
contrary.

Rather, the overall aim is to address the kind of question with which this introduction began: how can we *know* whether or not the events in stories from the past ever happened, and whether or not the people about whom the stories are told ever lived? To pursue that aim, we shall examine the content and sources of a number of traditional narratives, and think about the purpose these and similar stories may serve, what meaning they had to those who first heard them, and what the meaning of this kind of narrative may be for us today.

Looking for answers to such questions is clearly quite different from asserting that these events and people are wholly fictitious.

It is to be expected that as the implications of these questions are considered, other questions will arise. That, after all, seems to be unavoidable: because for so much of the time, the conclusion (for now, at least) may well have to be, *we just do not know*. Also, there is a need to keep in the front of our minds that good old Quaker advice, Think it possible that you may be mistaken. It is to be hoped, therefore, that I will not be caught too often using words and phrases such as obviously … of course … the fact is … we can be sure that …

With this declared intention of keeping the questions open and attempting to avoid any dogmatic stance, the book is intended both for those who have rejected or never accepted religious concepts or practices (after however little or however much thought), but who none the less feel some affinity with the 'spiritual' — in whatever way they would define it — and are open to thinking about spiritual matters; and for those who would call themselves Christian (as a result of whatever experience they may have had) and yet in some way have become uneasy or disenchanted with aspects of belief or practice, and would welcome an opportunity of taking a fresh look at things.

Books on religious subjects can generally and understandably be relied upon to give their argument a theological structure, using theological language. My hope here is to position the biblical discussion and my overall argument within a *literary* context and to place the resurrection (used as a metonym) in a literary framework.

Possibly a number of the ideas that we shall be looking at and one or two of the sources that we shall be drawing upon will be new or unfamiliar to some. I like to think that this will stimulate wider reading and study, because I believe the enquiry to be both fascinating and worthwhile.

* * *

The book is in three parts. The first begins with some thoughts on what we call the past, that apparently irretrievable phenomenon in which mankind has always been so interested, and has attempted to recapture. Then follows a discussion of some of the types of narrative which developed to encapsulate great heroic pasts, and to provide a celebration of a people's origins or national identity. An attempt is made to define the concept of history, history is contrasted with myth and legend, and the trustworthiness of even the historical record is challenged.

In the second part, origins and sources of some British legendary (and possibly historical!) narratives are outlined; and, using those as a model, two much earlier epics, both from the Bronze Age — the Trojan war and the Israelite exodus from Egypt — are discussed in light of some of the questions raised.

In the final part, thought is given to the essentially religious characteristic of myth; from this flow questions about the mythic characteristic of religion. Aspects of biblical textual traditions are considered and challenged, and questions asked about the relevance of myth within today's world. Some tentative conclusions are offered, but in essence they remain as questions.

If at this early stage any reader baulks at the juxtaposition of myth and religion, this is the right place at which to emphasise that myth is not being used to mean untrue or fictitious, but rather to signify a form of explanatory metaphor or symbolism. More about that in due course. Furthermore, it is not being proposed that only the verifiable and strictly factual is to be thought worthwhile. My hope is that in the end, it will be clear that I believe there is a place for transcendence and values which may be said to lie outside ourselves.

One or two other points need to be made. In the second part of the book in particular, we shall be looking at texts from three very different traditions, all of them in translation. When using translations of ancient sources, it is an obvious and notorious difficulty, if not actually an insuperable problem, to know exactly what the original words were intended to mean, or how they were understood or, indeed, what the original words were. It is important, therefore, consistent with the book's approach, to regard interpretation and understanding of the translated texts as provisional.

In places, where the discussion touches on topics which many or most would agree are widely-held views or well-established positions, I try to use words such as 'perhaps' and 'possibly' more sparingly than in those parts where a more exploratory stance is required. This may suggest a greater degree of certainty than I feel, or imply a higher level of assurance of my facts than I am entitled to. In those contexts and indeed throughout the book, it will be quite in order for the reader to ask, 'What makes the author think that *that* is true?'

So, to begin at the beginning ...

PART 1

LOOKING FORWARD
TO THE PAST

Irritating style ('use of "we" or "our"')

Chapter One

Blue Remembered Hills

Where *did* the time go to? The question is familiar to every-one, and one obvious answer is that the vanished time has moved from the present into the past. Obvious as the answer may be, though, it does seem to imply — rather like the question itself, which uses words such as where and go — that the past occupies space somewhere, or is a place of some kind. Perhaps, then, there is another question: Where is this limbo called the past, into which present time vanishes?

Some may wish to pursue such metaphysical questions, theorising about time and space, as countless wise men have done across innumerable centuries, and will doubt-less continue to do. It may be wise of us, however, if at this very early point in our discussion we neatly side-step areas which are the province of philosophers, mathemati-cians and physicists, or at least spend no more than a little of our time on them. Perhaps it is enough for our purposes simply to accept that the past lies somewhere on a contin-uum called time, one of the elements or dimensions in which we live and move and have our being. Time is the location of those things that have come and gone, those things that are here now, and those things that have yet to be. In that sense, the lost time that our opening question went in search of has simply passed along a constantly moving conveyor belt of future, present and past.

It may not be as simple as that, though. In his theory of special relativity, Albert Einstein contended that any distinction between past, present and future is illusory. Furthermore, he proposed that there is no way of knowing which of any two events preceded or succeeded the other. Curiously enough, our time-space language can be equally baffling. The imagery that we use puts the past behind us, while the future is said to lie ahead of us: and yet, we would say that the next generation—that is, the people who live in the future—*follow* us, which seems to suggest that the future is not ahead but behind. For practical purposes, though, the conventional concept of sequences is much more manageable and is the one we will work with. We can be fairly confident that we have left the past behind, and can re-visit it only in our imagination.

Einstein constructed a four-dimensional mathematical abstraction, adding time as the fourth dimension to Euclid's three, and it is within this space-time geometry that we conceptualise time as the dimension of change. An infinite number of parallel and concurrent sequences of events have occurred and continue to occur in three-dimensional space, and the intervals between these successive events create the continuous line of elapsed time.

It can be questioned, however, whether it is true that an infinite number of sequences can be said to define infinite time, stretching back eternally, just as it stretches forward eternally. There was, it seems, a starting point for time, calculated at 13.7 billion years ago (although that 'point seven' does feel rather precise!) and perhaps time will eventually come to an end.

Mathematical models aside, this place which we call the past can not be said to exist in any concrete sense, or if it does, it is not available or accessible to us. We cannot go there: at least, at the time of writing no scientific or technological developments have made it possible for us to go there physically or literally. While recognising that as blindingly obvious, it is a critically important point to emphasise when thinking about the past and what we can know about the past. Ways have been devised for attempting to gain access to the past, but we are bound to concede that these devices have their limitations.

One escape attempt from the here-and-now is science fiction. It is interesting to note that time travel, the subject of much sci-fi writing, is usually futuristic and less often makes a journey into the past. Einstein believed that in theory at least, travel into the future is possible; but he calculated that should you make a trip into the future, you will not be able to go back to your starting point – that is to say, he believed travel to the past is not possible. Interestingly, if it were possible literally to re-visit the past, it would no longer be the past, but would have become 'now' once again.

In more recent years, other scientists have built on Einstein's work, specifically on his concept of the line of time being a curved one or a loop, and models have been developed to theorise how a time-traveller could take a short cut across the time loop and so arrive in the future. One day, perhaps. But as for the past, there seems to be no reason to believe that we are ever going there.

To an extent that can be neither measured nor imagined, far and away the greatest number of sequences of events which have ever occurred had already come and gone aeons before human beings arrived on the planet, with their capacity for inquisitiveness and inquiry. Indeed, innumerable sequences of events continue to occur without being observed by any human eye. By definition, therefore, there is no record or memory of those primeval events, and the visual images of that infinite number of occurrences have vanished at the speed of light into the dark silence of the space between the stars – just as the images of events in our own time vanish. And for the moment, we will leave those images of the past out there in space.

Shakespeare was clearly aware of the ephemeral nature of the stage on which life's dramas are enacted, as it all melts into air, thin air …

> And, like the baseless fabric of this vision,
> The cloud-capped towers, the gorgeous palaces,
> The solemn temples, the great globe itself,
> Yea, all which it inherit, shall dissolve

And, like this insubstantial pageant faded,
Leave not a rack behind. We are such stuff
As dreams are made on, and our little life
Is rounded with a sleep.
[*The Tempest* 4:1]

Similarly, the familiar Remembrance Day hymn, 'Our God, our help in ages past' demonstrates an acceptance of life's transient quality:

Time, like an ever-rolling stream,
Bears all its sons away;
They fly forgotten, as a dream
Dies at the opening day.

In a letter written from his Nazi prison cell, Dietrich Bonhoeffer spoke of mankind's longing for the past, which reminded him of a song: 'It's a long way back to the land of childhood, But if only I knew the way!' [Bonhoeffer 1953]. Bonhoeffer had to add conclusively and sadly that there is no such way.

It is Everyman's constant and inescapable experience that the fleeting moment of what we call the present, the 'now', immediately becomes the past; and the as-yet future inevitably and all too soon becomes the 'now', and is equally destined to vanish instantly into the irrecoverable past.

Whether or not our propensity for dividing time into past, present and future is illusory, all are doubtless aware that life's journey moves in one direction only, and there is no going back. Housman's Shropshire Lad [1989] knew it:

Into my heart an air that kills
    From yon far country blows:
What are those blue remembered hills,
    What spires, what farms are those?
That is the land of lost content,
    I see it shining plain,
The happy highways where I went
    And cannot come again.

Looking back at that lost, far country of the past seems to generate not simply a nostalgia for the blue remembered hills, but at best a resignation and at worst a resentment that we can not come again to those happy highways. It may be questioned whether the highways were indeed happy, something we shall discuss later; but what is certain is that we cannot return to the land of lost content.

What seems to be a futile quest, searching for and wishing to recover lost time, is the subject of much of Proust's monumental *À la Recherche du Temps Perdu* — a title perhaps inappropriately mistranslated by Shakespeare's words, 'Remembrance of things past'. Unlike Housman's wistful recollection of blue remembered hills, the theme that runs through this vast eleven-volume work is a rather despairing sense of how time has put our past experiences beyond recovery. The *Recherche* is a quest, a quest for time that is *perdu*, lost.

This rather fatalistic contemplation of time's 'ever-rolling stream' may serve as an unnecessary, and possibly unwelcome, reminder that yesterday has gone and today is going, but it is also an important first stage in a discussion of the meaning of history.

Our wish to rescue and preserve the past is an age-old quest, perhaps as old as humankind itself, and the questions begin to arise: What was our past, and when did it have its beginning? Just as individuals develop a keen interest in discovering their roots and seeing how far back their family tree can be drawn, so whole peoples and races have attempted to look back into time immemorial, and developed and perpetuated beliefs not only about their own origins but also about the origins of the world in which they live.

For some present-day physicists, the answer to the question, 'How and when did it all get started?' would be (for the present, anyway) 'In the beginning was the big bang'. At that point in an unimaginably distant past, the theory is — and possibly it will remain as open to question as any other creation theory — that a spark ignited a cosmic explosion which created matter, and time itself began in that instant. Theories and models have been devised and calculations made to describe an expanding universe, and expanding at an ever-increasing rate at that. Others envisage a universe which will not only cease to expand but also begin to contract, until in a future expressed by an incomprehensible row of noughts the whole thing will come to an end in some kind of vanishing point. It is conceivable that it will then start all over again, just as universes may have come into being and then ceased to be, countless times before.

It may be difficult for a modern, educated mind to conceptualise where a 'big bang' could have taken place, since there was not yet any space in which a cosmic explosion could occur; or to wonder when it could have happened, since time had not yet begun. It is intriguing, too, to think that we have words (if we do) to describe something that did not yet exist: chaos does not fit the bill — there was neither light nor darkness, no up or down, no vacuum, no emptiness. How much more, then, would primeval, if not primitive, people begin to strive to find explanations for all those phenomena which they knew to be outside their control or influence — a sun which rose and warmed and set, a moon constantly and consistently changing shape, birth and death, sickness in people and in animals, bumper harvests and crop failure, earthquakes and floods and droughts — and then to begin to think about how it all began?

Less scientific or not quite so dramatic, perhaps, but for all that intriguing in their own right, are those ancient peoples' concepts of how our world or worlds came into being, and how mankind came to people the earth, concepts which are to be found in cultures of many kinds in many parts of the world.

The Alcheringa or Dream-time of the Australian aboriginal peoples is surely one of the most fascinating of these traditions, in that it not only stretches back into the mists of unknown numbers of centuries — the aboriginal peoples are thought to have inhabited Australia for at least 40,000 years and probably more — but also continues as a vital, living element in these ancient peoples' present-day communities. For the native Australians, the vastness of their land is criss-crossed with 'dream lines' which map the travels of countless ancestral cultural heroes from the very beginning of time, and record primeval encounters between animals which became people and people who became animals, bringing human beings and places into existence. Those creative ancestors are seen more as spirits than as human beings, born of the earth to which they long ago returned, and those mythic locations — rocks and water holes, for example — are still revered as sacred by their descendants.

By more recent times, somewhere in the third millennium BCE, Egypt had developed a number of religious centres, each believing that its god or gods had created the earth in some far-distant First Time. Later still, around 1500 BCE, creation myths were evolving in Asia. The teachings of the Persian prophet Zarathustra included the narrative of the universe being created by Ahura Mazda, the supreme god who had existed from all eternity. In this Zoroastrian tradition, the newly-created universe was egg-shaped, a concept found also in Polynesian, African, Japanese, and Chinese creation myths, among others.

In India, at about the same time as Zarathustra, the emerging Hindu hymns of the *Rig Veda* included creation myths, one of them telling how, when there was neither light nor darkness, the god Indra or Vishnu separated the heavens from the earth, creating the universe out of chaos. That element of chaos is to be found within the creation narratives of many widely-differing cultures — among them, Chinese, Tibetan, Scandinavian, Greek and Hebrew.

Varying creation myths exist among African peoples and tribal groups, some resembling the Australian traditions of an origin brought about by spirits and creatures that are part animal, part human, other traditions having uncanny similarities to the pantheon of Greek mythology or the biblical story of the Hebrews' God making the first man from clay.

In the eighth century BCE, the Greek poet Hesiod sang about the foundation of the world. After invoking the Muses to inspire him to tell of the coming of the first gods, Hesiod opened his *Theogony*: 'In the Beginning there was only Chaos, the Abyss' and he goes on to tell how Gaia the Earth came into being, and out of the Abyss were born night and then day.

The Hebrew Bible, too, opens with the words 'In the beginning God created the heavens and the earth'. But everything was still primeval chaos: 'The earth was a vast waste, darkness covered the deep, and the spirit of God hovered over the surface of the waters' [*Genesis* 1:1–2]. In this as in so many other creation stories, matter already existed but its existence was chaotic and unformed, until the creator-god gave it shape and set everything in its place.

It was not only in the ancient Hindu myths, or those of Australian Aborigines, that there were to be found creatures and gods that were half human, half animal. Egyptian hieroglyphs show gods with the head of an ibis, a falcon or a jackal. In the ancient Greek myths, the gods frequently take on the form of animals — Zeus as a swan, for example, and Athene as an owl; and in the *Iliad* there is a single reference to a unique title for Apollo, 'Smintheus', mouse god, perhaps the bringer of plague.

The Bible's first story presents a serpent that can speak, not a god in the story, but later identified as the tempter, or Satan. Immediately following the biblical creation narrative comes the story of the temptation of Eve and Adam in the Garden of Eden. The serpent, the most cunning creature in all of God's creation, suggests to Eve that were she to eat the fruit on the forbidden tree in the middle of the garden, she would be just like God, and know both good and evil. Not only does Eve do as the serpent suggests, but also gives some of the fruit to Adam. God curses the serpent, and turns Adam and Eve out of the Garden of Eden, as punishment for their disobedience.

Even by New Testament times, animal imagery was still being used to signify divine presence. At Jesus' baptism, the gospel narrative tells, the spirit of God was seen to descend on him 'like a dove'.

Tucked away between the Bible's first stories, of Adam and Eve, Cain and Abel, of Enoch (who was said to have been taken up by God without dying) and Methuselah (who lived to be nearly a thousand years old), and the stories of the Tower of Babel, and Noah and the Flood, there is a fragment, just one verse, which refers to the Nephilim who lived on the earth 'in those days as well as later'. This apparently isolated verse explains that this race of demigod giants, who were fathered by the sons of the gods and born to the daughters of men, 'were the heroes of old, men of renown' [*Genesis* 6:4].

It is interesting to note in passing, that in considering possible meanings for what appears to be a tiny fragment from an ancient Semitic document, we have an example of the challenges that face translators and commentators, and it raises questions for us as we begin to think about mythology. For centuries, English translations of the Hebrew text (of which there have been many) have described the giant Nephilim as 'sons of God', whereas more recent translations render the text as 'sons of the gods'. Working within a monotheistic tradition, earlier translators could have been expected to keep an eye on orthodoxy and were almost bound to conform (as they did) with the standard singular, capital-G God. But who were the sons of this one God, who fathered the heroes of old, the men of renown? And if 'sons of the gods' is more accurate, where does a pantheon, with generations of little-g gods and demi-gods, fit into this ancient history, if it is a history?

It is one of the many questions we may have to continue answering, *We simply do not know*. Whichever is the more accurate rendering of the origins of the awesome Nephilim, though, we shall come across these giants again.

* * *

From all time, then, men and women seem to have had a fascination with their own origins and those of the earth and the heavens and all creation. Out of that fascination and wonder, they crafted stories and epics and sagas, which were handed down across countless generations.

Many of these narratives took on the characteristics of what today we call history. Most are essentially religious and tell of golden ages inhabited by demi-gods and heroes.

It is to some of the narratives of those men of renown that we now turn our attention.

Chapter Two

Let Us Now Praise Famous Men

To be told that one is living in the past may be felt to be an unjustified and unwelcome criticism. On the other hand, many people clearly enjoy reminiscing about the good old days, and take pleasure in telling anyone whom they can get to listen that things that aren't what they used to be, nostalgically claiming that *those* were the days.

It is possible, though, that an obsessive interest in yester-year, an unrealistic yearning for the return of once-upon-a-time, is a blind alley leading nowhere but to disappointment and disenchantment. It may be that the longed-for golden age is not going to dawn after all, and we may be left sitting there, looking forward in vain to the return of a glorious past that has vanished for all time (if it existed at all).

While one may enjoy the fantasy of sci-fi futures, day-dreaming about the past is likely to be more realistic even if more prosaic. For one thing, our own past is more specific than the future, if only because we have already experienced it. Whether our memories are accurate is another matter, of course, a question at the centre of our discussion here. Housman's Shropshire Lad looked back with nostalgia at blue remembered hills. It may be that we all recall the endlessly sunny summer days of school holidays, and dream of all the Christmases that were white when we were young. Is it possible, though, that those memories are idealised? Perhaps, like daydreaming about the future, recalling the past also involves imagination and creativity.

Just as individuals have a tendency to glamorise or idealise the past and long for the return of those good old days, so whole societies have created memories of their own long-lost golden ages. Some even had or have an expectation of the return of a great king or heroic figure, who will come back to restore his kingdom or herald the establishment of a perfect world.

The age-old quest to recover lost times, to know about a society's origins and what it was that the men of renown did in the mythic golden age, is evidenced by the creative activities in which mankind engaged across the millennia. Their art, which helps us in some measure to rescue the past from oblivion, encompasses all the things that they made and the stories that they told. The significance of the artefacts that continue to be unearthed from archaeological digs is a topic to which we will return when examining more closely just what it is that we mean by history.

Objects that have lain buried in the ground for many centuries and which suddenly come to light, and the hidden ruins of buildings and cities which excavation discloses for the first time in hundreds or thousands of years, tell the historian a great deal about ancient societies and cultures. Unfortunately they reveal little or nothing of the actual events which took place within those societies, or about individuals who may have been involved in those events. Digging at Hissarlik in Turkey has revealed layer upon layer of ruined cities which may have been Troy, but has not found Achilleus or evidence of Homer's Trojan war. Digging at Jericho in the West Bank has unearthed an ancient city long pre-dating the exodus, but has not found Moses or proof of an invading Israelite army. Digging at Cadbury Castle may tell us something about Britons and Saxons, but so far has not found King Arthur or Camelot.

To recover the epic heroes and to learn of their awesome escapades, we need to turn to the art of story-telling, the oral traditions found almost certainly in every culture around the world.

It is to be regretted that oral traditions and the art of story-telling have now largely disappeared from sophisticated western cultures, since these narratives are or were an intrinsic part of nations' identity and heritage. The legends and the folklore that would once have been familiar to most if not all, sung by bards and minstrels, told and re-told by itinerant storytellers, and passed from generation to generation, are now to be found (those that have survived) only in books, there to be read by any who are interested, but in the process destined to become less and less familiar as time goes by.

Words such as myth, mythology, folklore and legend are beginning to appear here more frequently and it is time to make at least an attempt to give them more meaning, if not actually to define them. It will quickly be seen that distinctions are not easy to draw; one kind of narrative may well, and almost certainly does, contain elements or traces of one or more of the others.

Fairy stories are as good a place as any at which to begin, as they so often start with 'Once upon a time'. Among the best-known fairy stories are those collected in the early nineteenth century by the German brothers, Jakob and Wilhelm Grimm. While such tales do not always include fairies, what does characterise fairy stories, both ancient and modern, is that they are about make-believe. The stories take for granted the magical, the supernatural, or at least some other world, where animals speak, human beings turn into animals (and *vice versa*), in a world of magic spells and magic wands, of miraculous happenings and improbable but definitely impressive deeds, a world of castles, woodcutters, and forests inhabited by the kind of being that none of us have met in the flesh and hope we never shall, such as goblins, dragons, monsters and giants. And the custom is for the story to end 'and they lived happily ever after'.

Folklore is more comprehensive than the fairy tale, though it includes such stories. Quite possibly as old as humankind, folklore consists of the whole body of traditional beliefs, legends and customs of the ordinary people, providing them with a kind of history. The oral transmission of stories as a part of a society's folklore was inevita-

ble among illiterate people, or in cultures which as yet had
no written language, or where writing was a religious or
political prerogative (writing in hieroglyphs, and the
power of hierarchies, had their origins *in hiereus*, the Greek
word for priest). The narratives within folklore, then, were
oral, popular and almost certainly not free from what
today we would label superstition or a tendency to exag-
gerate or idealise.

The legend lies within folklore. A society would have
regarded their traditional narratives — what we call legends — as historical. They told of heroic events in some
long-lost past, and celebrated the heroes' achievements
and victories in a way which enhanced the society's values
and national pride. The judgment of today's matter-of-fact, scientific world would be that while any specific legend may, and probably did, have some basis in
fact, it cannot (yet) be authenticated as historically true.

Sagas are a type of legend originating in Nordic lands,
some being legendary in the sense used here, others taking
the form of historical narratives. Ballads, certainly dating
from the late thirteenth century in England at least, were
songs based on what we today call fairy tales, or on legends, sometimes from pagan origins, and often with some
historical or quasi historical content.

Epics are a specific form of narrative, usually relating a
story or a series of stories about one or more legendary figures. An epic is characterised by its length and by being in
verse. For example, Homer's *Iliad* and *Odyssey* were in all
probability composed and recited in verse form and con-
sist of nearly sixteen thousand lines and more than twelve
thousand lines respectively. Even more impressively, the
Hindu epic *Mahabharata* is some seven times longer than
the two Homeric epics combined.

Finally, and in the context of this discussion, most
importantly, there is myth. In day-to-day usage, myth and
mythical tend to be taken to mean imaginary or untrue:
unicorns, perhaps, and old wives' tales. Myths may also be
ideas circulated in order to persuade or mislead; for example, a lobby group may dismiss global warming as a myth.

But myth also has a specialist, literary meaning, to denote stories from a people's pre-history, normally incorporating divine beings and supernatural events. A people's mythology may not be readily distinguishable from legend, but it is not to be dismissed as merely legendary. Such myth has an explanatory function, presenting images of another world in terms of this one, as a way of attempting to give meaning to ultimate truths, and to make sense of today by referring to once-upon-a-time.

Myth as sacred narrative accounts not only for natural phenomena, and the origins of the world and all creation, but also tells of the gods and their dealings with men and women. And it is in this context that myth had a vital societal role, performing a moral function as it defined acceptable and unacceptable behaviour. Over time, as a society's moral understanding grew and changed, that function began to come into question. By the fifth century BCE in Greece, for example, three or four hundred years after Homer and Hesiod were composing their epic narratives, Plato's view was that many aspects of their portrayal of the gods and of the gods' behaviour were unacceptable in a modern republic. Plato believed that divinity was the source of good things, and that a stop should be put to stories such as Homer had told about fickle and vengeful Olympian gods, since parents frightened and misled their children by telling them such tales.

Myth is a quality that adds a numinous dimension to legend. Essentially, it may be seen as an ancient authority for, or authentication of, a people's religion or at least the people's understanding of the 'otherness' of the spiritual. What has to be underlined very heavily at this point is a need to accept myth and mythology as anything but trivial, something to be dismissed. Today's western unbeliever will tend, perhaps, to regard mythic narratives as nothing more than fables or fairy tales, or legends at the very best. However, it may not be an exaggeration to claim that an understanding of a people's mythology gives essential clues to understanding their culture and history. Carl Jung considered myth to be a fundamental expression of human nature, somehow forming a kind of common currency within the 'collective unconscious'.

That concept of myth being universally present in mankind's development appears to be substantiated by the occurrence of similar mythic narratives in widely-separated and very different cultures. One example will illustrate this. The biblical story of the flood, told in the sixth chapter of the book of *Genesis*, is familiar to everyone and a favourite with children, if only because of the charming image of all those animals going two-by-two up the gangplank into Noah's ark. But it is by no means a uniquely Hebrew narrative. The Maya of Central America had a tradition of such a flood. In Hindu mythology, the god Vishnu rescued Manu, the founder of the human race, from a flood that swept away all other creatures, saving him in a ship. From archaeology in modern-day Iraq, a Sumerian cuneiform tablet tells of the man Atrahasis being warned by the gods of an impending flood. This Babylonian 'Noah' built a boat, saved some animals, and survived the flood when his ark eventually came to rest on a mountain top. The detail of this Chaldean myth parallels the biblical story very closely, right down to the dove being sent out but returning to the ark, having found no dry land on which to settle.

A common feature of mythic and legendary narratives is that they praise great heroes, sometimes demi-gods, always men of renown. The heroes performed feats which, if not improbable, were at least impressive, and sometimes magical or miraculous. In the biblical narrative, Moses' walking stick failed to impress the Egyptian pharaoh when it was thrown to the ground and became a snake; but Moses later used his stick to good effect, to part the Red Sea so that the fugitive Israelites could pass over dry-shod and escape the pursuing Egyptian army. Any one of the great Greek heroes Achilleus and Aias, or the Trojans Hektor and Aineias, could lift and throw a boulder which was 'a huge thing which no two men could carry, such as men are now, but by himself he lightly hefted it' [*Iliad* 5:303–4]. King Arthur killed a giant who had been eating his captives alive and sinking their ships by hurling boulders at them, just as the Cyclops Polyphemos had eaten some of Odysseus' companions and attempted to sink his ships, snapping off a mountain peak and throwing it at them.

While the ancient epic and mythic narratives accessible to us today are preserved in written form — and in most cases, the written form itself is of great antiquity — they were originally transmitted orally over many centuries and even millennia. Cuneiform tablets discovered in the mid-nineteenth century, in the excavated ruins of Nineveh, contain the Sumerian epic of Gilgamesh and date from the seventh century BCE; but the stories themselves go back to the second millennium BCE. Gilgamesh himself may have lived a thousand years before that. In one episode, Gilgamesh is invited by the goddess Ishtar to become her consort, with the bonus of immortality, but it is an offer he turns down. A similar story recurs in Homer's *Odyssey*, when the goddess-nymph Kalypso attempts to dissuade Odysseus from returning to his home, with a promise of immortality if only he would remain with her. Odysseus had lived with her for seven of the ten years that he was to spend wandering around the Mediterranean, after the sack of Troy and until his eventual return to his island home of Ithaka. Odysseus turns down Kalypso's enticing offer, however, and resumes his wandering, only to have another narrow escape from a similarly seductive but more destructive goddess, Circe. She not only wanted Odysseus as her bedfellow, but also had a worrying trick of turning men into pigs.

The Hindu *Mahabharata* was compiled over a number of centuries, and reached its present form in about 400 CE. The stories of this great epic continue to be told in India, where a tradition of story-telling lives on. Consisting of some two hundred thousand lines of poetry, the *Mahabharata* includes stories of the martial hero Krishna, a manifestation of the great god Vishnu. Krishna the god-man killed many demons that had taken human form, but was himself eventually killed, mortally wounded in the foot, the only vulnerable part of his body. This is the same story as that of the death of the Greek hero Achilleus, son of the goddess Thetis. Achilleus' only vulnerable part was his heel, and it was in his heel that he received his fatal wound during the sack of Troy.

The stories of the greatest of the Greek heroes, the mighty Herakles, son of the supreme god Zeus, parallel very closely those of the Sumerian Gilgamesh: both were seduced by goddesses, killed lions, overcame divine bulls, slew dragons, and found the magic herb of immortality. The legends and myths surrounding Herakles suggest that his life spanned a number of generations of ordinary men. In a legend within a legend, the *Iliad* celebrates the superiority of Herakles in earlier generations, when he attacked Troy with only six vessels and the few warriors required to man them—a truly heroic achievement compared with Agamemnon's later expedition against Troy, which involved more than a thousand ships and one hundred thousand men!

Odysseus seemed to be aware of his own heroic status: he was prepared to boast that he excelled all of his contemporaries, although he drew the line at comparing himself with Herakles, the mightiest hero of them all [*Odyssey* 8:221-4]. According to his own story-telling, Odysseus claims to have met Herakles when he visited the underworld during his decade-long return home from Troy—although by his own admission, he did realise that what he had seen was only the image of Herakles, since the hero himself was now enjoying immortal life among the Olympian gods.

The idea of men and women, gods and goddesses, descending to and returning from the underworld was perfectly acceptable to the Greeks, even in classical times, and later to the Romans. The two cultures shared the myth of a goddess who spent one third of every year in the underworld, and the rest of her time above ground—Persephone and the kingdom of Hades for the Greeks, Proserpina and Elysium for the Romans.

The founding of Rome appears in a number of myths. Perhaps the best known is that of Romulus and Remus, twin sons of Mars the god of war, who were left to drown in a basket in the River Tiber (a legend which occurs in other cultures). The twins survived, though, were nurtured by a she-wolf, and went on to found the city, supposedly in the eighth century BCE. Rather less well known, possibly, is the legend already in circulation in Rome by about 300 BCE, telling of the great Trojan hero Aineias, who, having survived the sack of Troy, came eventually to Italy and settled there. Some four hundred years later, his descendants founded the city of Rome.

The Trojans are said to have come to Britain, too. The legend is that the first king of the Britons was Brutus, great-grandson of Aineias. At the end of his wanderings, Brutus came to the island of Albion, inhabited only by a race of giants. Renaming the island Britain, after his own name, Brutus called his men Britons. Albion's giants attacked and killed many of the Britons, but were slain themselves, with the exception of an especially repulsive creature named Gogmagog. Brutus' companion Corineus was matched with Gogmagog in a wrestling contest. Corineus lifted the massive Gogmagog on to his shoulders, staggered to the top of a high cliff, and dropped the hideous giant into the sea. In this tradition, the Trojan Brutus was a forebear of King Arthur.

Many other northern peoples were familiar with tales of giants and the mighty deeds of heroes, which appear throughout both the pagan or pre-Christian oral traditions and those of the early years of our own era, such as the long Finnish epic, the *Kalevala* — a poetic name for Finland, meaning 'Land of Heroes' — and in the Icelandic and Nordic sagas. Teutonic mythology, too, was filled with stories of heroic warrior princes, giants, elves, dwarfs, and dragons, all the fearsome creatures that were later to people Tolkien's tales. Dating from the thirteenth century, the German *Nibelungenlied* had much more primitive origins; its heroic stories of Siegfried formed the basis of Wagner's *Der Ring des Nibelungen* and later provided an updated mythology for the new Germany of the 1930s. Ancient Irish sagas, too, such as the Ulster Cycle, have stories of other-worldly beings and of heroes with supernatural attributes: like the weapons of so many other heroes, CúChulainn's harpoon, the *gáe bolg*, was more than any other warrior could wield. Early Welsh bardic poems and stories, too, some of them collected and translated in the nineteenth century *Mabinogion*, contributed to the Arthurian legends.

The earliest English epic, surviving in only one manuscript, is *Beowolf*, dating perhaps from the eighth century. The poem, written in Anglo Saxon or Old English, tells of the exploits of the eponymous warrior, in a legendary time which is partly historical. Beowolf kills the monster Grendel, who had been seizing and eating men from the great hall of the Danish king Hrothgar. Later, captured by Grendel's monstrous mother, Beowolf discovers a sword that had once belonged to a giant, a sword so big that only Beowolf is man enough to wield it. With this sword he kills Grendel's mother. Beowolf then reigns for fifty years in his homeland, but is called upon to fight and kill a fire-breathing dragon (or *wyrm*, in that beautifully expressive Old English). In slaying the dragon, Beowolf himself is killed. His people build Beowolf's barrow,

> a mound on a headland, high and imposing,
> a marker that sailors could see from afar. [Heaney 1999]

It is a fitting memorial to a great hero. In almost the same words, Homer tells how the Greeks did exactly the same for their dead hero Achilleus: they built a great burial mound high above the Hellespont, which for all time sailors would be able to see, even when they were far out to sea [*Odyssey* 24:81–4].

*   *   *

There is, then, an ancient and universal tradition of story-telling, of narratives celebrating the men of renown and a legendary golden age. Although oral in origin, many of these narratives have been preserved in written form. Many more are known to have existed but have been lost, while untold numbers were never heard beyond their native culture and so remained unknown to the outside world. The people whose traditions these were believed that the heroes and their heroic deeds formed their history. Some cultures shared similar traditions, perhaps borrowed by one people from another, perhaps both from a common, now-lost source. A modern, scientific age concedes that these tales may have had some factual basis; but in the absence of evidence from outside the narratives themselves, they cannot (yet) be accepted as historically true.

But what do we mean by historically true? In order that we may more readily differentiate between fact and fiction — always assuming that there exists such a black-and-white distinction — it will be helpful now to consider some possible meanings for 'history' and 'historical'.

Chapter Three

And the Rest is History

For most people, the story of Jack and the Beanstalk would probably not be very high on their list of historical narratives. A more likely consensual view would be that this is a fairy tale, with a fee-fi-fo-fumming giant smelling the blood of an Englishman as he clambers down the beanstalk, intent on grinding someone's bones to make his bread. The same view would probably be taken (today, at least) of Homer's similarly cannibalistic Cyclops Polyphemos, a colossal giant who could stop the entrance to his cave with a rock so massive that two dozen wagons would be needed to bear its weight.

But then, the story of the Cyclops was told by Odysseus as he spun one of his many yarns; and we would probably agree that this is a fairy story set within a legendary epic which *may* in turn have had some basis in fact.

Then there is the ithyphallic giant cut into the hillside at Cerne Abbas in Dorset. Possibly dating from the Romano-British period, he may have been called Helith, and was perhaps connected in some way with Hercules, as he wields his huge club; or maybe he was identified with a local god and fertility rites of some kind. Because he is there for all to see and wonder at, the Cerne Abbas giant demonstrably has an historical origin, however misty his past may be, and perhaps he had some mythic purpose or meaning. But just what that was, is not (at present) known.

It can be seen, then, that giants feature in fairy stories, legends, myth and maybe even in history. But where on

that continuum, marked 'fairy tale' at one end and 'historical fact' at the other, is the biblical giant Goliath to be posi-
tioned? Admittedly he was of somewhat more imaginable
proportions (and so, supposedly, more realistic) than the
Cyclops, and he was certainly diminutive in comparison
with the Cerne Abbas giant, but he was fearsomely
impressive, none the less. The biblical translations vary,
but Goliath seems to have been about ten feet tall and, like
Homer's warriors, was armed with bronze weapons. Goliath's armour is said to have weighed sixty kilograms, and
the shaft of his spear was as big as the beam of a weaver's
loom, with the spearhead alone weighing seven kilograms. Is the story of Goliath to be regarded as an historical
record? On what basis are we to differentiate one giant
from another?

It is too easy, perhaps, to use words like historical and
phrases such as throughout history when we mean little
more than in the past. If we are to know whether past
events or the people said to have been involved in those
events can with any degree of certainty be labelled historical — that is to say, the named events actually took place,
and the named people not only existed but were involved
in those events — it is necessary to be clear what it is we are
searching for and what it is that we are looking at.

Shakespeare's Prospero describes the magnificence of
the illusory drama that he had created as a 'baseless fabric'; and while history is by no means a baseless fabric, it is
no rich tapestry either. Perhaps history is better seen as
rather threadbare lace. Here and there, parts of the pattern
can be clearly discerned, sometimes large, complete areas
of it; but there are also many loose ends, broken threads,
big holes. The historian comes along and fills in some of
the pattern, ties up some loose ends, or repairs some of the
holes, and in doing so may even change the pattern from
one design to another.

One simple example may suffice. Historians had long
been familiar with the Viking ritual of burying a chieftain
or a leader together with his long ship and other artefacts,
in preparation for his journey to the afterlife. A number of

such ship burials were known from excavations in Scotland, Ireland and continental Europe, but none in England. Early in 2004, however, a missing piece came to light, with the discovery in Yorkshire of what is thought to be the first example of a ship burial south of Hadrian's Wall. The site dates from the ninth century CE, and included clinch nails typical of Viking long ship construction, together with King Alfred coins and other items.

Even more dramatically, perhaps, our knowledge (or ignorance) of *pre*-history is constantly being extended — that is to say, we discover more and more of what we did not know we did not know. With the discovery of flint tools in Suffolk in recent times, thought to be at least 700,000 years old, what was previously believed to be the earliest evidence of European human history has been pushed back an astounding 200,000 years.

After all, then, it may be said that in studying the past, we are not so much stating that we do not know, as that we do not know *yet*.

Central to the historical quest, then, is the search for *evidence* of times past. It does seem surprising sometimes to hear or read scholars stating that we shall never know about this person or that event. They may be right, of course: it is the lack of authentic evidence which clearly presents a major problem. An engraved tombstone unearthed at Mycenae, inscribed *Here lies King Agamemnon*, would answer many questions, just as it would raise a number of new ones. So far, it has to be said, no such tombstone has been found.

Archaeological digs do suddenly reveal new and previously unknown factors, though. As recently as 2002, for example, artefacts were found almost by chance at what had been considered an insignificant archaeological site at Baldock in Hertfordshire, bringing to light a previously unknown goddess, Senua. Senua may have been a Celtic goddess, adopted and Romanised possibly around the fourth century CE, and her discovery illustrates not only how gaps in the fabric of history can be filled, but also how previously *unknown* gaps can suddenly appear.

Archaeological digs and the ancient history that they uncover, feature prominently among popular television documentary programmes, affording one example of a continuing and widespread fascination with the past. History as entertainment does not please everyone, however. Some academics are concerned that such programmes, which they consider to be no more than exercises in story-telling, may undermine the intellectual quality of undergraduate courses, if students come to see this kind of programme as history, and lose sight of the rigorous scholarly discipline in which they should be engaging. A similar concern is shared by at least one eminent historian: Eric Hobsbawm has written that he does not consider himself to be 'part of the era of history as entertainment or as a section of the tourist industry, of celebrity dons presenting TV series of colourful visuals' [Hobsbawm 2003].

Whether presented in a television programme or in a book, it seems inevitable that to some extent history will be seen as an exercise in story-telling, but hopefully not only that. Simply for a book to be called a history does not make it one, of course: H.G. Wells's *The History of Mr Polly* is clearly not history in any scholarly meaning of the word, it is literally a story. On the other hand, *The Story of Art* by E.H. Gombrich is not a story in the conventional sense, it is a scholarly history. Gombrich makes clear that his book's purpose is to discuss works of art in their historical context; but he concedes that new discoveries render the story of the past subject to revision.

Is it possible, then, that one of the Raphaels that Professor Gombrich illustrates and enthuses over will one day turn out to be a dud? Artefacts which substantiate the historian's claim to have re-created the past must be shown to be authentic. After all, fakes may be found even in the great scientific museums. The skull of Piltdown Man, for example, was displayed for forty years in London's Natural History Museum before it was pronounced a fraud. A person, or persons still unknown, expertly placed in the Sussex earth a skull fragment and an orang-utan jawbone, together with other possibly 'contemporary' fossils, in a way designed to authenticate the dig. And the experts were taken in.

Even fakes have to be re-assessed. In 1900, what appeared to be a Roman coin was found in the Loire, showing an emperor named Domitianus. No other similar coin was known, and the only two brief historical references to Domitianus named him as a high ranking but rebel officer in the Roman army, punished for treason. It was concluded that the coin was a fake and it languished for a century in a local French museum. Then another similar coin was found, this time in England, embedded in a corroded hoard of other coins. The British Museum not only authenticated the coin, but also asked numismatists to check their collections, in case there were more of the same. History now has to be re-written, to take account of the rebel emperor Domitianus, who may have seized power briefly in third century Gaul.

Whether or not it is accurate to describe history as an exercise in story-telling, or to present history as a form of entertainment, it may safely be said that the task of professional historians is to exercise a rigorous intellectual and scholarly discipline. Their ultimate concern is to be in a position to find evidence of past societies, and analyse and compare that evidence with other contemporary and independent sources, in order to establish the truth about the past. Unfortunately, the relics of the past, the artefacts which find their way into the museums, are in large measure random and chance survivors. To some extent, therefore, historians are left not knowing what they do not know, and it is this apparently selective and random aspect of the availability of evidence which accounts for the ragged or tattered fabric of history.

History as fabric suggests fabrication, although that is not to suggest that we should assent to the view that 'History is more or less bunk'. The extent to which history is made up becomes another central theme here, if we pursue the original question: how can we *know* that these events really happened, or that these people really existed? In spite of the academics' criticism, the presentation of history is in narrative form, and it is a narrative *about* narratives. Our question, though, has to be, How trustworthy a narrative is it?

The historical record is prepared and presented in written form, and writing is an exercise in the exchange of ideas: authors express ideas in words, and readers give meaning to those words. It may therefore be said that history is created and re-created both by its writers and by its readers. Readers understand words differently, each in a unique way, and bring to a text their values, assumptions, prejudices, life experience, religious or political beliefs, and so on (and we all do). Given that this is true, it can be said that history is created by its readers, since every time a text is read, it is also being re-written.

History is constantly being re-written, then, not only by its readers in light of their unique experiences and values, but also by the historians, in the light both of new evidence and of changing political attitudes and social values. A history of the British Empire written at the height of Queen Victoria's reign, for example, may need to be revised very substantially for a twenty-first century readership. Moreover, such a revision would doubtless have different emphases were separate versions to be written by Indian and British authors.

That wonderful spoof history *1066 and All That* comes to a sudden end, with the conclusion that once America had become the top nation, history came to a full stop. If there was indeed a date on which history came to a full stop, George Orwell was sure that he knew when that was. When Orwell reflected on his experiences as a combatant in the Spanish Civil War in the second half of the 1930s, he concluded that it was then that history came to an end. Newspaper reports of events at the time, he noted, bore no resemblance to the war in which he had taken part, fighting on the side of the Republicans. It was Orwell's view that intellectuals and political commentators at home had constructed a 'history', not by recording events that had actually happened, but by concocting events which 'ought' to have happened, according to their differing

ideological standpoints, Left or Right, anti- or pro-
Franco's Fascist insurgency [Orwell 1968]. It is said that
when war is declared, the first casualty is truth. It would
be naïve to suggest that newspaper reports, whether in
wartime or in peace, are so accurate that they can in themselves be trusted as historical documents. In Britain anyway, newspaper editors have an ethical code of practice,
which requires them to take care not to publish inaccurate,
misleading or distorted material. However, one has only
to look at a number of different newspapers on any one
day, to see in how many varying and conflicting ways it is
possible to describe the same event — which raises questions about the code of practice, as much as anything. In
spite of that, newspapers are of course referred to by historians as just one source of primary evidence about the past
that they are attempting to reconstruct or interpret.

Orwell's claim was that history, as objective reporting of
fact, had now given way to propaganda, rewriting history
to suit a political or ideological agenda. But there was
nothing new in that. Examples of one group presenting
what they claim to be facts in a way that suits their own
ends, while their opponents present a quite different if not
opposite account, to suit their political or national interests, stretch back far into the distant past.

The first western historian is said to have been the
Greek, Herodotus, writing in the fifth century BCE. He
began his *Histories* by stating his reason for publishing his
researches, which was that he hoped to preserve from
decay the memory of what men had done. More specifically, he set out to examine the age-old enmity between the
Greeks and the Persians, and to put on record what it was
that had given rise to their wars.

Herodotus detailed the background to the bitter and
long-standing hostility between the two peoples: according to the Persians 'best informed in history', he wrote, it
was the Phoenicians who began the quarrel; but then he
adds, not surprisingly, the Phoenicians' account varies
from that of the Persians. Herodotus went on to say that
whether or not the Phoenicians' account was true, he

intended to write about those who 'within my own knowledge' first attacked the Greeks.

So here, to all appearances, we have an historical record based on an individual's first-hand testimony — or, 'within my own knowledge', as Herodotus put it. But to what extent should we be prepared to accept first-hand testimony without question? There does seem to be some reason for treating with caution the statement 'This is the way it was. I know, because I was there'.

Perhaps we are faced with a paradox: if we are to believe the historical record, there should be sufficient objectivity, and freedom from subjectivity, to tell us that we are looking at reliable evidence. On the other hand, there must be a place for witness statement.

Subjectivity inevitably leads to judgments being made or conclusions reached from a biased standpoint: unwittingly, we all carry around our social, cultural and experiential baggage, assumptions which we apply all too readily in commenting on events. Wittingly, Orwell's 'eager intellectuals' grind their axes.

What, then, are we to say history is? For some, the very word may trigger memories of schooldays, when history lessons were not exactly gripping, perpetuating the feeling that history is boring and lacking in excitement. A case can be made, though, for believing it to be interesting and stimulating, certainly that it is important. The case can also be made that although there may be some limited substance to the charge that history is made up, historians use methods and techniques that bear comparison with those of the scientist.

In making this case it is necessary first to attempt a definition. Although history may mean simply what happened in the human past, or refer to a variety of records and stories accumulated over time, the definition proposed here is one hinted at already. For our purposes, we will take history to mean the scholarly discipline of interpreting and reconstructing the past, through stringent, objective and wide-ranging analysis and comparison of contemporary and independent sources. Conclusions may be tentative and subject to revision, but they must differentiate the factual from the mythical.

The vaguely-recalled school history lessons which we thought to have been boring may well have been those that required us to memorise seemingly endless lists of dates, battles, kings and queens. The tedium may have been less had the narrative been supported by analysis and description, that is to say, discussion and explanation of why these events took place, what the inter-relationships were, and, most importantly, how societies changed over time. It may also have been both interesting and instructive had there been more emphasis on how we *know* that this or that aspect of what we call history is true. Merely listing dates, people and events, which is not history as defined above, may understandably be thought to be boring.

By contrast, as we have noted already, many people today take an active interest in historical television documentaries, and may find stimulation in reading historical novels or watching films which have historical themes. Some present-day novelists and film-makers take a great deal of care and spend a great deal of time and effort on researching the background to their fiction, in an attempt to ensure the accuracy of the historical content (or context) of their work – not that they always succeed, and howlers worthy of a schoolboy are not unknown. Even so, whether or not stories depict historical people and known events, and however accurately they may do so, novels and films remain fiction. Using the names of real people and real places does not qualify them as history.

Here we have an interesting example of the merging of fact and fiction: novels are by their very nature 'made up' and yet their authors use historical dates and known events. However, none of this matches our definition of history: it defines the historical genre of the novel, but it is not history. And the question of 'known events' remains unanswered.

More significantly, it can be argued that history is necessary both to individuals and to societies, imparting a sense of their identity, and providing a chart from which to take their bearings, discerning the origins of their communities and culture. In that context, history takes on added interest and importance. If historians enquire into our past and make a methodical attempt to produce an objective interpretation or reconstruction of it, it can surely be no surprise that we are curious about their findings.

Given that history is a necessity, it is important to ensure that the historian's interpretation and reconstruction are done well, and this requires a methodical and scientific approach. But to what extent can history be termed scientific? And if history is scientific, what place is there for invention or creativity?

Up to the beginning of the nineteenth century, no scientific methodology had yet been developed within historical study, and history could not yet be described as a discipline. In the opening decades of the nineteenth century, however, this was to change. The German historian Leopold von Ranke emphasised the imperative of using primary sources such as documents and artefacts from the period being studied, together with the systematic use of footnotes and bibliography, to authenticate the origins of research. Thus history moved forward very substantially as a scientific discipline.

Elsewhere a different but equally scientific approach was being taken by Auguste Comte and others. In the 1830s it was proposed that the human past could be studied in just the same way as scientists study the physical phenomena of the natural world. An attempt was made to establish what these laws of historical development might be, with the intention of giving a shape or structure to history as an intellectual discipline.

A little later, and for much of the remainder of the nineteenth century, Karl Marx too wrote extensively on themes of structure. He theorised that, based on the past, predictions might be made concerning future changes in society. Developments such as these began to bring history into line with scientific theory and practice.

An historian cannot undertake controlled experiments as, say, a chemist is able to do, nor do historians work with

proven formulaic principles, as do physicists. More significantly, the historian cannot make predictions as a scientist
may be able to do, as a result of his controlled experiments.
On the other hand, an analysis of events that have taken
place over time in a specific context may facilitate forecasts
of what *may* happen in the future.

In seeking to work scientifically, the historian does not
work in isolation. On major archaeological undertakings
today, it is common practice for historians to operate in
partnership with professionals from a wide range of disci-
plines — economics, sociology, geology, demography,
geography, and even psychology, among others.

Behind these arguments for scientific objectivity,
though, there remains the question of subjectivity. Historians also have their personal baggage, their individual
beliefs and values — including concepts of what form history should take — and the challenge is for all of this to
remain on the outside of their analysis.

While it is essential for historians to exercise their curi-
osity, as they engage in the detective work of searching for
evidence of the past and putting it together to form an
objective interpretation or reconstruction of it, they are
also called upon to use imagination, and occasionally to
play the hunch. There is an obvious difference, however,
between using creativity or imagination to fill in the gaps,
and inventing information. There is also a difference
between looking at primary sources and drawing objective conclusions from them — sometimes having to admit
that earlier conclusions may have been wrong or unsatis-
factory — and using or going in search of primary sources
to support pre-conceived theories or as proof of conclusions already reached. Historians must scrutinise the origins of their sources, asking questions to establish their
authenticity. In this investigative process there is an element of what might be called guesswork; but it would be
unreasonable to equate that with invention.

Perhaps the problem with history is less a question of
subjectivity — which may give rise to the charge of history
being, at worst 'bunk', or at best, made up — than one of its

being inconclusive. Fresh discoveries answer questions but raise new ones all the time, and any work done by historians is necessarily inconclusive or tentative. Well-established positions require re-thinking and firm ground sometimes begins to feel shaky.

History affords a rich source of discovery and knowledge. In spite of a place for imagination and creativity, the scholarly discipline relies on objective and methodical research and analysis. For all that, with at best fragmentary evidence, and in many cases no evidence at all, there inevitably remains a place for conjecture, and out of this can arise unwarranted claims for historicity.

With all the attempts at clarification and definition, however, the edges remain blurred. Truth, they say, is stranger that fiction, and there are times when they overlap or merge, making it difficult to distinguish one from the other, even in apparently factual works of history and biography. All authors, all storytellers, have their agenda, whether aware or unaware, which informs their writing. There may be no better demonstration of this than the life and work of Ernest Hemingway, Nobel-awarded author and perhaps the most outstanding novelist of the twentieth century.

Without any doubt, it is true to say that Hemingway was a legend in his own lifetime; but it is also fair to say that the legend was in large measure one of his own making. A master of narrative, his reputation rested as much on his image as a man's man, as on the quality of his fiction. While it is by no means unusual for a novelist's work to be autobiographical to one extent or another, in the case of Hemingway's fiction this was writ large, meaning very much larger than life. His private life and his public behaviour were intertwined with the subject matter of his books, and he was tireless and energetic in creating and promoting his macho image. And if the man and his fiction were intertwined, that was to some extent because the image that he portrayed was in part a fabrication. This can be deduced from a perusal of Hemingway's war-time correspondence in 1918 and reference to any of the more heavy-weight biographies. Michael Reynolds observes in *The Young Hemingway*, 'Sometimes it was difficult to keep the jokes separate from the life he was inventing … [but] The age demanded heroes, and if his experience did not quite fit the mold, then Hemingway would expand a bit here and there until it did fit' [Reynolds 1986].

There can be no question that Hemingway was a courageous man, not just as bull-fighting *aficionado* or as big-game hunter, but also as a reporter in at least four wars, briefly as an illicit combatant in one of them. However, as Michael Reynolds makes clear about Hemingway's brief involvement in the first world war as a young volunteer ambulance driver, he was not above 'inventing his fantasy war, the war he would have fought if only he had been given the chance' [*ibid*]. Hemingway's flair for invention and fantasy did not fade with the years.

If in modern-day narratives there can be this commingling of truth and fantasy, a merging of witness testimony ('I know, because I was there') with imaginings and exaggerations, with fiction presented as fact and fact as fiction, how much more might this have been true in ancient times? It is for this reason that Gunn and Fewell argue, in *Narrative in the Hebrew Bible*, that

> There is no such thing as 'what actually happened'; there are only stories (or histories) of what happened, always relative to the perspective of the storyteller (historian). [Gunn and Fewell 1993]

Considering that possibility, the possibility that some of the stories which we shall be examining do not record 'what actually happened', is the underlying theme of all the discussion that follows.

Chapter Four

Knowing or Believing?

In an attempt to give his definition of knowledge, American Defense Secretary Donald Rumsfeld was ridiculed for speaking in what his critics claimed to be gobbledegook; and he was awarded a mock accolade by the press for using what was said to be a world-beating example of unintelligible English. His proposition — and not only was it not original but it seems barely worthy of the derision — was that there are four kinds of knowledge:

> what we know, *and know that we know*
> what we know, *but don't know that we know*
> what we don't know, *and know that we don't know*
> what we don't know, *but don't know that we don't know*

The first is clear enough: we know that William Duke of Normandy arrived in England with an invading army in 1066 and we know that we know it — or, for sake of argument, we will for the moment accept that we know that we know it.

The second is perhaps better defined as the things that we know, but are unaware that we know; or to put it another way, we may have forgotten that we know them. Over the years, each of us has accumulated many thousands upon many thousands of bits of information and they now lie stored somewhere in our brains, temporarily half-forgotten, but hopefully retrievable when the right button is pushed.

An example of the third kind of knowledge is this: we do not know where Moses was buried, and we know that we do not know that. And if you did not know that you did not know that, be patient; we will return to it later.

The fourth may be illustrated by the discovery of the goddess Senua. We did not know that we did not know about her, until the evidence was unearthed. This fourth category is not knowledge at all, really, but ignorance; and it is a reminder that there are areas of ignorance of which we are not even aware.

That four-fold classification of knowledge may be crystal clear, but for Professor Nicholas Rescher there is a puzzle: '[the] issue of the extent and limits of human knowledge is a perplexing one. There is no way of establishing a proportion between what we know and what we do not' [Rescher 1995]. Another professor, Stephen Hawking, has now countered his earlier theory that one day it may be possible to know everything that there is to know. He has come to accept that some things will always remain unknown and the search for understanding will never come to an end. This unending search for knowledge, Hawking suggests, will keep scientists motivated, and prevent them stagnating.

Whatever the ratio may be between knowledge and ignorance, there is a kind of knowledge, or what we claim to be knowledge, which is important to a discussion about historicity: *the things that we know which ain't so*. This is not to say that our knowledge is in every instance faulty or necessarily to be questioned, obviously enough; that would be a foolish claim. But it is to say that much of our knowledge is open to challenge: what makes us think that *that* piece of 'knowledge' is true? In some cases, what we believe to be true may not be true at all; or at the very best, it may be said that *it was not quite like that*.

Henry Ford is famously quoted as saying that history is more or less bunk (a quotation slipped into an earlier chapter). But is that really what he said, or is it really what he meant? What is the historical context?

In 1916, the USA was preparing to enter the war which had already been raging for two years in Europe. Henry Ford was interviewed by the *Chicago Tribune*, and asked whether there was an historical basis for his being in favour of disarmament. Ford replied, according to the paper:

> What do we care what they did five hundred or a thousand years ago? History is more or less bunk. It's tradition. We don't want tradition. We want to live in the present and the only history that's worth a tinker's damn is the history we make today.

In the controversy which followed the publication of his remarks, Ford claimed to have been misquoted and tried to sue the *Tribune*, but without success. He was anxious to show that he did in fact have an interest in history, and to demonstrate his interest, founded a museum.

A modern writer, Clive James, has been wise enough to call his autobiography *Unreliable Memoirs*, and perceptive enough to note in his preface that 'the whole affair is a figment got up to sound like the truth ... The ego arranges the bad light to its own satisfaction' [James 1980]. While Clive James's stock in trade is humour, his wry comment raises yet again the question, How much reliance can we place even on first-hand 'evidence'?

In the early 1960s I listened to an octogenarian reminiscing about his long life. Among his memories was a recollection of his grandfather telling him that he had seen a flag flying on the parish church in our home town, to celebrate the victory at Waterloo. As I listened, I realised that here we had living memory of 1815, *viva voce* evidence of an event that had taken place a century and a half before. When in turn I related that to my grandchildren, at the opening of the twenty-first century, it was possible that I was now repeating oral evidence dating back very nearly two hundred years — or, to use Herodotus' words, 'within my own knowledge'.

But I had just the faintest of worries. What justification did I have for accepting that the old man's memory was accurate and to be trusted? I do not imply that he was not telling the truth, of course, but simply wondering whether these might be unreliable memoirs. Some time later I was given a book written by the old man's granddaughter and in it I found the same story. Was this corroboration of the facts? Or was the author doing no more than repeating her grandfather's half-remembered, half-forgotten story about *his* grandfather, and in the process perpetuating an inaccurate record? In a wider context, we doubtless have enough independent evidence, and sufficient cross references, to state with certainty that there was a British victory at Waterloo, and that it took place in 1815. We can also believe that in those circumstances, there would have been a flag flying on that church tower at that date. But what more do we *know*?

If we are to get anywhere near answering these proliferating questions about knowledge and belief, another, rather obvious, question can no longer be avoided: What do we mean by knowledge and belief? Certainly this is a weighty philosophical question and if whole libraries of learned works are devoted to it, we shall be hard pressed to settle on a definitive answer within the limits of this book. But at least there is a need to attempt a definition of our terms. You may wish to reach for your dictionary; but perhaps this is as good a starting point as any: knowledge may be taken to mean awareness or possession of facts which are founded on experience or verifiable evidence, and which are demonstrably true; whereas belief is a conviction or an opinion about something (concept, person, event), accepting it as true without tangible proof.

Having travelled to Europe, America, Asia and Africa, I can with confidence state that I know that they exist. To be more accurate, I know that those parts of the continents which I have visited exist; so the objection could be made that since I have not seen the whole of Europe or the other continents, the extent of my knowledge is limited. Still, on the basis of admittedly limited experience, I am prepared to accept that I have sufficient facts and information, gained through experience, to constitute knowledge, and I am justified in saying that I know about the existence of these continents.

Direct experience, then, forms one verifiable source of knowledge. But if the criterion of personal experience is to form a basis for knowledge, I cannot say that I know that Australia exists, because I have never been there. On the other hand, I have friends who tell me that they have visited Australia, and since I trust them to tell me the truth, I can say I know that the country exists.

There seems to be a problem with this, however. Suppose that, like me, my friends have not been to Australia themselves, but have told me that they have been reliably informed by people who have been there, that Australia exists — can I claim knowledge on that evidence? Probably not, although I could well have belief, an acceptance that the statement is true.

Similarly, do we *know* that William and his invaders came to our shores in 1066, on the basis of our having been told that by our history teachers, who were in turn told it by their history teachers, and so on? To what extent do some areas of knowledge present us with what the philosophers term an infinite regress? At what point back in time does an oft-repeated 'fact' finally come to rest, at the precise time and place when and where it actually happened?

In practice, there can be little doubt that there have long been sufficient sources and references to assure us of the truth of the Norman conquest, just as there is more than adequate evidence to enable me to say that I know that Australia exists. So it appears to be true that if one has a justified *belief* in x, as a result of experience or education, and provided there is sufficient evidence to underpin certain understanding (as opposed to opinion), one can be said to *know* x. On the other hand, in the absence of hard facts and verifiable information, one can be said to have only a *belief* in x — no more than an acceptance that x is true or that it exists, however firmly the opinion is held. I may graduate from a belief in Father Christmas to a belief in flying saucers, but I cannot with justification claim to have knowledge of either.

The same has to be said of history: one cannot claim as historical any people or events for which there is insufficient verifiable, independent evidence. Varying shades of belief are admissible, of course, and a range of possibilities were illustrated in the chapter on legends and myth.

Wondering to what extent all of this may apply to commonly-held ideas about the two main areas of my original enquiry — questioning the historical content of the Homeric epics and of the biblical exodus narrative (and by extension, of the resurrection stories) — I undertook some research, of a limited and not very scientific nature, admittedly. A simple questionnaire asked three questions about each of three subjects: the Trojan horse, Moses, and King Arthur.

In framing the questions, I was making a number of assumptions. The first was that the Trojan horse might fairly be regarded as general knowledge, that is to say, requiring no specific classical knowledge or education. My second assumption was that while Moses would be familiar to those with a religious education or religious interests, as a pivotal figure in the history of both Judaism and Christianity, and by no means unknown to Islam, he may perhaps be less familiar to those without that background. My third assumption was that King Arthur would be a familiar figure to British people anyway, and nicely introduced concepts of history versus legend.

Initially, King Arthur was included both to broaden the apparent scope of the questionnaire, and as a blind, to neutralise a potential (but correct!) perception of the loaded nature of the questions. But I came to see that Arthur deserved a place in the discussion, alongside Odysseus and Moses. Some may object that the tales of Arthur are not in the same league as the Homeric epic poems or the Old Testament's books. Others, though, who think it possible that the Arthurian tradition stands together with *Odyssey* and Pentateuch as a part of our cultural heritage, can be content to know that they are in the company of eminent commentators, including Winston Churchill.

The three questions asked respondents to say in a few words what they knew about each of the three subjects, to give a date to each, and to position each of the three on a scale ranging from historically factual at one end to without any historical basis at the other. (You may care to spend a few minutes now, to give some thought to those three questions yourself.)

Interestingly, bearing in mind the meaning of knowledge given above, no one questioned my use of the word 'know'. Every one of the nearly fifty respondents was prepared to make statements about the three subjects, sometimes in quasi-historical terms, even though in some cases they judged the subject to be without any historical origins.

From this very basic, toe-in-the-water research, Moses emerged as the subject on which there was the greatest degree of accord, both in terms of what the respondents claimed to know about him, and the extent to which the replies matched the biblical exodus narrative. To summarise the main points made in the returned questionnaires: as a baby, Moses was abandoned by his mother in the bulrushes, was found by a pharaoh's daughter and brought up as an Egyptian, led the Israelites out of Egypt through the wilderness to the promised land, but did not himself enter the promised land. The ten commandments also featured, as did manna, the parting of the Red Sea, and, a key point, Moses talked with God.

There appeared to be no consensus, however, on the historicity of Moses, or on when he might have lived. The responses were spread across the scale from legendary to historical, although the effect was that two thirds believed Moses to have been historical to some extent. It was noticeable that those with a strong church connection were the respondents who believed Moses to be historically factual. The dates for Moses were spread from 2000 to 200 BCE, with a concentration within the range 1500 to 1000 BCE.

The Trojan horse did not fare as well as Moses. There was both a greater disparity between respondents' ideas on the subject, including a number of erroneous ones, and a greater mis-match with the classical narratives. The common thread was that this was a hollow wooden horse, in which soldiers were concealed as a ruse to enter a besieged city. Most replies correctly stated that the soldiers were

Greek and the city Troy, but variants included Athenian soldiers, Romans, Trojans (attempting to get into Troy), and even Vikings, and the city was thought to be Sparta. Some thought the horse to be some kind of escape plan, and one or two connected Helen with it, either wishing to escape from a city or to get into one. One person thought the wooden horse to be a story from the *Iliad*, which it is not, but more of that later.

The great majority of replies indicated a belief that the Trojan horse was more historical than legendary, with a small number choosing historically factual. About one fifth of respondents, however, thought the wooden horse either more legendary than historical, or without historical basis. There appeared to be some uncertainty about dating the Trojan horse; possibilities ranged from 1000 to 100 BCE, with a concentration in the range 500 to 300 BCE.

Ideas expressed about Arthur suggested a much greater feeling of ownership of the narratives — as was indeed expected — and there was a sense that respondents felt (literally) more at home with this subject than with the other two. Arthur was almost universally identified as a fighting man: words such as warrior, tribal warlord, and military general were not uncommon. Most named him as king, or legendary king, variously of the land bordering Wales, east England, Camelot, Cornwall, south west England, Wessex, and Glastonbury. Only one person mentioned the Holy Grail, but other standard elements from Arthurian narratives were common: knights, the Round Table, Excalibur, Merlin, and Guinevere.

Far and away most respondents believed Arthur to have been more legendary than historical, with a few considering him to be without historical basis. However, there was a small number who saw Arthur as more historical than legendary, but only one believed him to be historically factual. Of the three subjects, Arthur proved to be the most difficult for respondents to date, with responses ranging from 200 to 1600 CE, although most chose dates between 400 to 1100 CE.

In the opening chapter, this book's central question asked: How can we *know* that the events in what we call history actually happened? As the argument develops, it appears that it may not to be unreasonable to continue to question what it is that we mean by knowledge. Given the philosophical soundness of the dictionary definitions that we looked at earlier, there seems to be a clear enough distinction between knowledge and belief. That distinction is vital to the argument. Even what we might choose to define as knowledge may more correctly be said to be belief. It was noticeable, for example, that in my admittedly unscientific and rather inconclusive research, those who readily nominated Moses as an historical figure, just as readily named Arthur as a legendary one. Further questioning might reveal the basis on which they made that judgment. The past that we think we can rely on may not be reliable at all.

To pursue that possibility in detail, let us look now at narratives about all three, King Arthur, the Trojan war, and Moses. In the next part of the book, they will be related in turn, some of their sources examined, and consideration given to the extent to which they may form a basis of historical record. The three traditions are told in summary but hopefully in enough detail to enable any who may be unfamiliar with them, or who feel a need to revise, to gain sufficient knowledge to follow the argument. Readers who decide that they are familiar enough with one or more of the stories may wish to speed-read or skip any or all of chapters five, seven and ten.

PART 2

ONCE UPON A TIME

Chapter Five

King Arthur: The Stories

The Roman legions had been recalled from Britannia, to reinforce the empire's defences nearer home, and the unprotected province now took the interest of marauders from across the Germanic Sea. Britain was never at peace. Native Celt fought native Celt, as warring British chieftains competed for possession of the land. The Britons fought a common enemy, too, struggling in vain to protect their homeland against invading Saxons. The Saxons in turn were in conflict with other invaders who also had an eye on the prize of the abandoned Roman province.

The Coming of Arthur

In those days, Utherpendragon was the great British king. He fell in love with Igraine, wife of the rebel Cornish Duke of Tintagel; and his desire for her was consummated through the special powers of his counsellor, Merlin. It was this Merlin who had had the great stones of the Giant's Ring brought from Ireland and placed on Salisbury Plain. He was said to be the son of an incubus, the devils that sleep with mortal women. Merlin schemed one night to deceive Igraine into believing Utherpendragon to be her husband. Unknown to Igraine, the Duke of Tintagel had just been killed in battle, and she thought Utherpendragon to be her husband as he came into her bed. A child was conceived that night.

Utherpendragon married the widowed and pregnant Igraine. When their boy child was born, elves came to enchant him and bring him gifts. One gave the promise that he should be the best of all knights; the second, that he should be a rich king; and the third, that he should have a long life. Merlin had arranged for the baby to be baptised, and he was named Arthur. The baby Arthur was put in the care of Sir Ector, one of Utherpendragon's lords, to be brought up as one of his sons.

Strife continued in the land, and eventually Utherpendragon was killed. The knights fought and quarrelled as to who should be king, and the leaderless realm was in great peril from the Saxon foemen.

Merlin counselled the archbishop that all the lords of the realm and gentlemen at arms should be summoned to London, so that God might reveal who should be king. That Christmas, all gathered at London's greatest church. After matins and Mass, the assembled knights saw in the churchyard a huge slab of marble, on top of which stood an anvil, and in the anvil there was impaled a beautiful sword. An inscription in gold letters read *Whoso pulleth out this sword from this anvil is rightwise born King of all England.*

All tried in turn to pull the sword from the anvil but none could begin to move it, in spite of their eagerness and great strength. 'The man whose sword this is is not here with us today,' declared the archbishop, 'but in due season God will reveal him to us.' And so it was agreed that at New Year, when it was the custom for the lords to meet for a tournament, the contest should be held again.

On New Year's day, as Sir Ector was making his way to the tournament with his son Sir Kay and Arthur, by now a fifteen year old lad, it was found that Sir Kay had left his sword behind. Arthur was sent back for it, and as he went, he recalled seeing the sword in the anvil in the churchyard and thought to take that for Sir Kay. With no effort, Arthur pulled the sword from the anvil and returned with it. Seeing the sword, an astonished Sir Ector asked Arthur how he had come by it. Arthur in all innocence explained, and the incredulous Sir Ector knew that he must see the feat for himself. When Arthur had replaced the sword in the anvil and effortlessly withdrawn it once more, Sir Ector fell to his knees, acknowledging Arthur as the rightful king. He led Arthur to the archbishop to relate the miraculous things that had come to pass.

The lords assembled again as agreed and none but Arthur was able to draw the sword from the stone. In anger and shame, the lords declared that they would have no boy to reign over them and the contest was deferred until Candlemas, and then again until Easter, and yet again until Pentecost, but on every occasion the result was the same: Arthur and Arthur alone could pull the sword from the anvil. By acclamation then the people recognised God's will that Arthur should be their king, and without more delay, Arthur was crowned.

King Arthur gathered together a great band of knights, both those who had served Utherpendragon — whom he now knew to have been his true father — and younger men too, who were ambitious to gain the honour of knighthood. With his new army, Arthur regained his father's lost lands and established Camelot as the capital of his kingdom of Logres.

Arthur's supremacy was challenged, however, by hostile kings from other parts of the Isles, who questioned Arthur's right to reign over the noble realm of Logres. They would have no beardless, base-born lad as the great king, they declared. While Arthur was as Caerleon, a number of these kings came, each with many hundreds of knights, to bring him gifts, as they said, gifts of hard swords which they would place between his head and shoulders.

Merlin met the massed armies and announced that Arthur was Utherpendragon's son; and while some of the rebel kings acknowledged Arthur's claim to the throne, others made war on him. After much bloodshed, the remnants of the hostile armies retreated. Merlin counselled Arthur not to pursue them but warned him that six kings would join forces with others to continue the war. Arthur took Merlin's advice, and formed an alliance with two foreign kings, the brothers King Ban and King Bors, who would come across the Channel to his aid just as he would go to theirs, should the call come.

Excalibur, Guinevere and the Round Table

It was customary in those days that as knights encountered one another riding about the countryside, they would issue a challenge to joust and even fight to the death, as a part of their code of chivalry and defence of their personal honour.

Even Arthur, though a king and the greatest of the knights, was not exempt from such challenges. One day he came upon King Pellinore, who threw down the gauntlet to all knights passing his way. In the ensuing fight, Arthur was hurled from his horse, and Pellinore, who was the bigger man, was about to behead him when Merlin intervened. Putting Pellinore to sleep with one of his spells, Merlin took the wounded Arthur away to recuperate.

Having recovered from his wounds, Arthur realised that his sword had been broken in the fight with Pellinore. 'No matter,' cried Merlin, 'another sword is nearby which shall be yours.' With that, they came to a lake and Arthur saw in the middle a hand holding a sword above the surface of the water. Arthur and Merlin rowed out onto the lake and took the sword. This sword was named Excalibur, or Caliburn, a blade forged on the Isle of Avalon.

The kings who had challenged Arthur's supremacy came now to fight King Lodegreance of Camelard, a dear friend of Arthur. King Arthur called upon his allies, the brothers King Ban and King Bors, and with their combined armies of twenty thousand knights engaged the forces of the rebel kings and after bloody battle put them to flight.

King Lodegreance had a beautiful daughter, Guinevere, whom Arthur loved and wanted for his queen. Merlin counselled Arthur that although she was the most beautiful of women, it was not wise for him to take her as his wife, because the knight Lancelot would love her and she him, and this would spell disaster for all. However, it was

Arthur's wish to marry Guinevere in spite of Merlin's prophecy; and when Merlin told King Lodegreance of Arthur's wish, he was overjoyed and promised to make Arthur a gift of the Round Table which Utherpendragon had given him many years before.

King Arthur and Guinevere were married in the church of St Stephen in Camelot, attended by two archbishops. Many kings and lords came from all the lands and provinces and principal cities, invited by Arthur who was renowned and loved for his unrivalled generosity and hospitality.

The Round Table was brought from Camelard to Camelot, and there King Arthur's knights assembled, all but one hundred and fifty in number.

The Quest for the Holy Grail

King Arthur and the fellowship of the Round Table believed it their duty to assemble at the time of all the great church festivals. For the vigil of Pentecost they came together at Camelot; and after hearing Mass, the king and his knights sat at the table in the great hall.

It was Arthur's custom to delay the meal until he had heard of some adventure. Just then, a beautiful woman rode into the hall on a white horse, asking that Sir Lancelot accompany her to an abbey into the forest. Eventually they came to the abbey, where nuns from the mysterious castle of Carbonek brought a young man to Sir Lancelot, saying that he was of royal lineage, and requesting that Lancelot make him a knight. Sir Lancelot recognised the youth as his son, Galahad.

As chivalry required, the young Galahad kept his all-night vigil and on the next day Sir Lancelot endowed him with his knighthood, asking that he return with him now to Arthur's court. Galahad wished to delay, however, saying that he would come there at a later time.

On his return to Camelot, Sir Lancelot joined Arthur and his knights in their set places at the Round Table. One place was always kept vacant, called the Siege Perilous:

none could sit there except the one for whom it was intended, and any other man choosing to sit there would die. On this feast of Pentecost, newly-written gold lettering was seen on the table: *Four hundred and fifty four winters after the Passion of our Lord Jesu Christ ought this Siege be fulfilled.*

Sir Lancelot was the first to realise that that was the very day referred to, and advocated that the lettering on the Round Table be covered with a cloth until the person appointed to sit at the Siege Perilous should be made known.

At that moment, an old man came into the hall. Lancelot recognised him as the hermit Naciens from Carbonek. Naciens had with him the young knight Sir Galahad, whom he introduced to the assembly as a descendant of Joseph of Arimathæa, who had buried the crucified Christ. Naciens led Galahad to the Siege Perilous, drew back the cloth and there revealed the words *This is the Siege of Sir Galahad, the High Prince.*

After dinner, a woman on a white horse appeared and in tears addressed Sir Lancelot: 'You are the best of men, of sinful men,' she wailed, 'but now this Galahad, a greater, a purer man is here. Weep, then, Sir Lancelot, for what you have lost.'

As the fellowship sat at the Round Table, there came a great wind into the hall, with thunder, followed by a shaft of brilliant sunlight. The Holy Grail appeared, covered in a cloth of white samite. No hands carried it, but it seemed to float in the sun's ray. All there were dumbfounded, but filled with joy and peace, thankful that the Lord Jesus had given them this blessing at the holy feast of Pentecost.

As suddenly as it had come, the Holy Grail vanished. Sir Gawain lamented that though they had been granted this glorious vision, they had been denied a full sight of the Grail, as it had remained covered. Then he made a vow that for a year and a day he would go in quest of the Holy Grail, and not rest until he had achieved it, or was found to be unworthy. Other knights made the same pledge; and in the morning, having renewed their vows of knighthood in the great minster, they set out on the quest.

Many are the stories that are told of the adventures and perils with which the great knights met, and the hardships that they endured as they went in search of the Grail, but it was the destiny of only three to achieve the quest.

The young Sir Galahad, Sir Percival and Sir Bors came in the end to Carbonek, and there it was granted to the three that the Holy Grail should appear. But it was only to Sir Galahad that the figure of Jesus came and spoke, and proffered the sacred vessel that he had used at the Last Supper. After the resurrection and ascension of Jesus, the Grail had been brought to Britain by Joseph of Arimathæa, together with the Roman spear that had pierced the side of the crucified Jesus.

Joseph himself came now to Sir Galahad, bringing a message from Christ. Knowing that his life's purpose was now fulfilled, Galahad died and his soul was carried to heaven by a multitude of angels. As Galahad's two companions watched, a hand came down from heaven and took up the Holy Grail and the spear, and neither has been seen by any man since that day.

In another part of the forest, meanwhile, Sir Lancelot had received just a glimpse of the Holy Grail in a chapel, as the vision appeared and healed a wounded knight. It was then that Lancelot knew, with a sense of foreboding, not only that his sinful love for Guinevere had prevented him from achieving the quest for the Holy Grail, but also that some dread disaster lay ahead.

King Arthur and the Roman Emperor

It is told that after many campaigns and battles, King Arthur had recovered Utherpendragon's lost lands, and was now lord not only of the former provinces of Britannia and Cambria, but also of Scotland and Orkney, the Isles, Ireland, Flanders, and the greatest part of the provinces of Gaul and Germany.

Arthur was at Carlisle for the festival of Christmas and it was there that he received an envoy from the Emperor of Rome, demanding tribute. The messengers from Rome brought insulting words from the senate, amazed at Arthur's insolence not only in withholding the tribute which had always been paid since the time of Julius Caesar, but also in wresting Gaul and Germany from the empire. Arthur's presence was now demanded in Rome, the emperor's messengers informed him, and if he did not present himself there by the due date, the emperor would invade Arthur's kingdom, punish him and recover the lands that he had stolen from Rome.

King Arthur sent back the envoys with defiance to the emperor, and his knights counselled war against Rome. Heeding the Round Table's counsel, Arthur set sail for France with his army, having appointed his nephew Mordred as regent. The treacherous Mordred is said by some to have been the son of Arthur, fathered unwittingly on his half-sister, and more than once he plotted against the king.

Arthur had hardly arrived in Normandy than news came to him that a giant, who lived on St Michael's Mount, was attacking and eating Arthur's subjects in Brittany: more than five hundred had perished in this way in the last seven years. After evensong, the king set out and met the giant, a most foul creature who was feasting on a spit of a dozen new-born babies. It is said that the giant measured five fathoms from head to toe; but after the bloodiest of encounters, Arthur prevailed against him and cut off his head.

Arthur's army met the Romans in battle and although they sustained many casualties, eventually routed them. The enemy dead were sent back to Rome with a message to the emperor from Arthur, that while his line ruled, Rome should not trouble itself to invade his territories.

Arthur then set about attacking and taking a number of city states and dukedoms throughout Germany and Italy, until the Pope pleaded to be spared, offering Arthur the emperor's crown. Some say that he accepted the crown, glorying that with his newly-conquered lands he would be overlord of everything on earth. Others say that he declined the offer of the crown, wishing rather to go on pilgrimage to Jerusalem.

In a dream, however, Arthur learned that his reign had come to an end, and that Mordred had taken both the realm and Guinevere. Arthur hastened back to Britain, and there engaged Mordred's rebel army. Mordred retreated to the west, where the final battle took place. Some say that this fateful encounter between Arthur and the traitor Mordred took place at Salisbury, but others say that the two armies came face to face at the River Tamar.

The Passing of Arthur

So all day long the noise of battle roll'd
Among the mountains by the winter sea;
Until King Arthur's table, man by man,
Had fall'n in Lyonnesse about their Lord.
[Tennyson, 'Morte d'Arthur']

Arthur had slain the treacherous Mordred but had himself sustained a mortal wound. Sir Bedivere carried the dying king to a nearby chapel, and there Arthur bade the knight take the sword Excalibur and cast it into the lake. Bedivere took the sword, but seeing how beautiful the weapon was, hid it under a tree and returned to the king. 'What did you see?' asked Arthur and Bedivere replied that he had seen nothing but wind and waves. 'That is not the truth,' cried Arthur, 'go and do as I have bidden you.' Bedivere went again but once more could not throw away the marvellous sword. 'What did you see?' asked Arthur again, and again Bedivere replied that he had seen only water and waves. 'Traitor!' exclaimed the king. 'Do as I have commanded or I shall kill you with my own hands.' Bedivere then went and with his two hands whirled Excalibur about his head and hurled the sword into the lake. A hand arose from out of the still water and took the sword, brandished it, and vanished.

Bedivere told the king what he had seen; and Arthur, satisfied that all was now accomplished asked Bedivere to take him to the water's edge. There he placed the king in a barge which was to take him to the island valley of Avalon, where he would be healed of his grievous wound. Three queens and the Lady of the Lake cradled the dying Arthur, and with the wailing of these mourning women the barge moved from the shore and was soon lost to sight.

Arthur, the King who will come again

When she heard of Arthur's death, Queen Guinevere went to Amesbury and in penance became a nun. It is said that there was never a more repentant woman in all the land, and she lived out her life in fasting, prayer and alms deeds. All were amazed at the virtuous change in her.

As Sir Lancelot rode west, he came to Amesbury and there found the nun that was Guinevere. They acknowledged that it was because of their adulterous love that the war had been waged, the realm lost, the Round Table destroyed, and Arthur slain. Guinevere asked Lancelot never to see her again, and with that promise, he went to a hermitage and there became a monk.

Years later, Lancelot learned in a dream that Guinevere was dying. He hastened to Amesbury, but came there just as she had passed away. Her body was taken to Glastonbury and entombed there, and Lancelot thereafter wasted away until he too died.

Whether or not Arthur died in Avalon, it is not known. Some men say that he is not dead but will come again. Others say that he was buried at Glastonbury with his queen and that on his tomb is written *Hic iacet Arthurus rex quondam rexque futurus ... Here lies Arthur, who was once the king and will be king again.*

* * *

These fragments give no more than the briefest of glimpses into the rich treasury of stories of King Arthur and his Round Table. There are scores of others, telling of the deeds of King Arthur, and of Balin and Balan, Nenive and Morgan le Fay, of Elaine, Lancelot and Guinevere, of Sir Gawain and the

Green Knight, Sir Gareth of Orkney, Tristram of Lyonesse, and of the many other knights.

Where and when, though, did these narratives originate? Who was Arthur? Is this history or is it make-believe? To what extent are fairy tales and legend intermingled, and what facts may lie behind these ancient narratives? It is to the sources of these stories and their possibly historical origins that we now turn.

Chapter Six

King Arthur: Sources and History

There is broad agreement among historians today that there is reason to believe that the stories of Arthur are based on a warrior-king who lived somewhere at some time in some distant past. In spite of that very general agreement, though, no one is yet in a position to say with any certainty who this Arthur-like warrior was, when or where he lived, or what battles he fought.

For the present, then, what we like to think we know about King Arthur is gleaned from literature and not from historical evidence. Even so, the tales of King Arthur which we were either reading or having read to us as children—certainly up to the time of the second world war—were from a relatively recent source. These stories owed a good deal to values and standards that lingered from the long years of Queen Victoria's reign, not only in their content but also in the images which they portrayed and fostered. During the first few decades of the twentieth century at least, the sun had not yet fully set on the Empire. Britannia still ruled the waves. Britain maintained a sense of her own greatness, a Motherland to which school-children continued to address Kipling's song:

> Land of our Birth, we pledge to thee
> Our love and toil in the years to be;
> When we are grown and take our place
> As men and women with our race.
>
> Land of our Birth, our faith, our pride,
> For whose dear sake our fathers died;

O Motherland, we pledge to thee
Head, heart, and hand through the years to be!

Even in the middle of the twentieth century, children's books perpetuated anachronistic Pre-Raphaelite images of a chivalric Arthurian court, and films and stage musicals such as *Camelot* did the same for adults.

It is fascinating to consider the possibility that, while the historians provide some assurance that an 'Arthur' once lived in some legendary twilight, many Britons today continue to believe (and believe as historical) the stories that are told of King Arthur, and cherish rather sentimental images of a vaguely-dated age of chivalry, in the absence of any verifiable historical evidence. It is unclear to what extent our forebears accepted Arthur as a part of our history, if indeed they did. In earlier centuries, stories of King Arthur may have been familiar both to children and to adults, who had little wish or ability to separate fact from fiction, even if they were aware that this was a question to be asked. It has already been lamented here that modern Britons have lost their age-old tradition of story-telling, but it is probable that for some centuries British folklore featured Arthur the heroic warrior-king. In some way, this legendary figure — that is to say, this possibly historical figure around whom legends had grown — came to symbolise or personify England, if not Britain, and so became a source of national identity, even though (as we shall see) England could lay no specific claim to him.

One very influential contributor to the adoption of Arthur as a symbol of the nation was Queen Victoria's poet laureate, Alfred Lord Tennyson. It seems wholly appropriate that Britain's longest-reigning monarch should have been served by the poet laureate who held that office for more years than any other, from 1850 until his death in 1892. Tennyson's prodigious output during that half century included many patriotic poems for state and national events, as widely varied as the arrival in London of Cleopatra's Needle, royal marriages, the opening of international exhibitions, the deaths of the Duke of Wellington and Gordon of Khartoum, and commemorations of military heroism such as the familiar 'The Charge of the Light Brigade'.

On the occasion of the Queen's jubilee in 1887, Tennyson's celebratory (and, some may judge, sycophantic) laureate poem included the lines

Fifty years of ever-broadening Commerce!
Fifty years of ever-brightening Science!
Fifty years of ever-widening Empire!

His words epitomise the prevailing national pride in Britain's unrivalled achievements during Victoria's fifty-year reign, enjoying (for much of that time anyway) world dominance in trade and industry, science and technology, and the position of the world's virtually unchallenged political and military power.

That is not to say that Victoria's reign and the decade which followed was a time of war. Quite the contrary. In the century between Waterloo and Sarajevo there were no major conflicts other than the war in the Crimea. Between 1871 and 1914 there was no war in Europe at all. So when Tennyson composed and published his popular poems about the warrior-king Arthur and the knights of the Round Table, he seemed to be not so much glorifying war as symbolising and celebrating British power and supremacy. His poetry may have been making allegorical references to the spirit of the golden age that was Victoria's Britain, as he and his contemporaries believed it to be.

Lord Tennyson's son later wrote that his father had made the old legends his own, restoring their idealism, and not only imparting to them what he saw as the spirit of his time, but also giving them ethical significance.

The Arthurian poems by Tennyson portray virtue and high ideals, presenting a code of chivalry and an example to young gentlemen, reflecting the biblical precept 'What it is that the Lord requires of you: only to act justly, to love loyalty, to walk humbly with your God'. However, just as Victorian values were not by any means always lived out in practice, so Arthur and his knights were not always perfect role models. Even so, the king and his knights are seen to lay great store by the correct observance of the rites and

ritual of the church and the Christian faith. A literary for-
mula in many Arthurian narratives is that the most significant events take place at the great religious festivals of
Easter, Pentecost and Christmas. Arthur's knights showed
honour, loyalty and chivalry, not least towards women,
whom they were sworn to defend. And when Arthur
engaged in war or battle, it was in a just cause (in his eyes at
least), either to repel invaders or defend his empire.

The earliest of Tennyson's Arthurian poems were 'The
Lady of Shalott' (possibly the best-known), 'Sir Launcelot
and Queen Guinevere' and 'Morte d'Arthur'. All three
were re-worked by Tennyson during his years as poet laureate; and with a number of other poems on Arthurian
themes, they were published in the year before his death as
The Idylls of the King.

Tennyson dedicated *The Idylls of the King* to the late
Prince Albert, suggesting that in the poems might be
found 'some image of himself'

> And indeed he seems to me
> Scarce other than my king's ideal knight.

That Victorian idealisation of King Arthur and the Round
Table was confirmed in visual form by Tennyson's contemporaries, the Pre-Raphaelites and other Romantic art-
ists, and reproductions of their paintings have been
familiar ever since. Possibly one of the best-known images
is that of John Waterhouse's love-sick and tragic Lady of
Shalott, about to float down-river in her decorated boat.
William Holman Hunt painted the same subject but in a
different way. Many other Arthurian themes were romanticised in paintings such as *Queen Guinevere* by William
Morris, *Arthur at Avalon* by Edward Burne-Jones, *Mor-
gan-le-Fay* by Frederick Sandys, and in Dante Gabriel
Rossetti's *The Palace of Arthur* and *Sir Galahad at the Ruined
Chapel*.

Tennyson correctly observed 'How much of history we
have in the story of Arthur is doubtful'. And since his
poems were not intended to be historical records, any
more than Pre-Raphaelite paintings are to be looked at in

that way, the possibly allegorical anachronisms of shining armour and all the trappings of medieval pageantry may be forgiven.

If Tennyson's Arthur and Lancelot were 'Victorian' — at least, created in some Victorian image of medieval chivalry — they became by implication English. The cross of St George, England's national flag, is alluded to in 'The Lady of Shalott', with its reference to Lancelot's armour:

> A red-cross knight for ever kneel'd
> To a lady in his shield.

Today, a growing awareness of separate and distinctive national identities within the United Kingdom contrasts with the Victorian concept of Britishness, which tended to equate Britain with England, as many English people continue to do. But if there was an historical Arthur, he was not one of the English: they were Arthur's enemy, the invading Angles and Saxons. He was probably a Briton, living somewhere in the so-called Celtic fringe — in what is today Wales, for example, or in Cornwall — and speaking the Brythonic tongue, a language related to Welsh, Breton and Cornish. Cornwall has a strong presence in Arthurian legends, and the Cornishmen's traditions were shared by their Celtic Breton cousins. If such an Arthur did live, it is likely that he lived at a time not long after the Romans left their province of Britannia in 410 CE, and hundreds of years before an entity identifiable as 'England' emerged, perhaps at the end of the ninth or beginning of the tenth century, the time of King Alfred.

The pedigree of Tennyson's Arthur is not English, then, but Celtic; and the old legends that the poet made his own came from a long line of French and German sources rather than from a purely English tradition. Sir Perceval, for example, the hero of the Grail, appears in a twelfth century French poem by Chrétien de Troyes, as well as in the epic poem *Parzival* by the thirteenth century German poet Wolfram von Eschenbach. The romance of Tristan and Isolde, which were to become a part of the Arthurian cycle, also had German origins. The *Parzival* includes the story of

Lohengrin, Perceval's son: both Parsifal and Lohengrin became Wagnerian themes.

The French connection can be traced by turning first to Sir Thomas Malory's *Le Morte Darthur*, the primary source for Tennyson's *Idylls of the King*. Although he wrote in Middle English, Malory drew much of his material from medieval French texts. His long book (or set of books, some scholars suggest) was completed in 1470 and printed by William Caxton in 1485. Malory is thought either to have invented some of the stories in his *Morte Darthur* or to have used texts unknown to modern scholars, but the greatest part of this extensive work is readily identified with known earlier sources.

The most influential of Malory's sources, perhaps, were the Arthurian legends contained in a collection of French prose romances, *Lancelot*, the *Queste del Saint Graal*, and *La Mort le Roi Artu*. Known now as the Vulgate Cycle, these three romances date from the first two or three decades of the thirteenth century, and may be seen as the most significant versions of the Arthurian legends to be written between the time of Geoffrey of Monmouth (whom we shall meet shortly) and of Malory himself. The Vulgate Cycle is comparatively free from the supernatural elements, or what we earlier called fairy stories, which characterise other contemporary texts.

Malory gave the title *The Book of Sir Tristram de Lyonesse* to the middle section of his work and for this he drew on a major French prose romance, *Tristan*. Dating from the middle of the thirteenth century, *Tristan* provided material for the many tournaments and encounters between knights that Malory featured in this part of *Le Morte Darthur*. Moreover, although the legends of Tristan (or Tristram) date from the eleven hundreds, they were only now becoming linked with the Arthurian cycle: the love of Tristan and Isolde forms a parallel story to that of Guinevere and Lancelot.

Two fourteenth century English poems provided sources for Malory. The first, the Stanzaic *Le Morte Arthur*, had as its principal theme the death of King Arthur and the

disintegration of his Round Table, seen as a moral judgment on the adultery of Queen Guinevere and Lancelot.
The second, referred to as the Alliterative *Morte Arthure*,
tells of Arthur's campaign against the Roman emperor
and conquest of continental territories. One other possible
English source for *Le Morte Darthur* was a near-contemporary of Malory, John Hardyng. His *Chronicle* tells of Arthur
being crowned emperor of Rome, and Malory appears to
have copied this unlikely and wholly unsubstantiated
event.

Writing about a hundred years before Malory, Chaucer
was clearly aware of the Arthurian stories, possibly from a
contemporary work, *Sir Gawain and the Green Knight*. The
Squire in the *Canterbury Tales* refers to Gawain as 'coming
from fairyland' so it is entirely possible that Chaucer did
not attribute great historical meaning to Arthur and his
knights.

It was in the first decade of the thirteenth century that
the first stories of King Arthur appeared in the English
language, in Laghamon's *Brut*. This verse history of Britain, written in more than thirty thousands lines, opens in
the pre-Christian era, in what was thought to be an heroic
age, when the legendary Trojan Brutus became the first
king of Britain, and ends with Cadwalader in 689 CE. As
well as stories of Arthur, Laghamon's work includes references to other early kings, Shakespeare's Lear and
Cymbeline, and King Coel, the Old King Cole of nursery
rhymes. The style of the poem pre-dates that of the chivalric and courtly French romances, such as those of the influential Chrétien de Troyes, and seems to look back to an
idealised and patriotic pre-Conquest age.

In his turn, Laghamon depended on earlier writers for
evidence of his Arthur. His *Brut* was largely based on
Wace's *Roman de Brut*, an Anglo-Norman verse adaptation
of Geoffrey of Monmouth's *Historia Regum Britanniae* (*History of the Kings of Britain*). For Geoffrey, British would
have meant Welsh rather than English. Wace was writing
in the mid-twelfth century, and appears to be the first to

refer to the Round Table. He also speaks of a hoped-for return of King Arthur from Avalon.

Geoffrey of Monmouth's *Historia*, written in Latin, is thought to date from the fourth decade of the twelfth century, and covers the same period as the versions by Laghamon and Wace. Geoffrey claimed to have had access to a very ancient book, written in the British language, from which he took his 'history' of those early times, including stories of Arthur. There is no knowledge of what Geoffrey's ancient source may have been, although that does not mean that it did not exist, and it is widely accepted that his stories are inventions. He was prepared, however, to date Arthur's death in the year 542 CE, and his use of dates and cross-references to known events imparts a feeling of history to his writing.

While Geoffrey is considered to be a writer of fiction rather than of history, William of Malmesbury can lay claim to being the first English historian of any note since the time of Bede. William's *De Gestis Regum Anglorum* (*Acts of the English Kings*), written in the mid-twelfth century, was a history of what he was prepared to call England, from 449 CE to 1120 CE. His book contains two stories of Arthur, regarded as a great warrior; but he appears to discount other stories as being unhistorical.

In the late ninth century, Nennius revised the seventh century chronicle *Historia Britonum*. This work details twelve battles fought by the Celtic Britons against the invading Saxons, under 'the magnanimous Arthur and the kings of Britain'. Arthur is named as the leader, *dux bellorum*, in the battle against the Saxons at Mount Badon but is not described specifically as a king.

The battle of Badon mentioned in the *Historia Britonum* appears also in the tenth century Welsh *Annales Cambriae*, and is placed in the year 518 CE; and it is at the battle of Camlan in 539 that Arthur and Mordred are killed. The *Annales* are the first to associate Arthur and Mordred; and the dates appear to give some authenticity to the historical nature of the records.

In about 600, a Celtic poem *Y Gododdin* tells of the defence of Catraeth (Catterick) against the Saxons, and speaks of a well-known hero, Arthur. The poem also refers to another valiant warrior, but concedes 'he was no Arthur'.

Somewhere at the end of the fifth century, Gildas' *De Excidio Britanniae* (*The Ruin of Britain*) refers to recent history and some possibly Arthurian events, for example the siege of 'the Badonic hill', but makes no reference to the commander or to Arthur himself.

By the late fifth or early sixth century, we arrive in the period of the historical Arthur if he did in fact exist at all, somewhere between the departure of the Roman legions and the first depredations of the Angles and Saxons.

The Arthurian stories that were to be crafted later place great emphasis on the devout values and practices of a Christian king and his knights. However, in large measure those stories reflect the culture of the medieval writers rather than that of their sub-Roman *dramatis personae*. Archbishops and cathedrals, the Mass and evensong, all these were at home in later centuries, but anachronistic in stories of the fifth or sixth century. The Irishman Columba did not bring Christianity to Scotland until 563, and Augustine did not come to Kent from Rome until 597. It is true that when the Romans left Britannia, Britons had taken their Christianity with them into the far west, to Wales and Cornwall, and into Brittany, all places that lay claim to Arthur; but the tradition of great Arthurian celebrations of Candlemas, Easter and Pentecost must have come much later.

In this way, the Arthurian legends take on the quality of myth — bearing in mind also their emphasis on good overcoming evil — in the way that *Beowulf* does. The 'history' within *Beowulf* is perhaps that of sixth century Scandinavia, but the narrative has a very strong Christian ethic, even though this was still the age of the 'pagan' gods. The poem's composition dates from the time when Britain was converting to Christianity, and the morality of the new religion was written anachronistically into the narrative.

In all probability, Beowulf's slaying monsters was intended as an allegory.

Even if today we have to leave it as a question, whether or not Arthur was an historical figure, it seems certain that medieval kings of England continued to believe that he was. Henry II had commanded that a search be made for Arthur's burial-place; but by the time what was claimed to be Arthur's tomb, complete with inscription, was found at Glastonbury in 1191, Henry himself had already been dead for two years. Although the giant skeleton bore signs of many wounds, the tomb was never authenticated as that of Arthur.

In 1275 King Edward I had what was said to be Arthur's Round Table brought to Winchester, where it was placed in the Great Hall. The table, certainly not large enough to seat one hundred and fifty knights, can still be seen there today.

There were at least two occasions when the throne of England might have been occupied by a King Arthur. Richard Cœur de Lion had intended his nephew Arthur of Brittany to be his heir; but when dying, named his brother John as king instead, as Arthur was still only twelve years old. After Richard's death, John wasted no time in having Arthur put to death, just to make sure of his position.

The sixteenth century Welsh Tudors seem to have believed they were descended from King Arthur, or at best made that claim to legitimise their royal lineage. Arthur, the son of Henry VII, would have succeeded to the throne had he not died before his father, and so the younger son became Henry VIII. That Henry had the round table at Winchester decorated with the Tudor rose, to symbolise what he saw as the British Arthurian origins of his royal house.

* * *

In one way and another, then, there is in this great number of ancient traditions superabundant evidence of a centuries-old legendary figure, who may have had some factual origins in some far-distant and long-forgotten time but for whom we have (as yet) no reliable historical evidence. The ancient traditions may abound, but the facts have yet to come to light.

The ancient tradition has come down to us through a long line of romances and chronicles, some of them purporting to be histories. With our modern definition of history, though, there has to be some doubt about the reliability of even those writings which appear to be historical. Historians today question the value of the writings of Gildas, Nennius and even those of the 'venerable' Bede. The tradition paints pictures of a Britain that was sophisticated, affluent and rich in decoration, where 'every knight ... wore livery and arms showing his own distinctive colour; and women of fashion often displayed the same colours ... The knights planned an imitation battle and competed together on horseback, while their womenfolk watched ... and aroused them to passionate excitement with their flirtatious behaviour' [Thorpe 1996].

That tradition, presenting images of a chivalric court arranging colourful tournaments, where knights joust for the favours of beautiful women, must surely be at variance with the reality of the world of a sub-Roman British chieftain and his Celtic tribesmen, battling in the so-called Dark Ages.

Where, then, in all this is the history? Where was Mount Badon, or Camlan, and in what years were the great battles fought? Where was Camelot: was it at Winchester, or Cadbury Castle, or one of the many other contenders? Was Lyonesse really the country between Land's End and Scilly, and when did it vanish under the sea? Where was Avalon: at Glastonbury?

These may be thought to be sceptical if not facetious questions. But as yet, the archaeology has provided very few answers. Cadbury Castle is perhaps the nearest we have come so far, with clear evidence of occupation through many eras, including the period after the Roman legions had left for home. Perhaps the outline of the great hall will give us Camelot.

Another favourite contender as the original of Camelot is Caerleon, where a post-Roman fortification, from the supposed Arthurian age, has been found within an Iron Age hill fort. Tintagel has a long-standing romantic connection with Utherpendragon and Arthur; but the ruined castle on its cliff-top site post-dates the supposed time of Arthur by some seven centuries. It is true that archaeological digs there have unearthed pottery from the fifth and sixth centuries, but all that this indicates is that Tintagel had been occupied for some centuries before the castle itself was built. So none of these sites tell us anything about King Arthur himself, and for now, at least, we have to settle for the Arthur of literature.

And yet a question mark seems to hang over any suggestion that Arthur's historical role is less significant than his literary one. A critical point that has already been argued here is that a people's sense of their past, whether historically verifiable or only the stuff of which legends are made, can become a source of national identity. Narratives that tell of a golden age which was inhabited by great heroes from whom generations have descended to the present day, give a sense of continuity not only with the here-and-now but also with some hoped-for glorious future. That is to say, while the narratives inevitably take literary form, the stories are not merely stories. They may have a mythic quality, the explanatory function of telling how things came to be the way they are, and how a golden age may yet come again.

Tennyson's *Idylls* may be seen to have had the same purpose in Victoria's reign as Spenser's *Faerie Queene* had in the reign of the first Elizabeth, celebrating what they deemed to be the most glorious of ages. In the early 1950s there were dreams of the dawning of a new, golden Elizabethan age for Britain, though just how long it lasted, or whether it ever dawned, is a good question. It may be interesting, too (even if idle), to speculate whether a future king will elect to use one of his many forenames in order to style himself King Arthur, rather than attempt a restoration of 'good King Charles's golden days'. And if that should be his decision, will he choose to be King Arthur the First or the Second?

*   *   *

In conclusion, then: Arthur may have been a type of the sub-Roman British tribal chieftains who resisted invading Saxons; it is even possible that he may have been an historical individual. It cannot be denied that the legendary and literary Arthur demonstrated the qualities of a hero: of royal lineage, granted divine visions, possessing supernatural powers, achieving superhuman feats. He was also flawed, a reminder of another great hero king, Israel's David. Just as David was denied his dream of building God's temple because he was a warrior and an adulterer, so Arthur seems also to have been denied achieving the Holy Grail for similar reasons.

The hero Arthur is said to have descended from a long line of heroes, all the way back to Aineias, son of the goddess Aphrodite, and the only Trojan leader to survive the fall of Troy. The world depicted in the Homeric epics had much in common with the world of the Arthurian legends. They were heroic ages, when the principal characters sought and achieved personal honour through superhuman courage and martial prowess, earning the devoted loyalty of their followers. After the bitterest warfare, both Camelot and Troy fell, and their dynasties fell with them.

The two worlds shared a mythic quality; and it is easy to understand that English monarchs who believed in their divine right to rule would readily claim Arthur as their ancestor, a hero whose history was so closely linked with the Holy Grail. And yet, whatever historical content there may be in the Arthurian narratives, surely most modern readers are unlikely to confuse the myth of the Holy Grail with historical fact.

On what basis, though, will one be able to disentangle fact from fiction when reading the stories of the Trojan war, told in the next chapter?

Chapter Seven

The Trojan War: The Stories

The Seeds of Conflict

On Mount Olympos three goddesses were quarrelling about who deserved the award of a golden apple which bore the inscription *For the Fairest*. Each of the three, Hera, Athene and Aphrodite, believed she could justifiably lay claim to this accolade. Mighty Zeus wanted no part in resolving the argument, but had in mind a young man who would not only arbitrate in the goddesses' wrangling, but would also spark a war which (some say) Zeus had already planned.

This young man was Paris, one of fifty sons of Priam, king of Troy. Hermes the messenger god brought the three goddesses to Paris, and handed the golden apple to him with Zeus' command that he award it to the most beautiful of the three. Disrobing so that Paris might behold their naked beauty, each goddess in turn made him promises in exchange for the award of the golden apple. But it was Aphrodite who promised Paris the most beautiful woman in the world as his wife, if only the golden apple were to be hers, undertaking to ensure that Helen, queen of Sparta, would fall in love with him.

This was an offer that Paris could not refuse and he handed the apple to Aphrodite. In that moment, Troy's fate was sealed, as the embittered Hera and Athene conspired to bring about the destruction of Priam's kingdom in revenge for Paris denying them the prize.

Paris the prince of Troy crossed the Aegean Sea to Sparta, where King Menelaos lavished hospitality on his royal guest, feasting Paris for nine days. In all this time, however, Paris abused Menelaos' generosity, flirting with his wife Helen, giving her many signals of his love. Helen appeared embarrassed by this attention, but when Menelaos had to leave Sparta for business in Crete, she eloped with Paris, although some say that he took her by force. Coming eventually to Troy, Paris and Helen were married amid great rejoicing.

When Menelaos returned home and found his wife gone, and believing that Helen had been forcibly abducted by Paris, the enraged Spartan king went to his brother Agamemnon, the great king of Mycenae, imploring that an army be raised to attack Troy and recover Helen.

Agamemnon counselled that envoys first be sent to Priam to seek the return of Helen; and only if they returned empty-handed would an army and a fleet be assembled. And so it was. The envoys failed in their mission and came back to Mycenae without Helen. Then the call went out through all the lands and islands of the Greeks, enlisting the help of the many kings and princes. More than forty leaders pledged their support and a vast fleet of a thousand ships assembled, with an army of one hundred thousand warriors.

Before Helen's marriage to Menelaos, there had been many suitors for the hand of this most beautiful of women. Her father Tyndareus feared that once he had chosen a husband for Helen, one or more of the unsuccessful suitors would attack his kingdom, to steal her away. It was the wily Odysseus who came up with the solution: before Tyndareus named a husband from among the many suitors, all had first to swear to him that they would band together to defend the chosen man against anyone who might abduct Helen. It is said that it was to honour this oath, after Helen had been taken by Paris to Troy, that the princes assembled and the thousand ships were launched.

Before the Greeks were to be blessed with a favourable wind, however, the gods had to be appeased; and a seer declared that this required Agamemnon to sacrifice his young daughter Iphigeneia. The great king sent to Mycenae for the girl, and in answer to the divine wish, she was slaughtered at Aulis. With the gods placated by Agamemnon's ghastly and inhuman act, a wind sprang up and the fleet set sail for Troy.

Some say that Iphigeneia did not die, but was rescued by the goddess Artemis, who substituted a stag as the sacrifice; others, that Achilleus saved her and sent her away to safety. Yet others tell how Achilleus married the girl. If indeed Agamemnon slew his daughter, this sealed his fate; for on his return from Troy, his embittered wife Klytaimestra took her revenge, having Agamemnon murdered by Aigisthos, her treacherous lover.

Ten Years of War

The Greek ships crossed the Aegean Sea and beached within sight of Troy. Immediately the Trojans assailed the ships before any of the invading enemy could come ashore. But their missiles were futile and as the ferocious invaders began to pour from the ships, the first blood was spilt, both Greek and Trojan. But the Greeks had a taste for battle and the Trojans were put to flight.

As the passing months turned to years, prophecies that the war would last for ten years showed signs of coming true. Both armies clashed in horrifying hand-to-hand fighting, and warriors on both sides were butchered in bloody confusion. Sometimes one side prevailed over the other, and the Trojans would flee for the safety of their high-walled city; or the Greeks would be routed and retreat to their beached ships, secure behind a palisade.

At other times, as the opposing armies stood taunting one another, a champion would step forward from the ranks, challenging the enemy to send out a man to meet him in individual combat. Both Greeks and Trojans had their many champions, terrifying gigantic warriors who towered above their fellows, ferocious slayers of men, the very sight of whom made lesser men quake.

On the Greek side stood the greatest and most terrifying fighter of them all, the dreaded Achilleus, unmatched in every way. He wielded a spear which no other man could lift, a spear given to his father Peleus by the centaur Cheiron. The great hero Achilleus was the son of the goddess Thetis, and it seemed that no man would ever prevail against him.

Aias the son of Telamon was said to be a very close second to Achilleus in valour and in fearsome demeanour. Even Hektor, the greatest of the Trojans, quaked before Aias, who faced his enemies with a huge shield made from seven layers of ox hide overlaid with bronze.

The Trojans too had their great heroes. The mighty man-slaying Hektor, son of Priam, put sheer terror into any Greek warrior, however courageous, who had the misfortune to meet him in the fray. The sight of huge Aineias, too, was the worst nightmare of any Greek. Aineias was the son of the goddess Aphrodite; and his ally, the ferocious Sarpedon, was a son of Zeus.

There were many such mighty men numbered among both armies, and even though the Olympian gods played their part in the hostilities, some siding with the Greeks and others with the Trojans, the war dragged on and on, year after year after year.

The Wrath of Achilleus

In all those years, the Greeks went marauding throughout the lands and cities of the Trojans' neighbours and allies, slaughtering and plundering as they went.

In was in the tenth year of the war, after all this Greek rape and pillage, that there came a hinge point in the seemingly unending hostilities at Troy, an event that spelt the beginning of the end. During one of his raiding campaigns, the mighty Achilleus had amassed treasures, seized from the cities which he and his warriors had taken by storm, and these had been distributed among the Greeks. Highly prized among these spoils of war were the women carried away by the raiders from the cities that they sacked. The great king Agamemnon had been given the beautiful Chryseïs, taken from the city of Thebe. Achilleus had kept for himself the young Briseïs, whom he had captured when he sacked the city of Lyrnessos.

Chryseïs was the daughter of Chryses, a priest of Apollo. Chryses came to Agamemnon with a ransom for the return of his daughter but Agamemnon abused him, angrily turning him away, shouting that he had no intention of giving up Chryseïs. She would grow old as his mistress, he cried, when he returned to his far-distant homeland. Weeping, the old man Chryses went away, praying to Apollo for revenge. The archer god heard the prayers of his priest and for ten days the Greeks were assailed and slaughtered by Apollo's arrows.

Despairing of any success against the Trojans while their sponsoring god continued his assaults, Achilleus called for a holy man to say what had to be done. A seer declared that the Greeks' misfortunes were caused by Apollo's priest being dishonoured by Agamemnon. The only remedy was the return of Chryseïs to her father.

A heated debate followed, but the affronted Agamemnon remained adamant that Chryseïs would remain his property. Achilleus and he exchanged insults and would have taken up arms against each other had not Athene descended from the sky and held the mighty men apart. Finally, Agamemnon's solution was to give up Chryseïs, and seize Briseïs from Achilleus.

With his honour impugned, and uttering the vilest of insults against Agamemnon, Achilleus declared that he and his Myrmidon warriors would withdraw from the fighting and sail back to their homeland of Phthia. In silent rage he went brooding to his tent. So bitter was his fury that Achilleus prayed to his goddess mother Thetis, asking her to entreat Zeus to teach Agamemnon and the Greeks a lesson, so that they might recognize their leader's madness in dishonouring their greatest warrior. Thetis went as supplicant to Zeus on Mount Olympos and there did as Achilleus had asked. With some misgivings (dreading a squabble with his wife Hera, who sponsored the Greeks)

Zeus none the less assented to Thetis' entreaty and agreed to side with Troy.

Encouraged by rumours that the Greeks' mightiest champion and his feared Myrmidon warriors had withdrawn from the fighting, the Trojans renewed their assault on the Greek lines. Then followed the fiercest fighting yet, in which a number of the greatest of the Greek leaders, including Agamemnon himself, Diomedes and Odysseus, were wounded so seriously they were carried from the fray. The frenzied Hektor seemed unstoppable now. He broke through the Greek defences and set the beached ships alight, glorying that at last Zeus, god of the gods, had given the Trojans a day that was worth all the others put together.

Even Heroes Must Die

When he saw the dread sight of the Greek ships ablaze, Achilleus for a moment forgot his grudge. Not only did he rouse his Myrmidons to rejoin the battle, but also called upon his dearest friend Patroklos to arm himself and lead the counter-offensive. At his bidding, Patroklos put on Achilleus' armour, though he was unable to take the great hero's massive spear, which he alone of all men could wield, and leapt into the melee.

Mistaking the armed Patroklos for Achilleus, the Trojans scattered and fled. The raging Patroklos pursued the retreating enemy and slew the Trojan's hero, Sarpedon, a son of Zeus, thus sealing his own fate. For while Zeus was deterred by Hera from avenging the death of Sarpedon, it was Apollo who was to bring about the death of Achilleus' dear friend. The frenzied Patroklos would have stormed Troy alone and single-handed taken the city's high walls, had not Apollo, defending Troy's citadel, stunned him so that he could not move. As Apollo stripped from Patroklos the helmet and armour of Achilleus, a Trojan spearman, Euphorbos, hit the unprotected hero between the shoulder blades with a javelin.

Seeing Patroklos now wounded and defenceless, Hektor thrust him through with his spear; but even as his life ebbed from him, Patroklos taunted Hektor with the assurance that he himself was soon to die.

The dreadful news was carried to Achilleus that his beloved companion had been slain by Hektor, and that the vaunting Trojan was now displaying Achilleus' gleaming armour as his spoils. Such was the grief of Achilleus on hearing of Patroklos' death, as he smeared himself with ashes and lay weeping in the dust, tearing his hair, that his companions feared he would cut his throat. Achilleus' mother Thetis came to him, gently reminding him that this horror had come about because of his own entreaty, when he had prayed that Zeus would take sides against the Greeks. But now, she added, it was decreed that Achilleus would meet his own death, but not before his foe Hektor was slain. Prepared to meet his destiny, and eager to find and kill his arch-enemy Hektor, the grieving Achilleus was counselled to delay his return to the fighting until his divine mother returned to his side, with newly-forged armour crafted by the smith god Hephaistos.

Achilleus now saw the need for reconciliation with the great king Agamemnon. What madness it had been, he said, that their enmity had been caused by disputing over a mere girl. Rather had Artemis killed Briseïs with an arrow on the day that Achilleus had taken her from her homeland, than the Trojans should benefit from this quarrel. Agamemnon was glad to hear Achilleus repent of their dispute, in which the proud king grudgingly acknowledged that he had played a part—although, he said, he was not really at fault, since Zeus was to blame.

With the Greek leadership reconciled, Achilleus clad himself in the brilliant new armour wrought by the artificer god, Hephaistos. To a man, the Trojans quaked with terror as they saw the crazed Achilleus come rampaging among them, his fiery armour giving him the appearance of Ares the murderous god of war himself. He was pitiless in his butchery and even the greatest of the Trojan heroes, Hektor and Aineias, felt faint at the sight of him.

In one encounter with Achilleus, Aineias would have been slain had not Poseidon come to his aid. The god wrenched Achilleus' huge spear from where it had pierced Aineias' shield, and laid the great weapon back at Achilleus' feet. At the same time, Poseidon lifted Aineias and carried him to safety, beyond the reach of the Greek hero's murderous spear.

Now the gods were in the thick of the fighting, intent on protecting their favourites. Hektor confronted Achilleus and cast his spear at him, but Athene deflected it, and the spear fell back at Hektor's feet. Achilleus made a furious charge at Hektor, but Apollo caught up the great Trojan warrior and wrapped him in a mist so that Achilleus could see him no more.

Hektor was not to escape Achilleus for long. As Achilleus closed on him once again, in his blazing Olympian armour and brandishing his fearsome spear, Hektor trembled in terror and could no longer stand his ground but turned and fled. Achilleus followed Hektor in hot pursuit and chased him around the walls of Troy.

Fleeing in terror, Hektor believed he was to be saved at last, as his warrior brother Deïphobos suddenly appeared at his side. But it was a tragic deception. Athene had disguised herself as Hektor's brother; and as Hektor turned to confront Achilleus, in the belief that Deïphobos stood shoulder to shoulder with him, he realised too late that he had been deceived. The two mighty warriors circled one another, each watchful for an opportunity. Achilleus was the first to move, hurling his great spear at Hektor. The spear missed the Trojan hero, but Athene picked it up and returned it to Achilleus. Suddenly then, in one swift movement, Achilleus plunged his spear through Hektor's throat, inflicting a most dreadful mortal wound.

As he lay with his life slipping away from him, Hektor pleaded that his body be ransomed and returned to Troy, not savaged by marauding dogs. But Achilleus' rage was not to be assuaged by such pleading and he spat words at the dying Hektor, that even a ransom of his weight in gold would not save him from the degradation he intended for him. Hektor's last words foretold the end of Achilleus himself, at the hands of Apollo and Paris.

Achilleus roped the corpse of Hektor feet first behind his chariot and day after day raced round the walls of Troy, dragging the dead hero's body as it lurched piteously over the rocky ground and rolled lifeless through the dust. But each night, Aphrodite anointed Hektor's body with oil so that it should not be mutilated by this barbaric treatment, and Apollo guarded the corpse from the scavenging dogs.

The gods on Mount Olympos were dismayed at the savagery of Achilleus' revenge on Hektor, and urged Hermes to steal the body. Such action could not be agreed by Hera and Athene, still smarting from Paris' insult. Apollo counselled that a messenger be sent to Priam, suggesting he go to Achilleus with a ransom for the body. Thetis, in turn, was to go to her son Achilleus and urge him to accept a ransom from the Trojan king.

And so it was. At the greatest danger to himself, Priam accepted Hermes' guidance and divine protection as he made his way perilously through the Greek lines. Achilleus himself could not believe that the old man had put himself in so much danger. Could he not have expected also to be slaughtered by the merciless Greek? But each man grieved for the loss of a loved one; and as they shared their sorrow, Achilleus accepted the ransom that Priam offered. Hektor's body was returned to Troy, where it was given the funeral rites due to a great prince and hero.

The Wooden Horse

Now there was rejoicing in the Greek camps. They had seen the last of Hektor, Troy's most monstrous warrior, who had brought more grief to the Greeks than all other Trojans together. At last, perhaps, there was hope of victory. But the tragedy was not yet over. Their own great hero Achilleus was soon to meet his destined end. The gods had been angered by his vaunting over Hektor, and

as the fighting continued about the walls of Troy, Apollo
guided an arrow shot by Paris, which hit Achilleus in the
heel, the only vulnerable part of his body, and he fell
dying. Others of the Greek heroes protected the body of
mighty Achilleus just where he had fallen, and the day's
fighting was brought to an end by a storm sent by Zeus.
Achilleus' body was carried amid great mourning to the
ships. After the funeral rites demanded by his status, he
was cremated and his remains interred beneath a great
mound on a hill that overlooked the sea, as an eternal
memorial to this the most glorious hero of them all.

Now, as the Greeks began to despair of any success
against their Trojan enemy, Athene put into their minds a
deception which was to secure their victory. At her bidding, they built a huge horse of wood, pretending it to be
an offering to Athene, to secure the goddess's protection as
they sailed for home. But inside the hollow horse were
concealed many armed men, led by a number of the fear-
less kings, Spartan Menelaos himself, with the wily and
resourceful Odysseus of Ithaka, and the Argive lord,
Diomedes, who had fought and wounded the gods Aphrodite and Ares.

Leaving the wooden horse just where it stood outside
the city's gates, the Greek ships set out from the shore. The
Trojans mistakenly believed the fleet was sailing home to
Mycenae, but the Greeks went only as far as the nearby
island of Tenedos and there moored in its hidden harbour.

With a great sense of relief and freedom the Trojans
flooded out of their city to view at closer quarters the huge
votive offering left standing on the beach. There was much
discussion about what was to be done. Some said that the
horse should be towed into the city; others, fearing treach-
ery, said that it should be burnt or thrown into the sea. As
the argument went to and fro, the priest Laocoön shouted
warnings to his fellow citizens. Were they mad? When did
they ever trust a Greek? Did they not know the crafty
Odysseus better than that? What made them think that the
Greeks had gone home, anyway? Even now, he said, the
horse might well conceal armed men, or else it was some

kind of engine for breaking down the walls of Troy. 'I fear Greeks,' Laocoön cried, 'especially Greeks bearing gifts.' With that, he hurled his spear at the horse's flanks, and as it struck the wood the quivering spear made the Greeks' hidden weapons clash aloud.

Just then, all were distracted by the arrival in their midst of a young Greek, bound hand and foot, discovered by some Trojan shepherds. Unknown to them, he had been left behind by the Greeks, with the purpose of opening Troy's gates to them. Simulating fear and trembling, the young man admitted to his Trojan captors that he was a Greek, and that his name was Sinon. Convincingly showing great distress, Sinon tearfully spun the yarn that in return for a favourable wind to take the ships back home, Apollo had demanded the shedding of young Greek blood in retribution for the youthful Trojan blood the Greeks had spilt. He had been chosen to be sacrificed, Sinon said, but had escaped. Now he feared that the Trojans would be as bloodthirsty as the Greeks had been. Weeping, he continued with his lies, explaining that the horse was indeed a gift from the Greeks to Athene, to secure their safe return to their homeland. Priam took pity on Sinon, commanding that he be set free.

Then a fearsome event occurred. Two hideous giant serpents came over the sea and seized Laocoön and his two young sons, twining about them. First they devoured the boys, and as Laocoön struggled to free himself, he was strangled in the serpents' monstrous coils. The people cried out that Laocoön had deserved his fate, as the price for spearing Athene's gift, and with one voice agreed that the horse should be taken into the city and set high on Athene's citadel.

When night fell, the Greek ships returned unseen from Tenedos to Troy. At an agreed signal, Sinon released the hidden warriors from the hollow horse. The Trojan sentries, taken wholly by surprise, were cut down and the city gates opened wide to the Greeks who came streaming from the beached ships.

The sleeping city was taken by storm with unremitting slaughter. By daybreak, the Greeks had finished their bloody work. Priam and his sons lay dead, and only Aineias had made his escape. Troy's women were now the spoils of war: Priam's queen Hekabe and daughter Kassandra, and Hektor's widow Andromache, all went into captivity. And the great city was all a ruin, consumed in raging fire.

The Wanderings and the Returns

Through all those years of war, vengeful gods and the bronze of Trojan weapons had stripped the lives from many Greek warriors and denied them their homecoming. Achilleus was dead, and Aias too. Many another king and prince who had answered Agamemnon's call to take up arms against Troy had fallen there, and countless others would not see their homeland again.

The aged king Nestor, who had reigned over three generations of men and whose counsels had been so valued by Agamemnon, came home unharmed to Pylos. Agamemnon was not as fortunate. He returned to Mycenae only to be murdered by his wife's treacherous lover, Aigisthos. Agamemnon's brother Menelaos came home at last to Sparta, after years of wandering, in which time he amassed great treasures from his plundering, and lived out his life with his queen Helen, secure in her home once more.

But it is about the wanderings of Odysseus that the greatest stories have been told. When first leaving Troy for home, his fleet came to the land of the Lotus Eaters. His men were content to stay there, eating the honey-sweet lotus fruit, as their interest in returning home began to fade. Rescuing his men from their lethargy, Odysseus sailed to the land of the Cyclopes, losing many of his companions to the cannibal giant Polyphemos. On the island of Aiolos, Odysseus was given a bag of winds to aid his ships' safe passage; but his inquisitive men opened the bag and the winds were lost. Then in the land of the

Laistrygones, the giants speared Odysseus' men like fish, and ate them.

The enchantress Circe turned half of Odysseus' men into swine; but Zeus' messenger Hermes gave Odysseus a magic potion, enabling him to rescue his crew. Voyaging to the land of the dead, Odysseus encountered the souls of Agamemnon, Achilleus, and Aias, and heard a prophecy of his own death. In great peril, Odysseus' ships sailed past the Sirens, whose singing lured sailors to a gruesome death; but Odysseus blocked his crew's ears with beeswax, lest they be tempted ashore. They barely escaped the howling terror of Skylla, who ate yet more of Odysseus' men, and the boiling black water of Charybdis' whirlpool, which would have sucked them down to dread oblivion.

At length the one remaining ship beached on the island where Helios the sun god pastured his cattle. Here the fate of the last of Odysseus' companions was sealed. In spite of many warnings, the men slaughtered and ate the sun god's cattle. The enraged Helios prayed to his father Zeus to punish this recklessness; and when Odysseus set sail, Zeus brought up the most ferocious storm, the ship broke up and all of Odysseus' men drowned in the dark depths. Odysseus alone survived. Clinging to the ship's wreckage, he was nine days in the sea, but came at last to the island home of the nymph Kalypso.

For seven years Odysseus remained with the goddess but more and more he longed for his wife and his home. Then Athene spoke with the gods on Mount Olympos, making the case for Odysseus' return to Ithaka. Hermes was sent to Kalypso to persuade her to let Odysseus go; and she gave Odysseus the tools and the timber to build a sea-going raft on which he sailed for home.

He was not safe yet, however, for his great enemy the sea god Poseidon created yet another storm and Odysseus was shipwrecked once again. Hardly alive, he was eventually washed up on the shore of the land of the Phaiakians. There the princess Nausikaä took him to the palace of her father Alkinoös. After relating the stories of his wanderings, Odysseus was put aboard one of the Phaiakians' fast-running ships, and brought at last to his island home of Ithaka. There he took merciless revenge on his wife's suitors, who for years had been abusing his home's hospitality. And so, with this last homecoming of the Greek heroes, there is an end to the stories of the Trojan war.

* * *

In these briefly summarised excerpts from the epic narratives, there is another example of that sense of looking back into the mists and uncertainties of the kind of ancient past discussed earlier, those long-vanished golden ages of heroes who were in many ways mightier than men are today, men of renown who had dealings with the gods.

These narratives concerning Greeks and Trojans can be seen to typify the conflation of fact and fiction, describing events which may have had some factual basis in a very distant past, experienced by men and women who may have existed in those ancient days. At the same time, the stories include episodes which would not be out of place in a fairy story: a goddess protects her favourite warrior by retrieving his mis-cast spear, and a hero is clad in armour forged by a god on Mount Olympos. The adventures of Odysseus during his wanderings are hardly credible as historically factual, either.

These stories of the Trojan war may therefore be said to be legends, and the people and their achievements justifiably described as legendary. Beyond that, though, the narratives' supernatural content qualifies them as myth, in that they have the moral or ethical explanatory function defined earlier. But where is the history? We will turn now to look at some of the original sources for the stories of the Trojan war and the extent to which they provide, if they do, historical evidence for these events.

Chapter Eight

The Trojan War: Sources and History, Part 1

It may be fair to assume that for many people, the Trojan war is synonymous with Homer; and it may well be true that more would be prepared to name Homer as the source of the stories of Troy, than would venture to identify sources of (say) the Arthurian narratives.

Quite clearly, the two Homeric epic poems have a great deal to say about a war waged by Greeks against a city called Troy. The *Iliad* especially and the *Odyssey* to some extent—that is to say, in different ways—deal with the main participants and many of the key events, either explicitly or by allusion.

It may be of value to make one or two points of clarification at the outset. Strictly speaking, the Trojans' enemy were not Greeks. The word *Hĕllēnĕs*, meaning Greeks, post-dated Homer. For him, the warriors who made war with the Trojans were Achaians, Argives or Danaans, and Hellas was still only a small part of the region that is Greece today. Although it may be anachronistic to do so, the word Greeks is used here simply because of its common coinage.

The Greek title for Homer's first epic, *Ilias*, means a poem about Ilion, the Greek name for Troy. It is not *the* story of Troy but *a* story of Troy. The title of the second epic, *Odusseia* means simply 'The story of Odysseus', not 'odyssey'. Our modern English word odyssey, used to describe a long and adventurous or arduous journey, was not coined until the late nineteenth century of our era.

Significantly, were it not for Homer's poems, we would have remained blissfully unaware of Troy (if it existed at all), and would not have known that we did not know about either the city or the war (if it ever happened). As a result, it could not have occurred to anyone to ask any of the questions which continue to surround the legends and whatever history may lie behind them.

Who, then, was Homer, and when did he live?

To take the 'when' first: for a number of reasons which we shall touch on shortly, the composition of the two epics is thought to date from the late eighth century BCE. So if Homer was the composer or compiler of *Iliad* and/or *Odyssey*, it may be true to say that he flourished at some time in the seven hundreds BCE. However, as with so many of the Homeric questions, this remains unclear and unresolved, as scholars continue to argue and develop their theories. Indeed, in the same way as there are questions about the historical basis of the stories that he told, there is continuing uncertainty about the historicity of Homer himself (or *themselves*!).

For the classical Greeks there was no doubt that Homer was an historical figure, possibly a blind rhapsode or bard, just as it was believed that his poems tell of the deeds of historical warrior-kings and their campaign against Troy. The fifth century Greek historian Herodotus accepted without question that Homer and Hesiod were the first composers of theogonies — poems relating the birth and genealogy of the Olympian gods — and did not hesitate to date both poets four hundred years before his own time, although we have no way of knowing on what he based his (probably inaccurate) assumption.

There is uncertainty, too, about Homer's birthplace. A number of claims are made, with a broad consensus that he may have come from Smyrna or Chios or one of the other Greek colonies of Asia Minor, on the Aegean coast of what is today Turkey, but was not yet Greek at the time of the events related in the *Iliad*. This itself raises a number of interesting points, as we shall see when we come to questions about the location of Troy.

However, whether a poet named Homer ever lived, or when or where, or whether there were two or more 'Homers', or whether there was none, with the name Homer simply standing as a metonym for an accumulation and amalgamation of varying traditions over generations or even centuries of oral composition and performance — all of this remains unknown.

The controversy over one Homer or two marks the opposing standpoints taken by those who are labelled unitarians on one hand, and the analysts on the other. In 1795 the German scholar Friedrich Wolf put forward what was at that time a wholly controversial view, that *Iliad* and *Odyssey* were not composed by one poet. Wolf's theory was that they derived from an accumulation of many strands of tradition which had merged over a long period, probably centuries. In the two hundred years or more since Wolf, the controversy has continued and broadened, with the analysts sharing his view that *Iliad* and *Odyssey* were not written or composed by the same person.

The analysts' argument for separate authorship includes questions about linguistic style, anachronisms, textual inconsistencies, and the incongruity of social customs and practices from widely-differing eras presented side by side, as though they were contemporaneous.

Differences of linguistic structure and vocabulary, the unitarians' counter-argument would run, may be simply accounted for by one poet naturally choosing to vary his style as he composed two poems with dissimilar subjects and purposes: the intensity of the brooding, violent and tragic *Iliad* is clearly differentiated from the romance of the *Odyssey*, with its fancy and fantasy, its fairy tale narratives and its occasionally comic passages. The swineherd Eumaios in the *Odyssey*, for example, would be very much at home among the rustics in a Shakespearean comedy, but uncomfortably out of place in the *Iliad*.

It is true that at a number of points within the epic narratives the social contexts appear to be those of differing ages, and it is possible to identify anachronisms. For example, the description of Odysseus' home on Ithaka seems more closely to resemble buildings of Homer's own time than those of the palace culture of Mycenae and Pylos, which is the supposed world of the *Odyssey*; and Nausikaä's description of her father's city is more like a city of Homer's time than one that Odysseus could have been expected to visit.

In the *Odyssey* there is mention of temples, which did not begin to appear until something like four centuries after the Mycenaean world portrayed in the two epics, when the gods would have been worshipped at open-air altars.

The *Iliad* is rich in frequent and striking similes. Many of them use rural or agricultural imagery, suggesting warrior-farmers, and this feels curiously at odds with the heroic status of such ferocious warriors as Achilleus: at one point even he speaks of his harvest and of his cattle. Another simile uses the image of a fisherman sitting on a rock, with his line and hook; and yet there is no mention of the Greeks eating fish as they camped for all those years on the seashore near Troy: rather they can be visualised tucking into their beef and lamb kebabs.

The bronze armour and weapons described in the *Iliad*, and methods of fighting which were outdated by literally centuries, could not have been known or experienced by Homer or his contemporaries, other than through word-of-mouth repetition over generations of oral tradition. Gold at Mycenae, a helmet somehow adorned with boars' tusks, Mycenaean shields, all are mentioned by Homer. Thousands of years later, they have been found in archaeological digs, but would have been quite unknown to the poet. The hill-top citadel of Mycenae had been in ruins for centuries by the time Homer was born.

The Greek hero Aias is three times described in the *Iliad* as carrying a massive curved, body-length shield, made of seven layers of ox hide overlaid with bronze. Such a shield would not only have pre-dated Homer by many centuries, it would also pre-date the supposed time of the Trojan war. Possibly Aias was a legendary hero from an even earlier age, and was inserted by Homer, complete with shield, into the Trojan narrative.

In the *Iliad* there are references to heroes being cremated and in one passage a hero's ashes are collected after cremation, to be taken home to Greece. In the Mycenaean era, on the other hand, the slain warriors would have been buried; cremation is generally thought to have been an eighth century practice.

Homer does appear to have difficulties with his text and trips himself up in ways that a single originating poet could be expected not to do, and it might be reasonable to look for greater consistency and accuracy if the two poems are indeed from one source. On the other hand, with more than one thousand names of people and places in the *Iliad* alone, it should come as no surprise that there are slips and inconsistencies. On the whole, the personalities of the principal characters remain persuasively the same in both poems, creating a very real sense that they have come from the same composer.

If the mortals behave in ways that are consistent between the two epics, the same cannot be said about the gods, and this is seen by analysts as another area of discrepancy. This is especially true of Zeus. In the *Odyssey* he is portrayed as the champion of justice. Zeus has it in his mind to punish some of the Greeks on their return from Troy — if they are to return at all — since not all of them by any means had been righteous or considerate in their behaviour [*Odyssey* 3:132–3]. Similarly, the massacre of the greedy and self-seeking suitors at the hands of Odysseus on his return to Ithaka was seen to be divine justice [*Odyssey* 22:413–5].

Whereas in the *Odyssey* Zeus shows justice and even-handedness in his dealings with men, in the *Iliad,* by contrast, he induces men to do wrong, urges the other gods to take sides either with Greeks or with Trojans, changes sides himself, and is thoroughly partisan.

Analysts argue that these anachronisms, and the textual discrepancies and inconsistencies, point to the poems having been composed by different authors. It is equally possible to argue that these and other differences are indicators of how one poet drew upon long lines of different oral origins, stretching back across centuries before his own time. In the *Iliad* especially, Homer alludes to incidents from the earlier Theban Cycle, and borrows brief portions of stories of Herakles and of Jason and the Argonauts. Within Homer's main text, the *paradeigma* or legendary and mythical allusions which he makes, came from sources outside the principal cycles: his borrowed references to centaurs, to Bellerophontes, Meleagros, Phoinix, Oidipous and Niobe, it may be assumed, would already have been familiar to his audiences.

Just as archaeologists dig down through layer after layer of the earth and uncover evidence of series of civilisations and cultures, so too it may be possible to dig down through the strata of Homer's texts and find evidence of successive sources for his narratives.

When all is said and done, however, these and other questions about Homer and the two epic poems may well remain unresolved, yet at the same time provide continuing scholarly debate. With millennia of tradition for one Homer, though, it does seem reasonable, for the time being at least, to agree with Richmond Lattimore's contention that 'the burden of proof rests on those who would establish separate authorship' [Lattimore 1951].

What does appear to be true, however, is that the origins of both the *Iliad* and its sequel, the *Odyssey*, lie in an antiquity far older than Homer himself; and somewhere in the mists of that ancient past, that lost age of the heroes, lie the historical truths (if there are any) on which the legends were based.

Homer, as we have already noted, may have flourished in the late eighth century BCE and this possibility alone raises interesting points. It was only at that time that the Greeks were re-discovering the skill of writing, as they developed a new alphabet based on letters borrowed from the Phoenicians. Writing had been unknown to the Greeks for something like four centuries, having been lost with the collapse of the Mycenaean culture at some time in the twelfth century BCE. It seems to follow from this that even if Homer was able to write his compositions (and that remains uncertain), the ancient sources on which he drew, running back though the illiterate centuries of the Dark Age to the vanished Mycenaean period, must themselves have been oral.

It is known that the Mycenaean Greeks were able to write, because tablets written in what is known as Linear B script have been excavated in a number of Mycenaean sites. Disappointingly, the Linear B tablets seem to have been used for commercial and domestic records, and not for literary purposes or for recording events. There is only one brief reference to writing in Homer; perhaps this is a memory of the Mycenaean age buried deep in the layers of the oral tradition.

There is the obvious question about how such extensive poetic works could have been composed, memorised and recited without writing. The *Iliad* alone has nearly sixteen thousand lines and the *Odyssey* more than twelve thousand. The published research of two twentieth century American academics, Parry and Lord, gave some clues. They make the point that the original Homeric recitation was improvised, each performance being to some extent unique. Parry and Lord demonstrated that the Homeric language was made for improvisation, and that the oral bards had developed a huge repertoire of stock epithets and repeated phrases, lines, even whole scenes. These appear to have formed a sort of mnemonic, as well as providing the poet with landmarks or milestones to keep them on track. Some kind of structure would surely have been needed in the bard's mind, both to aid his performance during the twenty-four hours required for reciting each of the epics, and to ensure as much consistency as possible in successive recitations. Homer's audiences, like our modern-day children, would quickly spot any glaring errors in the re-telling of familiar stories.

Many standard epithets and phrases are used to describe the poems' *dramatis personae*: Odysseus is frequently called resourceful, but sometimes he is godlike, long-suffering, or sacker of cities. Agamemnon is variously described as powerful or shepherd of the people, and his brother Menelaos as either fair- haired or as a man who utters a great war cry. Achilleus is brilliant or swift-footed, Hektor is man-slaughtering or wears a gleaming helmet. The Achaians are flowing-haired or glancing-eyed. Zeus is the cloud-gatherer or delights in the thunder, his wife Hera has ox eyes or white arms, and Athene is grey-eyed or carries the aegis. Whenever warriors are killed, they fall thunderously. And every time day breaks, 'the young Dawn showed again with her rosy fingers'. And so on and so on.

Repetition is common, frequently just a phrase, sometimes a whole line, occasionally a complete scene. Many genre scenes are repeated word for word — for example, depictions of bathing or feasting — and even similes recur. Five lines are devoted to the image of a felled tree to describe the death of the Trojan Asios at the hands of Idomeneus, and that five-line simile is repeated verbatim when the Trojan Sarpedon is killed by Patroklos.

These linguistic devices also served an important function in enabling the bard to maintain the rhythm of the poem's lines. The Greek words for the alternative standard epithets and stock phrases had their own varying combinations of long and short syllables, which changed with the word-endings dictated by their grammatical function (Greek nouns, for example, change their ending, depending on whether they are the subject or the object of a verb). These structural devices provided the poet with a system of metrical options, enabling the varying stresses and changing grammatical endings of words and their position in the line to be matched to the rhythm of the verses' dactylic hexameter. In this way, the poet could select the adjective or phrase that would most accurately fit any part of the metre.

These many combinations and variants, resulting both from the poet's use of linguistic devices and standard phrases, and from the multitude of ancient sources from different eras and cultures, may answer some of the questions about apparent inconsistencies of language, evidence of anachronisms, incongruous references to mis-matched social customs and practices, and — what interests us here — those elements which might be termed historical inaccuracies.

*   *   *

The chapter began with the suggestion that for many, the Trojan war and Homer are synonymous. It was noted that without Homer's epics, it is probable that we would never have heard of Troy. It should have become apparent, too, that Homer's is not the whole story. The *Iliad* covers only a few weeks at the end of the final year of the decade-long war, and makes no mention of many of the incidents that characterise the Trojan story. The *Odyssey*, the *Iliad*'s epic sequel, is concerned principally with the wanderings of the Greek hero Odysseus during the ten years after the sack of Troy, and his eventual homecoming to Ithaka, and makes only fragmentary reference to the other major characters and events in the story of Troy.

So where have all the other parts of the story of Troy come from? And where in all this is the history?

Chapter Nine

The Trojan War: Sources And History, Part 2

Homer and Troy may be synonymous, but many of the incidents central to the Trojan narratives, or some which we associate with the story, are either missing from Homer, or at best are alluded to only briefly within his *Iliad* or *Odyssey*. Where then did these other stories come from?

Much of the Trojan narrative as we have it does in fact derive from post-Homeric writings, principally the poems referred to as the Epic Cycle. These are now lost, or are to be found only in a few fragments quoted by classical authors; but the poems were known well into our own era, and were summarised in the fifth century CE by Proclus, the last of the major Greek philosophers.

The Epic Cycle tells of events both before and after those of the two Homeric epics. A work known as the *Cypria* begins with the Judgment of Paris, which explains the origins of the Trojan war but is mentioned only in passing in the final book of Homer's *Iliad*. Of unknown date, the *Cypria* covers the period between the gods' decision to cause the war, and Achilleus' quarrel with Agamemnon – that is, up to the beginning of the *Iliad*. The *Cypria* also tells of the sacrifice of Agamemnon's daughter Iphigeneia, an incident not mentioned by Homer, but one which may have pre-figured Agamemnon's murder by his vengeful wife's lover, on his return to Mycenae after the war.

We learn about Achilleus' vulnerable heel in another work, the *Aethiopis*, which dates from the mid-eighth century BCE. The *Aethiopis* continues where the *Iliad* ends and takes the story up to the suicide of Aias, insulted and demeaned by the Greek leaders' decision to award the dead Achilleus' armour to Odysseus and not to himself.

The episode of the wooden horse occurs after the events described in the *Iliad*, and therefore could not appear there; and it is referred to almost incidentally in the *Odyssey*. The story is told in *Ilias Parva* (the *Little Iliad*), thought to be the work of Lesches, and in *Iliu Persis* (the *Sack of Ilion*), by Arctinus, both of which continue the narrative up to the final departure of the Greeks from Troy. Lastly, the *Nostoi* (*The Returns*) tells of the homecoming of the heroes, other than the wanderings and return of Odysseus, which are related at length in the *Odyssey*.

Given that Homer, or at least his surviving poetry, was not the source of much of the now-familiar detail of the Trojan war, but that it is the Epic Cycle from which we learn of those events, it is possible that there were other, more ancient sources and traditions that were drawn upon both by Homer and the poets who followed him. Another possibility, of course, is that Homer was the author of (for example) the *Cypria*, the *Little Iliad*, and *The Returns*.

Six or seven centuries after Homer, the Roman poet Virgil enjoyed the patronage of his friend, the emperor Augustus; and it is suggested that Virgil's epic poem, the *Aeneid*, which tells of the legendary origins of Rome, was written to celebrate the glories of the Augustinian empire. It is clear that Virgil was familiar both with Homer's poems and the narratives of the Epic Cycle. The *Aeneid* tells how the great Trojan prince Aeneas (Aineias in Greek) escaped from Troy after it had been sacked by the Greeks, and how he and members of his family, with a number of companions, sailed westwards through the Mediterranean, landing eventually in Italy. According to Virgil's account, it was Aeneas' descendants who founded Rome.

In the second of the *Aeneid*'s six books, Aeneas relates his adventures to Queen Dido of Carthage. He tells at length and in great detail how the Greeks left the wooden horse outside Troy, which had been besieged for ten years, and seemed suddenly and inexplicably to have sailed for home; how, after the fearful episode of Laocoön and the serpents, the horse was taken into the city; and how under cover of night the Greek ships returned, and warriors concealed within the horse let the Trojans' enemy into the unguarded city, slaughtering and burning until Troy was a smoking ruin. It is in Virgil that the most accessible account of the wooden horse and the fall of Troy is to be found.

One curious source of questionable knowledge about Troy was a very long poem, the *Roman de Troie*, by the medieval French *trouvère* Benoît de Sainte-Maure. This in turn was based on two other dubious sources, the writings of Dares Phrygius and Dictys Cretensis. The first of these, Dares, was a Trojan priest of Hephaistos (according to Homer) and was supposed to have been the author of an account of the sack of Troy. His record was translated into the Latin *De Excidio Troiae* (*Concerning the Destruction of Troy*), a manuscript of which is extant, dating from perhaps the fifth century CE. The second, Dictys, was said to have accompanied the Cretan leader Idomeneus to the Trojan war and kept a diary of events. There was a claim that a Latin translation of this 'diary' was made in the fourth century CE, from a Greek translation prepared for the emperor Nero, from a Phoenician original discovered during his reign. It is easy to see why these 'records' could be considered to be of dubious origin or even thought to be fabrications. Even so, Benoît's *Roman* was an influential source of stories about Troy throughout mediaeval times and right up to the sixteenth century.

Until the fifteenth century of our era, Virgil was regarded as one of the principal authorities on Troy. In western Europe at least, Latin was read by every educated person, whereas Greek was not. Greek had been practically unknown in the west for a thousand years until its re-introduction from the Greek-speaking eastern Roman empire, when Constantinople fell to the Turks in 1453 CE. As a result, Homer was literally a closed book for centuries.

As the sixteenth century turned into the seventeenth, George Chapman's verse renderings of *Iliad* and *Odyssey* suggest that classical education in England was still biased more toward Latin than to Greek. Although Chapman's title page proudly announces that the poems are 'translated according to the Greek', it is the Roman and not the Greek gods who appear throughout, and Latin names are used for the Greek heroes. It could be assumed that educated readers in seventeenth century England would be more familiar with Jupiter than with Zeus, more at home with Ulysses than with Odysseus.

The first printed edition of Homer was published in Florence in 1488, from a text prepared by Demetrius Chalcondyles, a Greek scholar studying and teaching in Italy. It is likely that there had been handwritten copies of the Homeric epics in Italy for some centuries before that; the oldest complete manuscripts of *Iliad* and *Odyssey* in existence today date from the eleventh century CE, and were found in a library in Venice. It is known that there were variants of the text being edited by the late sixth century BCE, and it is thought that at about that time the Athenian tyrant Peisistratos had a definitive text produced and recited at the panhellenic festival. Differing versions of the poems were progressively standardised by Alexandrian scholars from the third century BCE onwards.

* * *

So far, then, we have been able to consider literary evidence for Homer and what are traditionally called the Homeric narratives, even though that evidence is punctured with a number of holes, or at least punctuated with a series of question marks. But in all this, little historical evidence has been produced for any events or people, or facts which might lie behind these legends.

It has already been noted that the world described by Homer seems to be a combination of a number of different societies from a number of different ages. It is clear from the Homeric texts that the events depicted are supposed to have taken place in the Bronze Age: all of the weapons are made of bronze, and the word bronze appears over and over again, whereas iron is rarely mentioned, and then only in the context of a valuable metal. More specifically, the narratives seem to be placed in the period of the Late Bronze Age known as the Mycenaean Age, which lasted from the sixteenth century until some time in the twelfth century BCE. But Homer's own time is thought to have been somewhere in the Iron Age, and between the two there stretched the four or five centuries of the so-called Dark Age, following the collapse of the Mycenaean era.

Generations of archaeologists digging at Hissarlik in Turkey, now generally considered to be the most likely site of Troy, have excavated and identified layer upon layer of successive cities. Some, they believe, were destroyed and burned down; but so far there they have unearthed no evidence, either documentary or archaeological, to show whether these were the result of siege or marauding attacks of some kind, nor have they found any indication of who mounted the attacks on the city, let alone whether they were 'Greeks', nor indeed any confirmation that this was in fact Troy.

As with so much of the study of Homer and his Trojan war, there are more questions than answers. For example, two layers at the Hissarlik excavations which are favourites for Homer's Troy, known as Troy VI and Troy VIIa, pose a number of problems. The destruction of level VIIa of the city appears to date from the middle of the twelfth century BCE or later, but the Mycenaean Age, which is the supposed era in which Homer's Trojan war took place, had already come to an end by then. Troy VI seems also to have been destroyed by fire, at around 1250 BCE, which is a widely-accepted date for the sack of Troy; but the evidence suggests an earthquake rather than a siege.

What, if anything, in the epics is historical and what is fiction? Modern-day western non-believers will doubtless readily dismiss as superstition the episodes on Olympos, the gods' conversations with each other and with mortals, and their active intervention in the affairs of men. But what may be termed supernatural nowadays was every bit as real to the ancient Greeks as biblical miracles and other numinous elements are for many people today.

Homer's great heroic epics certainly give every appearance of being based on *something* historical; it is difficult to believe that even with his undoubted genius he could have invented the whole thing. It is possible that the narratives are based on actual events which were in themselves not major or historical landmarks. Centuries and centuries of telling and re-telling talked up these events, perhaps, exaggerating their importance or historical significance and in the process turned them into these great epics which recall a long-lost or imaginary heroic golden age.

Our modern scepticism may readily dismiss as a fairy tale the story of the Judgment of Paris, and regard as fantasy the idea that the jealousy of a duo of spurned goddesses sparked off the Trojan war. But if there was a war between Greeks and Trojans, there must have been a cause. And if the numbers are anywhere near correct, they require some explanation. If more than forty kings and leaders assembled a fleet of over a thousand ships, and amassed an army perhaps a hundred thousand strong, they must have had a common purpose. Could this really have been simply a loyal response to a call to arms made by the king of kings, Agamemnon? Were these leaders paying homage to the unquestioned supremacy of the great king of Mycenae, who wielded the sceptre crafted by the smith-god Hephaistos for Zeus and handed down to Agamemnon's ancestors? Were these kings and princes prepared to go to war to resolve someone else's domestic problem, because the high king's sister-in-law had been abducted by a minor foreign prince? Were they honouring a loyal oath sworn years before, to the bride's father, Tyndareus?

More prosaically, some historians today suggest that the hill-top citadel of Troy literally oversaw the important Mediterranean trade routes and controlled the Dardanelles, possibly even taxing entry to the Black Sea and its prized sources of commerce. It may be that an attack was made on Troy to gain access to these trade routes, perhaps a relatively minor piratical hit-and-run raid, which centuries of story-telling turned into a major decade-long campaign.

Other scholars theorise that Troy was not destroyed by an army from Europe at all, but that the siege or attack may have been a wholly Asian event, with Troy falling as only one city among many during the periodic and continuous waves of migration and invasion from the north.

What seems to be clear is that Troy did come to a violent end; and within a generation or two, stories about the city's destruction would doubtless already have been in circulation. Mycenaean power itself collapsed within a hundred years or so of the supposed date of the Trojan war, and through the succeeding centuries of the Dark Age stories began to be told of a vanished heroic age. As we have already noted, in the absence of writing these narratives were essentially oral in character and, over time, elaboration and individual variants affected any historical accuracy which may have been there in the first place, not least the knowledge of the true location of Troy itself.

The classical Greeks were familiar with many ancient sites but had no ability to date them, and many attained heroic status or association. Herodotus tells of the Persian king Xerxes visiting the Trojan ruins, having long wanted to see the place, and there he poured libations to honour the heroes who had fallen at Troy. Alexander the Great is said to have visited the tomb of Achilleus. Notions about the actual whereabouts of Troy remained vague, however.

If it is true that Homer came from one of the Greek colonies on the Aegean coast of Asia Minor, he may well have been familiar with the geography of the stories of Troy, and even known the ruins of what was thought to be Ilion. It is possible that among the Greek colonists in that region there were nostalgic memories of the homeland where their people had originated, or a romanticised tradition of voyages from Greece to the Troad and a dream of returning or homecoming to the mainland. Perhaps Homer built his stories around such long-lost or half-remembered tales.

In our own era, from the sixteenth century onwards, European travellers began visiting the Aegean and parts of Asia Minor around the Hellespont, attempting to locate possible sites of the tombs of the Greek heroes who died in Homer's Trojan war, even hoping to find the site of Troy itself. These early efforts were in effect literary sleuthing, scanning the Homeric texts for clues, rather than searching for evidence literally on or in the ground.

For many years, increasing interest was shown in identifying the site of Troy, but it was only at the end of the eighteenth century that a number of German archaeologists believed they had successfully narrowed the search within an area of Turkey near the Dardanelles. For decades, Balli Dag was the favoured contender but in 1870 Heinrich Schliemann turned his attention to a small hill at Hissarlik. He began excavation there with a huge army of workmen, and sometimes upwards of a hundred men were digging at any one time. In the space of a few months, Schliemann's bull-in-a-china-shop excavation had cut a huge trench down through millennia of history and exposed layer upon layer of what proved to be a previously unknown Bronze Age civilization. The dating appeared to match Homer's Trojan war.

Schliemann had also dug at Mycenae and there had found bronze weapons, gold masks, and the ruins of palaces and mighty fortified walls. This could well have been the world that Homer *sang* about but it was not a world that he could have *known* about. Mycenae had been in ruins and largely hidden from sight by the time Homer was reciting his poems.

Schliemann led a number of further expeditions to Hissarlik, until his death in 1890, and his work formed the basis for continuing archaeological digs to the present day.

Happily, modern archaeological methods are more scientific and painstaking than Schliemann's. Today's major multi-disciplinary expeditions are undertaken by teams of specialists from perhaps a dozen or more academic and professional fields. However, Schliemann led the way. When he unearthed a golden death-mask at Mycenae, he may have been justified, even if mistaken, in imagining that he had gazed upon the face of Agamemnon. Most scholarship has since then agreed that at Hissarlik Schliemann had indeed found the most likely site of Troy.

For all that, though, there remains no historical evidence for Homer or for his Trojan war. Hissarlik/Troy has yielded a great deal of Mycenaean pottery, known to be from the same period as similar pottery found in Egypt which has been dated, and the site can therefore be said to be contemporaneous with the Mycenaean Age. But that is only evidence of a period in time, it does not reveal people or events. Moreover, it does not afford any proof that this was in fact the site of Troy.

Tablets found when excavating Turkish sites of the near-contemporary Hittite empire in Asia Minor, and dating from perhaps the thirteenth century BCE, include references to a number of names resembling those which appear in Homer. For example, a people named as Ahhiyawa may have been Homer's Achaians (*Akhaoi*) but there seems to be no way of knowing. However, some scholars now believe that the Hittite tablets are from an even earlier date, perhaps the fifteenth century BCE, which was long before the time traditionally ascribed to the Trojan war. There is good reason to believe that the Ahhiyawa, whoever they were, engaged in some centuries of warfare in that region of the Aegean, sometimes against Hittite cities, but there is no specific mention of Troy. So we are left with historical silence, and a virtually blank page.

*   *   *

Again, then, as with King Arthur, we have a wealth of literary sources for Homer and the Trojan war, but little or no historical evidence.

In the closing years of the sixteenth century, George Chapman prefaced his translations of *Iliad* and *Odyssey* with: 'Of all the books extant in all kinds, Homer is the first and best. No one before [him] was there any whom he imitated; nor after him any that could imitate him'. Three and a half centuries later, T.E. Lawrence wrote in the preface to his curious prose translation of the *Odyssey* that he considered Homer's epic not only the oldest book worth reading for its story, but also that it was the first European novel. Later, E.V. Rieu introduced his more scholarly translation in similar vein, with a claim for the epic as 'the true ancestor of the long line of novels that have followed it'; and went on to say, 'though it is the first, I am not sure that it is still not the best' [Rieu 1946]. The present-day Homeric scholar, P.N. Furbank, has dismissed that claim: 'of course, Rieu does not mean a word of it; and it would be the silliest way imaginable of praising Homer to declare him a better novelist than Dostoevsky or Proust'; but he continues: 'the influence and authority of Homer has been staggering, and the attempt to translate him and rewrite him ... has, over nearly three thousand years, produced a body of magnificent writing' [Furbank 1992].

While it may be questionable to equate or compare Homer with a novelist, it is demonstrably true that Homer has had a 'staggering' effect on millennia of literature, both in classical times and in the centuries of our own era. Many works take up the theme of a hero's wanderings, perhaps the best-known even if not the most widely-read being James Joyce's *Ulysses*.

Following George Chapman's fine English verse translation in the late sixteenth century, Homer's texts were further translated by Alexander Pope in the early eighteenth, although there were questions as to just how 'Homeric' his verse was. These were followed in turn by a number of Victorian prose translations by Lang, Leaf, Myers, Butcher and others, which were the forerunners of present-day verse translations. Modern Homeric scholarship has facilitated the excellence of poetic work such as the outstanding translations of both *Iliad* and *Odyssey* by Richmond Lattimore.

It is not an option for many to read Homer in the original Greek. Faced with a wealth of versions of the Homeric texts, it is important to remember that we are reading in translation, however faithful it may be to the original, or however technically competent. When Alexander Pope pressed Richard Bentley to comment on his translation of the *Iliad*, Bentley is said to have replied, 'It is a pretty poem, Mr Pope, but you must not call it Homer'.

Bentley's put-down makes the point: Pope's translation may itself have been a fine poem, but Homer's originals were far more rugged and robust than that. In these monumental epics, the Greeks found what they believed to be the history of their people and what were for them eternal truths about the dealings of the gods with mortals. The transcendent, mythic qualities of both *Iliad* and *Odyssey* have made their mark on millennia of western societies, and continue to do so today, even if now we find ourselves questioning their historicity.

If the ten years of the Trojan war were waged in the mid-thirteenth century BCE, then (according to the stories which are told) there were possibly near-contemporary and significant events taking place in Mediterranean lands further to the east and south. What are we going to make of these narratives, the stories of the Hebrew people?

Chapter Ten

Moses: The Stories

Corn in Egypt

Long, long ago in the land of Canaan, among the Hebrew nomads following their flocks in search of fresh pastures, there was a small clan whose chieftain had two names. He had been called Jacob by his father Isaac, but he was also known as Israel, a name meaning 'Striver-with-God'. This nickname had been given to him in his younger days by a mysterious stranger, an angel perhaps, who had attacked Jacob one night while on his travels. Failing to overcome Jacob, the stranger gave him the name Israel, because, he said, 'you have striven with gods and with men, and have overcome'.

Now an old man of one hundred and thirty years, Jacob Israel was desperately anxious for his clan, suffering from a prolonged famine in Canaan. When he heard that there was corn in Egypt, Jacob began to wonder whether he should move his people there, if they were to avoid starvation. One night, the god of his father and of his father's father appeared to him in a dream, and told him not to be afraid to go to Egypt. This god of Jacob's ancestors said that he would go to Egypt with his clan, and promised to bring his people back safely, and make them into a great nation. So, encouraged by the god's promise, the little clan of Israel packed up their tents, gathered their flocks, and set out on the long journey to Egypt. There were just seventy people, Jacob Israel and eleven of his sons, with their wives and children.

Many years before, Jacob had had another son, a much-favoured—and some might say spoilt—youngest boy called Joseph. But Joseph had been sold by his jealous brothers to some passing slave traders, and nothing had been heard of him since. But things had in fact turned out well for Joseph. After years of adversity and many adventures, but still only thirty years old, Joseph had the great fortune to become viceroy of all Egypt, accountable only to the pharaoh. When he discovered that his family had arrived in Egypt, Joseph made himself known to his incredulous father, who was overjoyed to find his son still alive, and to his estranged brothers, with whom Joseph was now reconciled. So, with such a highly-placed friend at court, the clan of Israel was assured of security and prosperity and was given land in which to settle.

Jacob Israel remained in Egypt for seventeen years until his death; and as the years went by, the whole generation that had come from Canaan had passed away too. However, Israel's descendants had prospered and become very numerous. When a new pharaoh came to the throne, one who had not known Joseph or his family, he felt that the ever-growing numbers of this immigrant population posed a threat to his land. So he appointed slave masters over the Hebrews, and used them as forced labour to build new cities at Rameses.

Moses, Prince of Egypt

The new pharaoh, determined to eliminate this potential threat to his people's security, gave orders that henceforth all newborn Hebrew boys be thrown into the Nile. However, when a baby boy was born to a Hebrew woman named Jochebed, wife of Amram, a great-grandson of Jacob Israel, they determined to keep him safe, and hid him. After three months, though, they could hide him no longer. Jochebed found a basket, made it water-tight with tar, and placing her baby in the basket put him in the bulrushes at the side of the Nile.

When a daughter of the pharaoh came to the river to bathe as was her practice, she found the baby, and realised it was a Hebrew child. The baby boy's sister, who had been standing watching nearby, asked the princess whether she should fetch one of the Hebrew women to nurse the baby. The princess agreed; but unknown to her, it was Jochebed, the baby's own mother, who was called to nurse the baby, and she was paid by the princess to do so. When the baby was weaned, the daughter of the pharaoh adopted him and raised him as her own son. She called him Moses, a name that sounds like the Hebrew word for 'removed', because, she said, she had removed him from the river.

Many years later, Moses went out to Rameses to see how his fellow-countrymen, the enslaved Hebrews, were faring. There he saw a Hebrew being ill-treated by an Egyptian slave master, and in anger he hit the oppressor, killing him. Thinking that no one was looking, Moses hid the body in the sand. Next day, he came across two Hebrews brawling, and asked one why he was attacking his fellow-countryman. 'Who are you to be a judge over us?' retorted the man. 'Do you intend killing me, the way you killed that Egyptian yesterday?'

Terrified by the knowledge that if news of what he had done should come to the ears of the pharaoh, he would have him executed, Moses fled and crossed the wilderness of Sinai until he came to the land of Midian.

Moses in Exile

As Moses sat resting by a well in Midian, some young women came to water their father's sheep, but were driven away by local shepherds. Moses came to the young women's assistance and watered the sheep for them. They returned excitedly to their father, a priest named Jethro, telling him how an Egyptian had helped them. Jethro was surprised that they had shown so little hospitality to a foreign stranger, leaving him sitting by the well, and they called Moses to come and eat with them. Moses remained with Jethro and his family, and married one of the daughters, Zipporah.

For forty years, Moses looked after Jethro's sheep. One day, as they pastured near the holy mountain of Horeb,

Moses' attention was taken by a sight which totally amazed him: a bush had caught alight but was not being destroyed by the flames. As he approached to look more closely at this extraordinary sight, Moses was astonished and then terrified to hear his name being called from the middle of the burning bush.

Moses was told to remove his sandals, because he was standing on holy ground. Then from out of the bush the voice said, 'I am the god worshipped by your forefathers, Abraham, Isaac and Jacob. I have seen my people suffering in Egypt and am going to release them from slavery and return them to a land that I promised to your ancestors long ago. And you, Moses, are going to help me.'

Unknown to Moses, his forefather Abraham had not been above arguing with this god of his. Moses was all set to do the same. He could immediately think of a number of reasons why it might not be a good idea to return to Egypt. He began to argue with the Voice: 'Go back to Egypt? Would that be smart? I go back, the pharaoh kills me. So then where am I?' No answer came from the bush. Moses tried again: 'All right. I go back. I tell these Hebrews their god has sent me. Why do they care? Some foreign stranger they don't know from Adam, why do they believe me?' Still no reply from the bush. 'And another thing ...' (Moses was not giving up) 'Am I such a good choice to speak to your people, with a stut ... stut ... stutter like mine? Someone else should go, far better.'

Now the Voice spoke again, sounding impatient. This was none other than El-Shaddai, God the Almighty One. Everyone who had wanted to kill Moses was now dead, God the Almighty assured him. 'And in any case,' he added, 'I shall be with you. As for my name, I AM is who I am. Tell my people that I AM has sent you, the god of Abraham and Isaac and Jacob. The men of old knew me as El-Shaddai, because I had not yet told them my name. But my name is Yahweh, and that is the name by which I shall now be known for all time. As for your ability to speak, I have arranged for your brother Aaron to be your mouthpiece, and he is already on his way here to meet you.'

Moses had not given up yet. He was not so sure that the Hebrews would believe him, if he told them that their ancestors' god had sent him. Yahweh patiently assured Moses that he would give proof of his authority, and proceeded to show Moses what he meant. 'Put your hand inside your cloak,' Yahweh said, and when Moses did and took his hand out again, it was eaten away with leprosy. When Yahweh told him to put his hand back inside his cloak, it was healed. Moses was then instructed to throw his staff down on the ground, and it turned into a snake. Yahweh told Moses to pick up the snake by its tail, and it became his staff again.

Now Moses could see that Yahweh was determined that he should return to Egypt. So he went home to his father-in-law, asking leave to go back to see whether his relatives were still alive; and with Jethro's blessing, Moses began to retrace the long journey he had made many years before. On the way, he met his older brother Aaron, as Yahweh had said he would, and told him all that their ancestors' god had in mind for them to do once they were back in Egypt.

Let My People Go

In his conversation with Yahweh, Moses had been warned that there would be some difficulty in persuading the pharaoh to let the Hebrew slaves go free. Moses and Aaron were about to discover how true this was going to be.

The brothers went to the pharaoh, telling him that the Hebrews' god Yahweh wanted his people to go into the desert for three days, to observe a religious feast. The pharaoh's response was instant: he knew nothing of any gods called Yahweh, and anyway what were Moses and Aaron thinking of, taking the people away from their work? So now the slave-drivers were to make life even harder for the Hebrew slaves: the straw needed for brick-making was no longer to be supplied, but they were to gather their own straw. The slaves still had to meet the same daily production tally, though, and if they did not, the Hebrew foremen were to be flogged.

The Hebrew foremen were dismayed by this news, cursing Moses and Aaron and this god of theirs for making even worse their already intolerable lives. Moses in turn had words with God: 'You tell me to come here. I do as I'm told. Now see what trouble we're in! Your people were badly treated before. Now they are treated worse. Your people would be set free, you said. So when will that be, tell me?'

Yahweh replied that he intended to keep the promise made to Abraham, Isaac and Jacob, that Canaan, where they had lived as strangers, would be their land in which to settle. Moses and Aaron were to tell the Hebrews that Yahweh would free them from captivity, adopt them as his people, that he would be their god, and would lead them to this promised land. But the people were so cowed and defeated that they would not listen to what sounded like pious nonsense.

Once more Moses and his brother returned to the pharaoh, to make their request. To demonstrate that they came with Yahweh's authority, Aaron threw down his staff and it became a snake; but the Egyptian sorcerers were able to do the same with their staffs, although Aaron's snake ate their snakes! The pharaoh remained unmoved by this sign, insisting that the Hebrews were not going into the wilderness for any religious festivals, and that was that.

Over the coming days, more dramatic signs followed. The Nile and all the drinking water throughout Egypt were turned to blood, although the Hebrews' water was spared. Then the land was plagued with frogs which crawled and hopped everywhere. The invading frogs were followed by countless maggots that got into everything, and then the land was infested with swarming flies. With each plague, the pharaoh relented, but as soon as Moses arranged for everything to return to normal, he reneged and refused to let the people go.

So the plagues continued, one after another. All the livestock in the land was suddenly diseased, then boils broke out on all the Egyptians. After that the most violent hail-storm destroyed crops and property, a hot wind blew and brought a plague of locusts, and that was followed by three days of pitch darkness, when no one could see a thing. In spite of all these disasters, the pharaoh remained adamant: the Hebrew slaves were staying where they were.

Finally, Yahweh told Moses to prepare the Hebrews for the final terror, an event that would not only persuade the pharaoh to let them go, but also one that was to be remembered and celebrated for all time, by them and by all succeeding generations.

The Hebrews were told to prepare for departure. Each family was to take a lamb or a young goat and kill it, smearing some of its blood on the doorpost of their house. The meat was to be roasted and then eaten hastily with unleavened bread. Everyone was to be dressed and ready to leave. On that night God would pass over Egypt and every first-born male would die; but the destroying angel would not enter any house where there was blood smeared on the doorpost. God commanded that this momentous event, the deliverance of his people from slavery, was to be observed for all time as the feast of unleavened bread, because this was the Passover of Yahweh.

At midnight, this terror descended on Egypt: the eldest son in every family was killed, and every first-born of their cattle, and only the Hebrews were spared, as Yahweh had promised. There was not an Egyptian home without a death, even the palace of the pharaoh. In panic he summoned Moses and Aaron, demanding that they get the Hebrew people out of his country, this very minute.

And so it was that the descendants of Jacob Israel left the land where they had been in bondage for more than four hundred years, and began their journey to the land promised to them by their God.

The Exodus

To the sound of the wailing of grief throughout the land of Egypt, the Hebrews set out into the darkness of the desert, six hundred thousand men, together with women and children and all their herds and flocks. Yahweh led the way, guiding them with a column of fire as they journeyed through the night, and with a pillar of cloud as they travelled by day.

When the pharaoh realised what he had done in letting the slaves go free, losing all his construction workers at a stroke, he assembled chariots, cavalry and infantry and set out in hot pursuit. The Hebrews were camped near the Red Sea, and were horrified to see the approaching army. Rounding on Moses in fury and dismay, they exclaimed, 'There were graves in Egypt, and you bring us here to die? So we were slaves, but which is better — being in chains or dying in the desert? How can we escape — a vast army on one side, the sea on the other?'

Moses now showed his leadership. 'Do not be afraid,' he cried out. 'Now you will see how Yahweh has promised to deliver you.' Doing as he had been instructed, Moses stretched out his staff towards the sea, the water rolled back, and the seabed became dry land! The Hebrews were able to pass over dry-shod, with sea water heaped up like a wall on either side of them. The Egyptian army followed in hot pursuit, but God commanded Moses to stretch out his staff again, and the sea returned, drowning those who sought to recapture God's people.

Safe at last from the pursuing Egyptians, the people of Israel travelled for three days across the desert but had no water. They came eventually to some springs but their relief was short-lived: the water was so bitter that it was impossible to drink it. Again they complained to Moses, and once more he asked Yahweh for help. Yahweh pointed out a kind of wood which, when thrown into the springs, made the water sweet and drinkable and the people were satisfied.

This was not to be the last time that the Israelites were in uproar, blaming Moses for leading them into a waterless desert. Later, when they came near Mount Horeb, the thirsty people again demanded action from Moses. Yahweh told him to strike a rock with his staff and fresh water came pouring out. It is said by some that this rock then accompanied the Israelites for the remainder of their desert wandering.

Now Yahweh gave his people their first rule of life: if they listened to his voice and followed his commandments, then they would suffer none of the afflictions that had befallen the Egyptians, and Yahweh would ensure their wellbeing.

Manna from Heaven

The people were not content for long, however, and Yahweh was about to test their readiness to obey his commandments. As the Israelites complained of hunger, Moses went yet again to get his instructions from God. God told him that he was about to rain bread on the desert, and Moses was to tell the people to go each morning and gather as much as they needed for that day. On each sixth morning they were to collect a double quantity, because the seventh day was to be a day of rest, the sabbath. Moreover, they were not to keep any bread overnight, except on the sixth night, prior to the sabbath, or the bread would rot.

When the Israelites awoke next morning, it was as Moses had said. The ground was covered with something white, and the people picked it up, asking '*Man-hu*, What is it?' Tentatively, someone put a little of this manna into his mouth, and found that it tasted like a wafer made with honey. So the people gladly collected the day's supply, some picking up more and some less than others; but it was found that those who had picked up more did not have too much, and those who had collected less had enough for the day.

Some people, though, kept some of the manna overnight, and in the morning found it was putrid and foul-smelling. Moses was furious with this disregard for Yahweh's new law. Others, on the seventh morning, went out to collect manna but found none. It was Yahweh's turn now to be angry and he demanded of Moses, 'How long will you Israelites go on refusing to obey my commandments?'

Although his people did indeed continue to disobey his laws, their god provided manna throughout their forty years of wandering in the wilderness, until they reached the promised land. Not that they were always satisfied with this unfailing providence. More than once their patience ran out and they complained against Yahweh and against Moses, asking why they had been brought out of Egypt, only to die in a waterless desert where there was no proper food.

Yahweh's patience too was tried, and he sent venomous snakes among this ungrateful people, and those who were bitten died. Once more, the Israelites acknowledged their disobedience and pleaded with Moses to ask God to take the snakes away. Moses crafted a huge bronze serpent and set it up high on a pole, and anyone bitten by a snake recovered if they looked up at the bronze image.

But still the Israelites had not learnt the lesson. A man named Korah led a revolt of several hundred men against Moses, accusing him of having no more special relationship with this god than anyone else had. Moses announced to the people that a sign would be given to prove that he had indeed been called and sanctified to serve Yahweh: if the earth split open and swallowed the rebels, Moses declared, then all Israel would know the truth. At that moment, the ground opened and Korah and the hundreds who had rebelled with him went down alive to Sheol, the underworld, and the ground closed again over them.

The Battles Begin

As it advanced in a distant cloud of dust, a seemingly unending column of what appeared to be invaders moving toward their country was inevitably seen as a threat by the people living in the lands of Sinai and the Negev.

The Amalekites, descendants of Jacob Israel's estranged brother, Esau, were the first to venture out to fight against the approaching Israelites. Moses ordered his second-in-command, Joshua, to enlist men to meet the enemy. Moses stood on a hilltop, urging the Israelites on. While he held high the staff of the Lord, the Israelites prevailed over Amalek. When Moses' arms tired and he dropped the staff, the Amalekites gained the advantage. Aaron and Hur found a rock for Moses to sit on and they held up his hands, one on each side, and they stayed there until sunset. And so the warriors of Israel won their first battle, defeating the Amalekites.

Sometimes Yahweh led the people on a detour to avoid hostile cities and one of these detours brought the Israelites back very near to the Red Sea, where years before they had narrowly escaped recapture by the Egyptians. But conflict was unavoidable. One of the Canaanite kings, Arad, whose lands were in the Negev, came out to fight the Israelites and took some of their number prisoner. But the Israelites, believing that God was on their side, defeated Arad and destroyed all his towns.

There were times when the advancing people of Israel sought safe passage through a country, promising to keep to the main highway, taking nothing from the fields and leaving the wells alone. King Sihon of the Amorites would not listen to such undertakings and led his whole army against the Israelites. That was his mistake: the Amorites were defeated and the Israelites occupied all their towns. King Og of Bashan was the next to oppose the Israelites but he and his whole army suffered the same fate as the Amorites.

The people of Israel were no longer a rabble of migrant ex-slaves, but a feared fighting force. The Canaanite and Hittite kings became increasingly terrified by the invading horde, and they had every reason to be afraid. One after another, their cities were destroyed, and their land occupied by the Israelites. Midian, which had been in alliance with Moab and the Amorites, shared their fate. Nor were the battles to end even when the people of Israel finally crossed the River Jordan to enter the promised land. The spectacular defeat of Jericho and the destruction of Ai were yet to come, and all the conquests of the Canaanite lands under the leadership of Joshua still lay in the future.

The Ten Commandments

It was after only three months in the wilderness that Yahweh had led the Israelites as far as Mount Sinai and there established his covenant with them. Some say that these events took place at Mount Horeb. Yahweh called Moses up into the mountain and there declared that if Israel would listen to him and keep his covenant, they would become his special people, a kingdom of priests, a holy nation. Moses carried this momentous news of this god's promises down to the people and with one voice they cried out that whatever Yahweh said, they would do. Back up the mountain went Moses, to relay the Israelites' response to God.

Then Moses began to receive the first of Yahweh's laws, ten concise and unambiguous commandments, followed by many more detailed precepts. Once more, Moses descended Mount Sinai and relayed to the people all that Yahweh had commanded. Once more, they cried out that whatever was required of them, they would do.

Moses was called back to the mountain again, this time with Aaron and his sons, accompanied by seventy elders, and they saw their god standing there, on a pavement of sapphire, as blue as the sky. Moses made a number of return visits to the holy mountain of Sinai, and continued to receive detailed laws concerning every aspect of the Israelites' lives, how they were to worship, festivals to be observed, regulations for the family, how to behave with neighbours, dietary and hygiene laws, sexual and other moral precepts, punishment for crimes, hospitality to strangers, how to treat their slaves, and many other commandments.

Yahweh handed Moses two stone tablets on which the law was engraved, written on both sides by the finger of

God himself, and Moses carried them down the mountain. But he had been gone for more than forty days, hidden in the smoke and fiery cloud on Mount Sinai, and the people had grown restless. Not knowing what had become of Moses, they called on Aaron to make a god to lead them. They collected their gold jewellery, melted it and crafted the image of a golden bull calf, and cried out, 'This is the god that brought you out of Egypt!' Then they set about celebrating, with feasting and singing and dancing.

As Moses arrived back in the camp, he was enraged by what he saw. In his fury, he threw down the tablets of stone, which shattered. Realising that the people were out of control, he called out, 'Those who are on the Lord's side, come here to me.' It was the men of the tribe of Levi who rallied to Moses' side and he commanded them to take their swords and go and slay the idolatrous people. More than three thousand people died at their hands, and Moses blessed the Levites for their loyalty, appointing them as the people's priests.

Moses returned to Mount Sinai and there sought forgiveness for the people's waywardness. In forgiving the Israelites, Yahweh renewed his covenant with them, and replaced the broken tablets, on which he wrote the law. If only they would keep his commandments, he promised, he would cast out all the nations in the land that he had promised to them, and Israel would be known for all time as God's chosen people.

At Last, the Promised Land

When the people of Israel came to the land to the east of the River Jordan, Moses sent out twelve men, one from each of the tribes, to spy out the land beyond the river. He instructed them to see how strong the inhabitants were, and how numerous, what the terrain was like, and whether the cities were fortified. They were to see how fertile the land was, and whether it was wooded, and they were to bring back some of the fruit of the land.

After forty days, the spies returned, bringing both good news and bad. The good news was that the land was flowing with milk and honey, and the twelve showed the grapes, pomegranates and figs that they had gathered. The bad news was that the land was inhabited by people of formidable stature, among them the giant Nephilim. In the presence of these huge beings, the spies trembled to relate, they felt no bigger than grasshoppers. Then the Israelites were dismayed and once again demanded to know why they had spent all these years wandering about in the desert, only to face annihilation by a nation of giants. They even began to speak of choosing leaders to take them back to Egypt!

However, Yahweh was to be as good as his word, and the time was now very close when his people would enter the promised land. Moses stood on a hill above the Jordan valley, looking westwards toward Jericho, and Yahweh showed him all the country that the people were to occupy as their own. But God had long ago sworn that because of the people's disobedience and many rebellions, none of those who had seen his signs in Egypt or in the wilderness would enter this new country, apart from Joshua and a man named Caleb. Even Moses was not to enter the promised land, though he had now at last been able to see it from a distance, and he died there and was buried, though to this day no one knows his burial place. Moses was one hundred and twenty years old when he died, still a vigorous man and with good eyesight, in spite of his great age.

The people of Israel mourned for thirty days, and then their new leader Joshua was told by Yahweh to get them ready to cross the River Jordan. The river was in full flood, but as soon as the priests stepped into the water, it stopped flowing and the river was banked up like a wall, and all the people crossed dry-shod. And so the people of Israel entered the land that their god had promised so long ago, to their forefathers Abraham, Isaac and Jacob.

*   *   *

These, then, are the stories of a captive people, freed from slavery and led into a land that they believed had been promised to them by their ancestors' god, the Almighty God, to whom they were now bound by an everlasting covenant.

But to what extent and on what grounds can this be described as an historical narrative? In what ways is it different from the stories of the Trojan war, for example, with its apparent mix of legend and myth, with origins in a very ancient past? What is to be made of a sea that parts to provide a dry road for fleeing refugees? Or a god seen standing on a mountain ledge as blue as sapphire, who gives to his chosen spokesman stone tablets hand-engraved with divine law? And what of a voice from a burning bush, or manna from heaven, or terrifying giants?

Where did these stories come from, and where among it all is the history?

Chapter Eleven

Moses: Sources and History, Part 1

To speak of plural sources of the stories of Moses and the exodus may be something of an exaggeration, because to date we have only one source — the Hebrew Bible, or more specifically its first five books, known collectively as the *Torah* or The Law, and referred to as the Pentateuch.

As we give thought to the stories of Moses, we will do what we did with the stories of King Arthur and the Homeric epics: first look at the source of the narrative and its possible origins, before coming to questions of historicity. Central to that enquiry are questions about the history of the source itself, asking what kind of document it is and where it came from. While there is only this one documentary source for the stories of Moses, its study has occupied countless philosophers and theologians for many centuries, and continues to form a probably unparalleled body of wide-ranging and in-depth scholarship. Clearly, against such a background, it is decidedly presumptuous to attempt any kind of summary here, but that is what we shall try to do.

A reminder may be in order here: the Hebrew Bible's content, though not the way in which its books are arranged, is the same as that of the Christian Bible's first part, the Old Testament. However, whereas Judaism holds this collection of texts to be complete in itself, Christianity believes that it prefigures and is fulfilled in the New Testament, the Christian Bible's second part.

The five books of the Law, the *Torah*, where the stories of Moses and his forebears are to be found, form the first of three collections which make up the Hebrew Bible: the second, *Nebiim*, The Prophets, consists of eight books, and the third, *Kethubim*, The Writings, contains a further eleven. The Bible was written in classical Hebrew, although just when that might have been is a question we need to examine more closely a little later.

The earliest manuscripts of the Hebrew Bible known so far date from some time in the last two centuries BCE, and were among the Dead Sea scrolls discovered in 1947 in desert caves at Qumràn, east of Jerusalem. The scrolls range across the whole Hebrew Bible, although in most cases only in fragments. These Qumran manuscripts are something like a thousand years older than the earliest surviving document known prior to their discovery, which was a ninth or tenth century CE copy of the Masoretic Bible (*masorah* is Hebrew for tradition). The Masoretes were Jewish scholars who established an authorized, canonical version of the Hebrew Bible in the early centuries of our era, editing ancient texts which had survived the Romans' destruction of Jerusalem in 70 CE.

During the third to second centuries BCE, the Hebrew Bible was translated for Greek-speaking Jews. This Greek version is referred to as the Septuagint or LXX, as it is said to have been translated by seventy scribes — seventy-two, to be more precise, six from each of the twelve tribes of Israel.

In the early centuries of our era, the spread of Christianity, the new religion which had grown out of Judaism, gave rise to a need for a Latin version of the Bible. In the fourth century, a Latin translation was commissioned by the Pope, and this was undertaken by a biblical scholar, Jerome, who worked not from the Greek Septuagint but direct from the Hebrew text. Jerome's version collected the Hebrew Bible's twenty-four books and re-arranged them as thirty-nine, separating, for example, the contents of *The*

Book of the Twelve into the twelve minor prophets. To this
so-called 'Old Testament', Jerome added the books of the
Apocrypha, a number of deutero-canonical books which
are not in the Hebrew Bible. He also included for the first
time a number of Christian writings, which now form the
twenty-seven books of the Christian church's New Testament. Referred to as the Vulgate—a book in the common
tongue—Jerome's Latin Bible remained the original on
which later English translations authorised by the Roman
Catholic church were based, whereas Protestant translations have had their origins in the Hebrew Masoretic text.

A problem will be readily recognized here. Most present-day readers of the Bible read the text in their own modern language, other than those able to read and
understand classical Hebrew, Greek, or Latin. In all probability, that modern language version will itself be just one
of a series of versions, translated and updated a number of
times over literally centuries, deriving from a number of
variant texts, with their origins in collections of manuscripts written in what are now dead languages. In other
words, it has come a long way from the original. Therein
lies the problem for modern-day translators. Without
question, centuries of study have ensured a good understanding of those dead languages, although certainty
about meaning gradually decreases as one moves down
through the layers of a language's structure, from gram-
mar to vocabulary, to the idiosyncrasies of idiom and
finally to the subtlety of nuance; but translators can never
be absolutely certain that they have got back to the true
and authentic meaning of the original author's text. It can
be seen that the processes of translating from Hebrew into
Greek into Latin and finally into a modern language, and
then updating that version as modern language gradually
changes, must raise questions about a faithful rendering of
the original, whatever the original may have been.

In Judaism, the five books of the *Torah*, The Law, are
accorded the authority of Moses, who is believed to have
received this law direct from God. However, even the
most ancient manuscripts available to date appear to make

no specific claim that the five books were literally written, or at least written in their entirety, by Moses. The few texts that make direct reference to Moses actually writing seem to relate to specific and limited passages within the books. Rather, the transmission of the law appears to be oral. Formulaic phrases appear over and over again throughout the Mosaic narratives, such as 'The Lord spoke to Moses and said, Tell the Israelites ...'. This makes clear the expectation that the Israelites would pass down their tradition by word of mouth, from generation to generation:

> When in time to come your son asks you what this means, say to him, 'By the strength of his hand the Lord brought us out of Egypt, out of the land of slavery'. [*Exodus* 13:14]

References from the first century of our era show that the early Jewish Christians retained the traditional belief that Moses was literally the author of the Bible's first five books. The New Testament writers, the great majority of whom were Jews, not only stated their own unquestioned acceptance of the Mosaic authorship, but also put the words into the mouth of Jesus. The belief in Moses as the author of the Pentateuch is maintained within the tradition of Judaism, and is shared by probably the majority of Christians today.

In English translations, the books' main titles derive from the Greek Septuagint: the first is *Genesis*, the second *Exodus*, and so on. To the title *Genesis*, early Protestant translations added 'The First Book of Moses'; *Exodus* was 'The Second Book of Moses', and so on. More modern translations, in English anyway, have discontinued that practice; but in German Bibles, Luther's names for the books, as 'Das erste (zweite, dritte, etc.) Buch Mose', tend still to be used. The discussion here questions whether there is any evidence for accepting as historically sustainable the idea that a man named Moses was literally the books' author, although Mosaic *authority* is a different question.

What, then, do these 'books of Moses' contain?

The first of the five books, *Genesis*, opens with two intertwined accounts of the creation. Then follow the stories of

Adam and Eve, Cain and Abel, and a number of surprisingly brief references to a succession of shadowy figures, all of whom, the stories tell us, lived for many hundreds of years, but who were clearly regarded as a part of this primordial history. Methuselah, for example, seven generations after the first man Adam, is said to have lived for nine hundred and sixty nine years; but for all that, he is given no more than three or four verses in the narrative, referring only to the names of his father and his son, and to his great age. In reading these fragments, one seems to catch glimpses of other, longer narratives about these legendary figures, of which we now have no trace.

Methuselah's grandson was Noah. Contrasted with the short shrift given to his forebears, Noah is accorded several whole chapters in *Genesis*. This ancient narrative tells how God saw that human beings had become wicked, and he bitterly regretted creating mankind. But there remained just one righteous man, Noah. Together with his family and two of every kind of bird and animal, Noah was saved from the flood that God sent to devastate the whole earth. It was with Noah that God first established his covenant, pointing to the rainbow in the sky as the sign of the covenant that he had established with all of his creation. God's covenant with mankind is the most fundamental element within Judaism, and is the thread which runs throughout the whole of the *Torah*.

The stories of Noah's ark and the flood are followed briefly by what again appears to be a fragment of another, longer narrative. No more than nine verses tell the story of the tower of Babel, when God intervened to bring an overly-ambitious humankind literally down to earth, frustrating their plans to build a tower up to heaven. All at once, the tower builders found themselves speaking different languages, which prevented their understanding each other, and God dispersed these diverse people across the whole earth.

At this point, there is suddenly a very real sense that *Genesis* has at last come to its main theme. The greater part of the book, the remaining thirty-nine of its fifty chapters, is in effect an epic cycle, telling the stories of the great family of patriarchs, Abraham, Isaac and Jacob. This cycle, told at length, introduces the concept of a promised land, and prepares the ground for the great Mosaic narratives, which tell how Abraham's descendants are enslaved, then freed and chosen as God's people. It was to Abraham that God promised:

> I shall maintain my covenant with you and your descendants after you, generation after generation, an everlasting covenant: I shall be your God, yours and your descendants'. As a possession for all time I shall give you and your descendants after you the land in which you are now aliens, the whole of Canaan, and I shall be their God. [*Genesis* 17:7-8]

The Abraham narrative in *Genesis* is followed by stories of his son Isaac, and finally by the epic of Isaac's son Jacob Israel and his emigration to Egypt at the time of famine in Canaan. The Bible's first book closes with the death of Jacob.

The scene is now set for the encyclopaedic sweep of the four remaining books of the *Torah*, which not only tell the stories of the exodus and of Moses the Lawgiver, but more significantly record at length and in precise detail the law that God gave, through Moses, to his chosen people, with whom he had established an everlasting covenant. That promise is confirmed for all time, in the stories of Moses, when God called to him from the mountain at Sinai:

> If only you will now listen to me and keep my covenant, then out of all peoples you will become my special possession ... You will be to me a kingdom of priests, my holy nation. [*Exodus* 19:5-6]

It is the everlasting covenant of God with Israel, and the law for all time, handed down by God to his chosen people, which give meaning to the stories of Moses, found in this great five-volume source, the Pentateuch, the Jewish *Torah*.

* * *

There is, then, an obvious sense in which the Pentateuch does indeed constitute five books of Moses, if by that we mean books about Moses. The first book, *Genesis*, sets the scene, literally from the beginning of time, for the coming of Moses; and the other four books, *Exodus*, *Leviticus*, *Numbers* and *Deuteronomy*, narrate the stories of Moses: how at God's bidding he led the captive Israelites out of Egypt, guided them through forty years of desert wanderings, was the medium through whom God established his law and covenant with Israel, and eventually brought them to the promised land, or at least to its borders.

The question remains, however: were these books written by Moses? Modern scholarship — indeed, scholarship for the best part of two centuries — seems all but unanimous in answering no, but on the other hand has so far been able to offer only theoretical alternative explanations.

Even a cursory reading of the Pentateuch's five books gives a very clear impression of multiple authorship, not least because of their very different literary styles. On the other hand, it was argued when discussing the origins of Homer's *Iliad* and the *Odyssey*, that different styles do not in themselves necessarily indicate more than one author.

There does seem to be evidence within the Pentateuchal text, however, of widely differing origins for the Mosaic narratives: indeed, in some places, more than one origin for a single narrative, and frequently different sources appear to be intermingled. There are also a number of seemingly unrelated textual fragments, inconsistencies, and sections of text repeated in quite different contexts, similar to those that characterise the two Homeric epics, and suggest ancient, multi-stranded oral traditions as a source. J.N. Schofield has suggested that the earliest of the *Genesis* narratives were 'probably taken from Palestine's *Canterbury Tales* — the folklore and legends sung at the sanctuaries to travellers on the pilgrim routes to the great festivals' [Schofield 1964].

The creation myth itself bears the marks of two different traditions. We have already noted that the stories which follow immediately after the Adam-and-Eve narrative appear to be fragments of what may well have been much longer but regrettably now-lost narratives, quite possibly oral traditions, about these rather shadowy figures, legendary men who may have been types rather than historical individuals.

Enoch, Methuselah's father, is possibly the best example. Representing the sixth generation after Adam, Enoch is given no more than half a dozen verses in *Genesis*. And yet he had the remarkable distinction of being a man who not only walked with God, but was also one of only two people in the Bible 'taken by God' and said not to have died. The prophet Elijah was the other.

This virtually unique significance attributed to Enoch is surely deserving of far more heroic treatment than a handful of verses tucked away at the beginning of *Genesis*. There is in fact evidence that in earlier times he was indeed accorded a status better suited to a man who walked and talked with God. An Aramaic manuscript of the extra-canonical book of *Enoch*, previously known only in Greek and Latin translations, was unearthed among the scrolls found at Qumran; and its existence seems to be one example of a vast array of ancient heroic traditions, probably oral in origin, later collected, edited and preserved in written form. In the Bible itself there are references to other such writings, some extant, many more lost: *The Book of the Wars of Yahweh*, a lost collection of ancient war songs, is one example; *The Book of the Just*, a collection of poems, and the *Book of the Acts of Solomon*, a 'history', are two others. The 'books of Moses' are just a part of this great tradition; but interestingly, it was these writings that were accorded canonical status, and not those others.

In the five 'books of Moses' there appear to be abundant clues to the probability of many-faceted origins — thus suggesting multiple authorship — including textual devices and factors which point to generations of oral traditions, and narratives which not only resemble each other but may themselves have come from a common source in different cultures. For example, it was noted earlier that the *Genesis* story of Noah and the flood matches similar

narratives from other traditions, and may have been borrowed from an ancient Mesopotamian epic. Also from
Mesopotamia comes the story of Sargon, later to be a great
ruler, being abandoned as a baby by his mother, who set
him afloat in the river, placed in a basket of rushes with a
lid sealed with bitumen — a story which is an obvious parallel to that of the infant Moses, but pre-dating it by perhaps a thousand years or more.

From 1929 onwards, following the discovery of the site
of the Canaanite city of Ugarit in Syria, an understanding
was gained not only of the culture of this ancient civilisation, but also the possibility that it formed a common background to both Hebrew and Greek civilisations.
Cuneiform tablets found at Ugarit date from about the
fourteenth century BCE down to the twelfth, the supposed
time of both the Trojan war and the Israelite exodus. Comparisons have been made between Ugaritic epics and biblical and Homeric epics, which they pre-date; and cultural
links have been proposed between Canaan and Mycenae.
Ugarit gave the Phoenicians their alphabet, and the Phoenician alphabet was borrowed both by Hebrew and
Greek — aleph/alpha, beth/beta, gimel/gamma,
daleth/delta and so on.

It seems entirely possible, therefore, that elements of the
Homeric epics and narratives within the early part of the
Hebrew Bible have common roots. A prime example may
be the stories of Abraham being commanded by his god to
sacrifice his son Isaac, and Agamemnon being required by
his gods to sacrifice his daughter Iphigeneia. At the crucial
moment, God the Almighty provided a ram to be sacrificed in place of Isaac; and in one account at least,
Iphigeneia was saved when the goddess Artemis substituted a stag as the sacrificial victim.

A standard device used in ancient epics was to tell of
gods causing the sun to set too soon or else delaying its setting, to give their chosen people time to gain an advantage
over their enemies in battle. In the *Iliad*, Zeus' consort Hera
causes the sun to set early in order to save her beloved
Greeks, hard pressed by the Trojans; on the day of Joshua's

battle against the Amorites, God ensures that the sun should not set until the Israelites have taken vengeance on their enemy.

As we saw while discussing Homeric origins, repetition of scenes is characteristic of oral composition. In *Genesis*, an identical story is told about both Abraham and his son Isaac, with the same events occurring in the same city of the same king, and substantially related in the same words, but first told about Abraham, and later Isaac. Clearly what may have been a legend or a traditional tale is the same story told twice, once about the father, once about the son.

A recurring theme in the patriarchal narratives is that of paired characters, one man going on to succeed within the divine plan, as an ancestor of God's chosen people, the other fading from the scene, or later re-appearing as a baddy: Abraham and his nephew Lot, Isaac and his half-brother Ishmael, Jacob and his brother Esau. This device, associated with oral verse composition, closely resembles that used frequently by Homer: for example, the courageous Hektor contrasted with his cowardly brother Alexandros, or the virtuous Penelope contrasted with the treacherous Klytaimestra.

God's call to Moses, bidding him return to Egypt, seems to be presented in two variants, again, reminiscent of Homer apparently tripping himself up by drawing on more than one source for his story. Moses' father-in-law has different names in different parts of the narrative, Jethro, Reuel and Hobab. Was it by coincidence that Moses found his future wife in precisely the same way as his ancestor Jacob Israel had done, as he sat resting by a well in a foreign land, helping a young woman water her father's sheep? Or was this some kind of traditional story that was borrowed and somehow duplicated in the telling? Was it by chance that Moses' father, grandfather, and great-grandfather all lived to be one hundred and thirty seven years old? Is this repetition fragmentary evidence of some lost, ancient tradition, or is it a device to aid recitation?

The stories of Moses parting the Red Sea and of Joshua parting the River Jordan are similar to those later in the Bible, when the prophets Elijah and Elisha both part the Jordan by striking the water with a rolled-up cloak. Was this a traditional story, a legend, and where or when did the story originate?

A strange but very brief interlude in the story of Moses appears to be curiously out of place and certainly out of style, giving the feeling that it has come from some other narrative. Following Yahweh's call, Moses is obediently making his way back to Egypt, when God met him and would have killed him. Quite why Moses deserved this fate is not made clear, but the narrative picks up again and Moses continues safely on his way, to accomplish God's plans.

It has already been conceded in our discussion that present-day readers may have to decide how to understand any numinous or apparently supernatural elements contained within a narrative. A number of miraculous events occur in the stories of Moses — the parting of the Red Sea, is perhaps the most obvious and spectacular one — and they may have perfectly rational explanations. Even given that possibility, it may not be as easy to explain or accept as fact the story of Balaam's talking donkey, complaining to her master that she objected to being beaten by him three times, just because she has been stopped in her tracks by an angel standing in the road, with his sword drawn [*Numbers* 22:22ff]. Or perhaps this story, told in a single verse later in the Bible, is difficult to accept literally: a burial party, frightened by the sudden appearance of foreign raiders, panicked and dropped the corpse they had been carrying, dumping it into an old grave, that of the great prophet Elisha. As the corpse touched the prophet's bones, the dead man sprang back to life [2 *Kings* 13:21]. These elements may more realistically be identified as coming from a legendary tradition, than forming an historical record.

One of the textual analysts' arguments for the possibility that oral traditions formed the origin of ancient writings such as these, is the presence of verse or song, either as the narrative's main form of composition or as fragments within a prose text. Again, making a comparison with the Homeric tradition: the epics were sung, and would therefore have been composed in a metrical form, not least because the rhythmic structure would have aided memory and performance. Similarly, there are many passages in the *Torah* which are in the form of poetry or song, suggesting oral origins. It is possible that all of the original text was in verse, but only snatches survived by the time the various traditions were collected, edited and finally written.

None of this, of course, begins to offer proof that the Pentateuch's five books were not written by one man, or that they were not written by Moses. Given that the original sources may indeed have been oral traditions, that they came from any number of earlier centuries and even from different cultures, it is entirely possible that one man could have collated them, edited them, and put them into written form.

The opposite view, the proposition that the Pentateuch was compiled and written by a number of different authors, dates back at least to the sixteenth century of our era. Over many years, a number of philosophers and theologians developed critical arguments for the probability that the five books were not written by Moses at all, but by a number of authors, and at different periods in history. The so-called liberal criticism of nineteenth century scholarship, notably the work of the Germans Graf and Wellhausen, undertook detailed textual analysis of the first books of the Bible. Their analytical work in fact encompassed the Hexateuch, as it included the Bible's sixth book, *Joshua*, which continues the narrative from the death of Moses, telling of the Israelites' crossing the River Jordan, and their conquest of Canaan. The scholars' findings, known as the Documentary Hypothesis, produced a theoretical structure which claimed not only to demonstrate multiple authorship for the books, but also to show that the various strands which were finally brought together to form the Hexa/Pentateuch had origins that lay in quite different eras, all of them later than Moses.

The Wellhausen hypothesis described four principal sources for the Pentateuch. The first two were identified through an analysis of the texts' images of God and how God is named in them. The first of these sources is referred to as the *Yahwistic* tradition, and is identified with the (German) initial J. In the J texts, God is named Yahweh, and is portrayed in anthropomorphic terms: he walks and talks with men and women, and is pleased by the aroma rising from burnt sacrifices. The *Elohistic* document, referred to as E, names God as Elohim (interestingly, a plural word); and in this tradition, God is a transcendent figure, making himself known through dreams and visions and in spectacular events. It is thought that the J document was compiled at some time in the ninth century BCE in the southern kingdom of Judah, and the E document a little later, in the northern kingdom of Israel. At the time of the fall of the northern kingdom (more about that in the next chapter), the two documents are thought to have been merged to form JE.

The third document, the *Deuteronomic* source D, is believed to have been a lost book of law discovered during repairs to the temple at Jerusalem in the early seventh century BCE, and may have been written about a century before that. This document was in turn merged with the others, to form JED.

Finally, after the return from exile in Babylon in the sixth century BCE — again, we need to leave that event until the next chapter — the *Priestly Code* P, which is largely made up of law, was combined with the earlier documents to form JEDP, the collection which later became the *Torah*. However, JEDP needs to be envisaged not so much as a neatly-defined and cohesively-edited volume, but more as the confluence of many streams of oral traditions, songs, stories and legends, dating back to time immemorial.

Although a source of controversy, the nineteenth century Documentary Hypothesis formed the basis of a widely-held consensus on possible origins for the Pentateuch, and continues to be quoted as *the* structural origin of the first section of the Bible. Like all such theories, though, it is likely to be superseded, or at least remain a topic of debate. What the theory does do, however, is illustrate the very real probability that these ancient sources of the stories of Moses came from a broad band of origins, both of time and place; and with all their variants of style, their inconsistencies and their duplications, these varied origins may well spell legend, certainly myth, rather more than history.

*   *   *

Once again, then, we have caught glimpses of extensive literary evidence for a number of ancient traditions, perhaps incorporating elements of an historical past, more likely drawing on legends and folklore, maybe passed down orally from generation to generation across many centuries.

At the heart of the *Torah* are the stories of the patriarchs and of the great lawgiver, Moses, and the all-important themes of God's deliverance of his people and his covenant with them. These great figures from Israel's past — at least, from a past portrayed by the books' author or authors — and the events in which they played a part, all have the appearance of recording the origins of a people. But is it history? We need now to consider that question in more detail.

Chapter Twelve

Moses: Sources and History, Part 2

So far, in taking a brief look at the one documentary source for the stories of Moses and of the Israelites' exodus from Egypt, the focus has been on the narrative's literary origins and characteristics. Now we come to other questions, questions of historicity. Do the books of the Pentateuch offer historical evidence of the patriarchs, of Moses, and of Israel's deliverance from slavery? Or are they documents of a quite different nature? Do these narratives tell of the beginnings of the history of a people? For it is very clear, surely, that the very existence of the Jewish people, with their distinctive ancient religion, culture, and their wealth of tradition, has to be taken as evidence of a past that is more than simply legendary?

As these questions are asked, it is important to keep in mind the definition of history which was proposed earlier. To gain anything even approaching a reliably historical view of the past demands a critical study of a wide range of independent sources. For that reason, the biblical record cannot be expected to authenticate itself, although for centuries the way in which the world depicted in the Bible was understood was indeed based wholly on the content of the biblical books. Today, every effort has to be made to employ critical methodologies, to challenge myths — that is to say, narratives which have a symbolic meaning rather than a strictly factual one — and avoid their perpetuation. Extra-biblical evidence will be required if that is to be achieved.

Creationists, which may be taken to include conservative and evangelical Christians, will without doubt wish to uphold the opening chapters of *Genesis* as historically factual, that is to say, recording events which actually took place as they are described: the six days of creation, Adam and Eve in the Garden of Eden, their expulsion by God after eating fruit from the tree of knowledge, Cain murdering his brother Abel, and the stories of generations of men of renown, leading up to the story of Noah and the flood.

The flood described in the *Genesis* narrative is believed by many to have been not only an historical event but also a global cataclysm. There seems to be little doubt that at some time there was such a massive flood, in the region of Mesopotamia at least. Excavation at Ur, in what is today Iraq, uncovered a stratum of clay up to eleven feet thick, calculated to have been laid by a sudden flood perhaps twenty-five feet deep. Whether it was a regional catastrophe limited to Mesopotamia or a disaster that engulfed the whole world, the biblical flood is the motivation for continuing archaeological expeditions to Agri Dagi on the border of Turkey and Armenia, in quest of the ark's resting place. Until remains of Noah's ark are discovered, though, we are bound for the time being to say that the criteria for authenticating the historical nature of the event are not yet met.

The flood narrative serves to illustrate how an event which may have occurred at some point in primordial times — that is, an event which may have happened even if there is no historical evidence for it — becomes the basis of a legend or myth, increasing in scale and significance through generations of oral tradition. The *Genesis* story of the Tower of Babel is another example. The Babylonian ziggurat or temple tower, a steep-sided pyramid, suggests the inspiration for the story of the Tower of Babel. Although the ziggurat at Babylon dates from only the eighth century BCE, similar pyramids were being built as far back as the fourth millennium BCE. Such massive structures would doubtless appear awesome to desert nomads and would readily form the basis of ancient legends about towers being built to reach the heavens.

It is interesting to note in passing that surprisingly detailed attempts have been made to allocate dates to the biblical narratives, beginning with creation itself. Perhaps the most notable 'historian' in this context was the seventeenth century Archbishop James Ussher. His painstaking deductions and calculations, working sequentially through the Bible's texts, arrived at 4004 BCE as the date of the first of the six days of creation. (He was even more precise than that: he believed it all began on 23 October in that year.) Ussher dated the flood in the year 2348, and the exodus in 1491 BCE. His conclusions were widely accepted at the time and his dates for all the biblical narratives were printed at the top of each page of some editions of the Bible certainly well into the nineteenth century.

Whether or not Noah's flood was an historical event, some may consider this story — or stories, really, since two versions from the E and P traditions are intertwined — to be a boundary, a marker between some kind of primordial age and the point where historical figures begin to emerge. Unfortunately, it has to be said that even for those major figures at the centre of the *Genesis* cycle of the patriarchs, there is no independent, verifiable evidence, and it may have to be accepted, for the present at least, that any attempt to establish dates for the patriarchs is set to fail. It seems likely that a centuries-long process of migrating Semitic peoples had become telescoped into the metaphorical three-generation myth of Abraham-Isaac-Jacob.

One of the claims made for the historicity of biblical narratives, and one that initiated the present discussion, is the fact that it is possible to visit places named in the Bible, and see the sites for oneself. One such site, named in *Genesis*, is the cave of Machpela. The cave can be seen at Hebron on the West Bank, and is said to be the burial place of the patriarchs and their wives, Abraham and Sarah, Isaac and Rebecca, Jacob and Leah. It is possible also to visit what is said to be the tomb of Jacob's second wife, Rachel, near Bethlehem. But it may be valid to ask how such sightseeing would be different from visiting (say) Mycenae in present-day Greece or, nearer home, Tintagel in Cornwall. They are historical sites, without doubt, but they are places named within legends and are associated with kings who are themselves legendary. To walk up Mycenae's paved ramp and pass through the massive Lion Gate does not prove that Agamemnon strode this way too; any more than to stand on the ruined ramparts of Tintagel's castle proves that from there Arthur once looked out over his kingdom of Lyonesse, bordered by the sea.

In the closing chapters of *Genesis* and the opening chapter of the Pentateuch's second book, *Exodus*, the pace and the intensity of the biblical narrative seem suddenly to shift up a gear or two. When reading the stories of Israel in ancient Egypt and the exodus narratives which follow, it is easy to gain the impression that here at last is something that can be called history. On the other hand, it may be that it is the references to Egyptian pharaohs, with whom we are already familiar from a multitude of other sources, which impart the sense that we have entered an historical world. After all, it seems hardly possible to read the stories of Moses without visualising the pyramids and the Sphinx in the background.

As we give thought to the possible historicity of Moses and the exodus, it would have been helpful if the author or authors of the Bible's first two books had named the pharaohs who ruled Egypt at that time. Elsewhere in the Pentateuch and throughout the rest of the Hebrew Bible, foreign kings and rulers are named, but these pharaohs are not. Since so much is known about the history of ancient Egypt, those names would have enabled us to gain a much clearer picture of when it was that Jacob is said to have left famine-stricken Canaan and journeyed to Egypt, how long the Hebrews were in captivity, and the date of the Israelites' exodus, desert wanderings and eventual entry to their promised land.

So when did Jacob Israel's clan first migrate to Egypt, how long were the Hebrews there, and when was the exodus? The inescapable answer seems to be that we do not know, or to put it another way, we have only the biblical references, which are themselves inconclusive, and no other very helpful independent evidence.

Let us look at the biblical references. In the Abraham narratives, his god tells him that his descendants will be aliens in a land not their own, that they will be oppressed there as slaves for four hundred years, but in the fourth generation will return to the land that was promised to them. From the exodus narrative itself we learn that the Israelites were settled in Egypt for four hundred and thirty years, although in another place it is stated that it was the fifth generation of Israelites that left Egypt. The genealogy of Moses shows that his was the fourth generation after Jacob; but even allowing for the longevity typical of the main characters within the Pentateuchal narratives, it is difficult to reconcile four or five generations with four hundred and thirty years. Curiously, the biblical references suggest that Moses' aide and successor Joshua, who finally took the Israelites across the River Jordan into the promised land, and led the conquest of Canaan, lived not in the fourth or fifth generation after Jacob Israel, as we would expect of a near-contemporary of Moses, but in the tenth.

The biblical record of the building of King Solomon's temple in Jerusalem, which is traditionally dated in the middle of the tenth century BCE, states that the exodus had taken place four hundred and eighty years earlier. That suggests a date somewhere in the middle of the fifteenth century BCE. How might that date be cross-referenced to what is known about the history of ancient Egypt?

The Egyptian pharaohs play a key role in the exodus narrative; but as has been noted already, they are not named. Although it is not clear how many pharaohs feature in the biblical narrative, there appear to have been at least three. The first was the pharaoh who permitted the immigrant Hebrews to settle in his land, as a favour to his viceroy Joseph. It is commonly supposed that Joseph's pharaoh was Amenhotep IV, also named Akhenaton, not least because his own renowned and revolutionary monolatry—a remarkable contrast with the customary Egyptian polytheism—may explain his sympathy with the near-monotheistic religion of Joseph's family. Amenhotep was pharaoh in the mid-fourteenth century BCE.

The oppression of the Hebrews began under a later pharaoh, who did not know about Joseph. It may be assumed that Moses was born and grew up in the reign of this pharaoh, who, the Bible says, ordered the Hebrews' baby boys to be thrown into the Nile. The book of *Exodus* records that the Hebrews were used as forced labour to build this pharaoh's store cities at Pithom and Rameses. It is known from other sources that these cities were built by XIXth Dynasty pharaohs, begun by Sethos I and completed by his son Ramses II, who reigned for sixty-six years, perhaps from 1279 to 1213 BCE. A letter from the time of Ramses is extant, in which an Egyptian official concerned with construction gives orders for the distribution of rations to those who were working on the great pylon of Rameses, including the 'Hapiru'. Possibly the Hapiru were the Hebrews, but that is by no means certain, and to base an assumption on similar-sounding names is none too safe. Ramses II may therefore have been the pharaoh of the oppression, but his thirteenth century dates are a long way adrift from the fifteenth century dates suggested by the Solomon reference to the exodus. On the other hand, the latter may itself be questioned.

When Yahweh called the exiled Moses to return to Egypt, he assured him that all those who had wanted to kill him were now dead. This seems quite clearly to imply that another pharaoh was now on the throne, and it was he who eventually let the slaves go free. The earliest extra-biblical reference to Israel known to date is on an inscribed stele or column, commemorating campaigns in Canaan undertaken by Ramses' son Merenptah, who reigned in the last decade of the thirteenth century BCE. It is possible, therefore, that Merenptah was the pharaoh with whom Moses and Aaron pleaded and that the exodus took place in his reign. Some scholars are of that view, while others think it more likely that the exodus can be dated at some point in the reign of Ramses II, probably around 1250 BCE.

So, we have some names and some dates, but none of them seem to take us much nearer to anything that can be claimed as history within this biblical narrative. There is nothing yet to provide clear links between any of the named pharaohs and the exodus narratives, and we are left engaging in guesswork.

If it is accepted for a moment that we are indeed looking at an historical exodus, there are many elements within the narratives, as written, which raise further questions. It is also interesting to ask questions about what is not written: for example, there is no bridge between the end of *Genesis* and the opening of *Exodus*, between the death of Joseph and the birth of Moses, some hundreds of years or a number of generations later. Did nothing worth recording happen in all that time? Were there no great clan leaders to succeed Jacob and Joseph? Why did the exodus have to be led by an exiled murderer, or manslayer at least? Could not Moses have risen as a local hero? Or did those who were later to write, or edit, these narratives seek to create Moses as a mystical 'saviour' figure, one who mysteriously appeared from who knows where, outside the world of the Hebrew slaves — a man with no name riding in from the desert, a figure materialising out of a shimmering desert mirage, to dispense justice to an oppressed people?

Perhaps most fascinating, if not surprising, is the question, why is there no shrine to Moses? As the Pentateuch closes with the death of Moses, it states that to this day no one knows where his tomb is. The traditional location of the patriarchs' tomb has already been alluded to, and the greatest of Israel's kings, David, was buried in Jerusalem; but there is no known tomb for the man about whom it was said, 'There has never yet risen in Israel a prophet like Moses, whom the Lord knew face to face' [*Deuteronomy* 34:10].

It also seems remarkable that after the Hexateuch (the first five books plus *Joshua*), there is infrequent allusion to Moses. Barely more than a dozen biblical texts refer to him by name, and half of those are more concerned with the law than with the man. Moreover, it is not easy, in reading the post-exodus biblical narratives, to recognise Israel as a nation that lived by the hugely detailed Mosaic law presented in the *Torah*. Most notable, perhaps, is the absence of mention of the festival of Passover, which at the time of the exodus Yahweh had insisted on as a *sine qua non*, the essential and perpetual celebration of Israel's deliverance from slavery. Although observance of Passover was (is) a domestic rite, and therefore may not merit specific mention, it might be expected to be referred to somewhere in day-to-day stories.

When Passover does appear in the biblical narrative, it seems to be because it is an unfamiliar or unusual practice. Its observance had great national significance at the time of the religious revival and reform introduced by kings in the eighth and seventh centuries BCE. Then, the celebration of Passover initiated by King Hezekiah brought people to Jerusalem from all over both the southern and the northern kingdoms, and it is said that this was the largest number of people ever to have celebrated the great festival. A similar record was claimed when King Josiah ordained a national Passover to celebrate the discovery of the long-lost law scroll in the temple at Jerusalem.

An obvious question may be, How many Israelites left Egypt at the time of the exodus? The Pentateuch states that there were about six hundred thousand men on foot, together with women and children. A large number of other people are said to have accompanied the Israelites, although just who these were the narrative does not make clear. Six hundred thousand men with women and children may give a total of two million people, or even more. Had the Hebrews' numbers really increased, in five generations or even four hundred years, to such a huge population, from the seventy who first went to Egypt with Jacob Israel? And if they had, their procreation had resulted from intermarriage between cousins, the children of the original twelve sons of Jacob. The number is stated even more precisely in the order of march detailed later, as six

hundred and three thousand five hundred and fifty men.
Perhaps the figure is as metaphorical as Agamemnon's
fleet of a thousand ships and the one hundred thousand
Achaian warriors who waged war on Troy, simply indi-
cating a very large number. Perhaps something has been
lost from the exodus narrative which would have clarified
this.

It has been calculated that a column of two million people, including children, walking five abreast across rough
terrain, together with their cattle and baggage wagons,
would take about ten days to pass. Even if that calculation
is wide of the mark, such huge numbers do present problems with, for example, the Israelites' quick getaway
across the momentarily dried-up Red Sea. What may be a
more realistic figure of something between two and six
thousand people has been proposed.

The archaeology of Sinai and the Negev indicates that a
number of cities were attacked and destroyed during the
mid-thirteenth century Bronze Age period which is suggested for the exodus and the period of the Israelites'
desert wanderings. In some measure, the sequence of
those attacks seems to match the route taken by the Israelites between Egypt and Canaan, as detailed in the Pentateuch. However, excavations indicate that these desert
cities were strongly fortified, a description which tallies
with the report of the scouts whom Moses had sent to spy
out the land: 'its inhabitants are formidable, and the towns
are fortified and very large ... we cannot attack these people; they are too strong for us'[*Numbers* 13:28 and 31]. But,
according to the biblical narrative, the people of Israel did
attack these towns and took them. We may well wonder
how these thousands of people, who once were shepherds
and had spent generations in slavery, had now become an
unstoppable fighting force. With what were they armed?
How did they go about destroying these mighty desert for-
tresses?

In one of its more dramatic stories, the Bible provides an
answer to these questions. After the death of Moses,
Joshua had led the Israelites across the River Jordan into

the promised land, and now they were confronted by the great cities of Jericho and Ai. As he reconnoitred Jericho's mighty walls, Joshua was met by a man with a drawn sword, who declared himself to be the captain of Yahweh's army. Then Yahweh himself spoke to Joshua, giving him his battle orders. The Israelites' fighting men were to march around the walls of Jericho, once a day for six successive days, led by priests blowing rams' horns. On the seventh day, they were to make seven circuits of the city walls, and when the army heard the blast of the rams' horns they were to shout aloud. Joshua and his army followed Yahweh's orders; and as the Israelites made the seventh circuit on the seventh day, and shouted aloud, the city walls fell down. Then the Israelites sacked Jericho, killed all of its inhabitants, set the city on fire, and carried away its treasures.

There have to be questions about whether Jericho met its fate in quite that way, though, not least because of the timing. Archaeological excavation at both Jericho and Ai indicates that the cities' fortified walls had been destroyed many hundreds, possibly a thousand, years before the putative date of Israel's settlement of Canaan, once again confusing the history of these events. It is possible that after its destruction, Jericho had been resettled and it was this later and much smaller town that Joshua attacked. It may be that the memory of his campaign included the sight of the thousand-year-old ruins, which were doubtless very impressive; and in generations of re-telling, Jericho's one-time mighty fortifications became a part of the heroic Joshua epic. One is reminded of the way in which the Homeric epics include memories of once great cities with their mighty walls, based on Homer's possible familiarity with their ruins.

Just where in the epic narrative of Moses and the exodus it is possible with any historical certainty to fit Jericho and the walls that came tumbling down must remain unresolved, at least until independent and verifiable sources come to light. Once more, in the absence of other evidence, it has to be concluded that the narrative examined here is

great literature — even greater, when its mythic value is
taken into account — but it cannot with any justification be
presented as history.

*   *   *

As the Bible's story of Israel unfolds in the books which
follow the Pentateuch, it remains difficult to discern with
any certainty where history actually begins. The book of
Joshua tells of the Israelites' conquest of Canaan and their
settlement in the land which had been promised to them
by their god. The period of the tribal leaders or 'judges' is
described in the book of that name, with stories of the
heroic leaders Gideon, Samson, and Deborah, one of the
Bible's few great women leaders. The narrative continues
in the book of *Samuel*, with the establishment of the monarchy. In spite of the warning given to them by their god
Yahweh, whom they rejected as their king, the people
clamoured for a supreme ruler to be chosen from among
their number, so that they could be like other nations. First
to be anointed king was Saul, and his reign was followed
by the unsurpassed golden age of King David.

David's son Solomon succeeded him, and it was in his
reign that the first temple was built in Jerusalem. On the
death of Solomon, the kingdom was divided: the northern
kingdom of Israel was centred on Samaria, while the
southern kingdom of Judah retained David's capital, Jerusalem. The books of *Kings* tell stories of generations of
monarchs, both those who ruled the northern kingdom
and those who ruled in the south. Many offended against
God's laws, encouraging pagan religious practices. Others, notably the great reformer Josiah, returned to Yahweh
and re-established the Mosaic law.

By this point in the story, it is possible at last to begin
allocating specific dates to events described in biblical stories, simply because of the wealth of verifiable extra-biblical evidence. The archaeology of the Assyrian and
Babylonian empires has provided extensive records of this
period, from the ninth century down to the sixth, which

not only tally with much of the narrative of the Old Testament books of *Kings* but also enable dates to be given to the events described there.

It is significant, however, that unlike the traditional sub-divisions of the Christian Old Testament, the Hebrew Bible does not arrange any of its books under the heading 'historical'. The book of *Kings* (*Melakim*) forms a division of *Nebiim* known as 'The Former Prophets', and its emphasis is not on history but on what might be termed theology — that is, the prophets' warnings of impending doom, unless a wayward people returned to a rejected God. The prophetic message to the people of Israel and of Judah was that disobeying God's laws and breaking their covenant with him would lead inevitably to invasion and conquest by foreign armies, because that is what God had promised. When *Melakim* records the 'events' which followed, it is not to record history but to show that the Almighty God is true to his word.

In 722 BCE, the northern kingdom of Israel was conquered by the Assyrian king Shalmaneser V and his son Sargon deported the Israelites to Assyria, replacing them with people from other subjugated lands. In 705 BCE, Sargon's son Sennacherib over-ran the southern kingdom of Judah, but mysteriously failed to take Jerusalem. According to the biblical narrative, the besieging Assyrian army was attacked one night by the angel of Yahweh, and one hundred and eighty five thousand warriors died, whereupon Sennacherib struck camp and returned home. This miraculous episode does not appear in the Assyrian version of events, however.

The Assyrian empire had passed its heyday, though, and fell to the Babylonians in 612 BCE. The Babylonian Nebuchadnezzar attacked Judah in 598, eventually sacked Jerusalem in 586, and took the people of Judah into exile in Babylon. And so, within the space of perhaps fewer than seven hundred years, the children of Israel had been delivered from slavery in a foreign country, had become a nation and settled in a land of their own, promised to them by their god, but now were captive once more in an alien land. Their two kingdoms had ceased to exist.

But this was not to be the end of the story. Indeed it seems entirely possible that this was only the beginning of the story — or, more significantly, the beginning of history. In chapter fourteen we will pick up the story again, and give some thought to what among all this may be history and what may be myth. And if myth, why?

PART 3

BACK TO THE FUTURE

Chapter Thirteen

In the Lap of the Gods

The last few chapters have examined three narrative traditions, clearly very different from each other in origin and content, but in other respects sharing some important features. One of a number of the significant characteristics which they have in common is that, in their various ways, they tell of quests.

For forty years, the biblical narrative tells, Moses and the Israelites were wandering around the wilderness and deserts of Sinai and the Negev, in quest of the new homeland promised long before to their ancestors. Meanwhile, for ten of those years, the Greeks were at war with Troy (so Homer's poems say) and for a further ten, the great Greek hero Odysseus was wandering around the Mediterranean, in quest of a return to his home in Ithaka. At long last, the Israelites entered the promised land, and Odysseus regained his kingdom. Thousands of years later, the legends tell us, King Arthur's knights left their Round Table and rode out from Camelot in quest of the Holy Grail. Most failed in their quest, but the vision was finally granted to a chosen few.

Perhaps 'the quest' is a metaphor for the life of men and women. Like John Masefield's 'Seekers',

> We travel the dusty road till the light of the day is dim,
> And sunset shows us spires away on the world's rim.
> We travel from dawn to dusk, till the day is past and by,
> Seeking the Holy City beyond the rim of the sky.

Another of the attributes shared by these three traditions is their mythic content or quality. That is to say, they can be seen as sacred narratives, with their essential theme of the intervention of a god or gods in the affairs of men and women, and the ways in which men and women respond to divine intervention. Moses and the Israelites are delivered by Yahweh, who enters into a covenant with them and leads them on their journeys through the wilderness. Odysseus suffers great tribulation at the hands of his enemy, the sea god Poseidon, but at the same time is protected by his sponsor Athene, the daughter of Zeus. Throughout the Arthurian Grail narrative there is an all-pervading sense of the holiness of the quest, with the knights' observance of the church's festivals, their vigils and visions of the Christ, the presence of the sacred relics from Calvary, and the soul of Sir Galahad, a descendant of Joseph of Arimathæa, being carried into heaven by angels.

In this third and final part, we return to the Homeric epics and the biblical exodus narrative, and consider the possibility that their value and meaning may lie more in their mythic or metaphorical qualities than in some unverifiable or questionably historical content. The argument for myth versus history is then extended to the Christian writings of the Bible's New Testament. Finally, some tentative moves are made toward proposing a place and relevance for myth and metaphor in the twenty-first century.

First, then, let us think about myth within the Homeric epic poems, before moving on to give similar consideration to the stories of Moses and the Israelite exodus.

Homer's *Iliad* and *Odyssey* present two major episodes from an early age, later accepted by the classical Greeks as the history of their own race. The world depicted in both epics is peopled not only by mortals — many of them not merely mortals but great heroes or supermen — but also by powerful Olympian gods, whose will and whim, and active intervention, directly affect the fortunes of mankind.

Transcription of Linear B texts suggests that the Mycenaean culture included a pantheon of perhaps twelve major divinities, closely resembling the extended family of gods who dwelt high on Homer's Mount Olympos. There were other gods under the earth and in the sea, as well as many lesser beings in streams and forests. Homer's poems and the *Theogony* of Hesiod, perhaps Homer's contemporary, confirmed belief in this other-worldly population of immortals. The origin of these gods is not clear, but they seem to have had eastern or near-eastern counterparts. The Greeks were descended from an Indo-European race, and their supreme god Zeus-pater may be identified with Dyaus-pitar, the god of the sky in the Hindu *Rig Veda*.

In Homer's portrayal of the heroic Mycenaean age, it is clear that both the Achaians and the Trojans believe that they cannot escape the will of Father Zeus, the most powerful of the gods. At the same time, men seem prepared to act in ways which suggest that they feel they are in control of events, or at least that they can take care of themselves. This is not to say that mortals' beliefs were polarized simply between a passive submission to a destiny that lay in the lap of the gods, and an assertive sense of freedom to make their own decisions and act with impunity. The genius of Homer's poems creates a far more complex picture than that.

In this chapter, we look at a number of aspects of these apparently conflicting sets of beliefs, to illustrate some of the ambiguity that mortals seemed to experience in their dealings with the gods: that is to say, while human beings seem to be essentially religious beings, they appear perfectly ready to believe that they can rely on their own resources in solving the problems that face them.

Homer's *Odyssey* and *Iliad* were a foundation of classical Greek education; but in Plato's view, the way in which Homer had presented devious and vengeful gods was very damaging when it came to teaching children. But for Greeks living three or four hundred years before Plato, the most likely first audience for Homer's recital, 'the gods appear to have been very real and ... a potent source of belief about the most important human values' [Emlyn-Jones 1992]. For men and women living even earlier, in the ancient Mycenaean world portrayed in the epics themselves, the gods were even more real than that. The overwhelming evidence, in Homer at least, is that they experienced the gods' presence in their everyday lives as a powerful but arbitrary source of help and reward, and of hindrance and punishment. There was no such thing as luck. Any piece of good fortune or an outstanding achievement was the result of one of the immortals' inspiration or help. What a modern-day sceptic might dismiss as magic was actually believed in as literally divine intervention.

Not that divine intervention was totally arbitrary. The gods had specific roles and functions and in that sense did not act at random. When Achilleus is in danger of drowning in Troy's river Skamandros, it is the task of the smith god Hephaistos to rescue him by threatening the river god with fire. The Trojan archer Pandaros, who wounds King Menelaos, had received his bow from the archer god Apollo. When Achilleus needs a new suit of armour and a shield, it is the artificer god Hephaistos who makes them. As Hektor and his Trojan battalions press back the Greeks —whose superiority would be assumed by Homer's listeners —it must be because the war gods Ares and Enyo are leading the attack.

This theme, that mortals' affairs are influenced and controlled by the gods, runs right through *Odyssey* and *Iliad*. Sometimes the belief is affirmed with an air of resignation, with an acceptance that there is nothing that can be done about the situations in which men and women find themselves.

After his many years of absence at Troy, it begins to be assumed in Ithaka that Odysseus will not be returning; and many suitors have assembled in his palace, abusing the household's hospitality, and vying for the hand of Odysseus' wife Penelope, now thought to be a widow. When the suitor Eurymachos taunts Odysseus' son Telemachos about who will be his father's successor as king in Ithaka, the young man accepts with resignation that this is simply one of those questions that lie on the knees of the gods, and there is nothing further to discuss.

At other times, the belief in the gods' intervention is expressed in the form of a prayer or supplication, demonstrating an active expectation or wish for the gods' will to be accomplished, hopefully in the supplicant's favour. With the *Iliad* approaching its climax, as mighty Achilleus' dear companion Patroklos is slain by the Trojan Hektor, Patroklos' charioteer Automedon recklessly leaps from the chariot, ready to take on the Trojans single-handed, apparently content that 'these are things that are lying upon the gods' knees'. With that assurance, and with a prayer to Father Zeus, Automedon prepares to hurl his spear at Hektor and Aineias, mighty warriors against whom he has little chance: 'I myself will cast; and Zeus will look after the issue' [*Iliad* 17:514–5]. Unknown to Automedon, Zeus had already determined to rescue him, a lesser mortal, from his mindless attack on these, the two greatest of Troy's hero-princes.

In their final confrontation, the Trojan champion Hektor comes face to face with the mighty Achilleus, and acknowledges his inferiority to his enemy. Even so, Hektor fearlessly engages with him, believing that 'all this lies upon the knees of the gods; and it may be that weaker as I am I might still strip the life from you' [*Iliad* 20:435–6]. Again, while Hektor accepts that it is for the gods to decide, he very naturally hopes that the decision will be in his favour.

There is, then, a recognition that not only are the gods in control of men's destiny but also there is no point in resisting the divine will. In Ithaka, the duplicitous Eurymachos assures Penelope that her son Telemachos has nothing to fear at the hands of the suitors — although, as the leader of the plot, Eurymachos knew full well that they planned to ambush and murder Telemachos. On the other hand, Eurymachos adds, if death is ordained by the gods, there is no way of avoiding it [*Odyssey* 16:447].

For mortals to resist the gods is a dangerous tactic: when the goddess Aphrodite is wounded by the great Achaian warrior Diomedes, she is consoled by the thought that the 'man who fights the immortals lives for no long time' [*Iliad* 5:407].

On returning to Ithaka, Odysseus remains incognito as a beggar, as he plans his revenge on the suitors. Just one of the suitors, though, Amphinomos, is hospitable to the 'beggar', who then warns him of the hero's impending wrathful return. The disguised Odysseus wishes that the gods will protect Amphinomos, and that he will be able to reach home safely before the slaughter begins [*Odyssey* 18:146–7]. Ironically, Amphinomos' destiny is bound up with the fate of the other suitors and with their morally justified slaughter, approved by the gods. He is the first to die at the hands of Odysseus' son Telemachos as he stands shoulder to shoulder with his avenging father.

It would, perhaps, be surprising if the gods' inescapable will is always accepted with equanimity or good grace. Agamemnon is able to rationalize his fateful quarrel with Achilleus by blaming Zeus: 'I am not responsible but Zeus is'. Agamemnon claims that the god 'caught my heart in the savage delusion ... what could I do?' [*Iliad* 19:86–90]. However, this realisation and acceptance do not prevent the great king from making full amends in his reconciliation with Achilleus.

Penelope, too, is convinced that the gods' intervention in mortals' affairs is the cause of suffering. The blame for the Trojan war and all the misery that it had caused should be laid on the gods and not on Helen, who had absconded with Paris. Helen was shameless in her actions, Penelope believed, but it was the gods who had spurred her on [*Odyssey* 23:222–4].

The Zeus of the *Odyssey* sees things differently: mortals, he says, blame the gods for the evils they suffer, but it is their own recklessness that brings sorrow. The view from Olympos is that if men did what they knew to be right, especially after receiving clear prompts or messages from the gods, all would be well. Athene cites Aigisthos as one whose death was well deserved. Aigisthos had defied the gods' warnings and married Klytaimestra, the wife of Agamemnon, murdering him on his return from Troy. As Zeus points out, Aigisthos had now paid the price: the gods had given him clear warnings and he had brought his destruction upon himself [*Odyssey* 1:37 and 43].

The Greeks' religion was one of orthopraxy, doing the right things, rather than orthodoxy, believing the right things. Right practice included *xenia*, the obligation to extend hospitality to *xenos*, the stranger. Failure to practise *xenia* incurred the wrath of Zeus, the guest-god, who was likely to punish any denial of hospitality to the stranger.

Another essentially right practice was that of *eusebeia*, piety, or giving due recognition to the gods, paying them full reverence. It was important that men kept in touch with the gods. There was no formal religious organisation or structure, but each of the gods had his or her priests. Dishonouring a priest was also to court disaster, as the Achaians discovered to their cost when Agamemnon spurned Apollo's priest Chryses. Seers, too, were able to 'see' the will or intention of the gods, usually through observing omens. It was open to, or expected of, individuals to make propitiatory sacrifice to the gods. Non-observance of the need for sacrifice spelt trouble.

The image of men's affairs lying on the gods' knees links to the Homeric concept of supplication, where the suppliant holds the knees of the person or god from whom he or she seeks help or a favour. Perhaps through the supplication of prayer, the gods' inescapable will could be influenced positively.

The orthopraxis of prayer and sacrifice did not itself ensure success, however. In his negotiations with his wife Hera, who has been demanding the destruction of Troy, Zeus objects that no city beneath the sun dwelt in by men has been nearer to his heart than this one:

> Never yet has my altar gone without fair sacrifice,
> The libation and the savour, since this is our portion of
> honour. [*Iliad* 4:48–9]

But Hera will not give in. In exchange for Zeus agreeing to Troy's destruction now, in spite of the city's piety, she promises not to stand in his way should he in future wish to destroy Mycenae, Sparta and Argos; and Zeus agrees.

Athene, the goddess patron of Odysseus, thinks Zeus harsh for delaying the hero's homecoming from Troy, not least because he has faithfully sacrificed to the great god. Zeus in turn acknowledges the virtues of Odysseus, who more than others has sacrificed to the gods. He now agrees that the immortals should take steps to ensure a safe homecoming for Odysseus. Prayers commonly included a reminder to the god of sacrifices made in the past, in the hope of increasing the likelihood of securing a positive outcome.

Neglecting sacrifice, on the other hand, was almost certainly a recipe for disaster, as the Spartan king Menelaos discovered. His return from Troy was delayed, the Old Man of the Sea tells him, because he had omitted to make due sacrifice to Zeus and the other gods [*Odyssey* 4:472–3]. Only when he has honoured the gods will he have his longed-for return.

The fault of Penelope's suitors is not simply that they ignore the rules of *xenia* and eat and drink extravagantly at their unwilling hosts' expense, at the same time spurning strangers and denying them *xenia*; but more, that they do not dutifully acknowledge the gods as a part of their feasting. Just once, at the behest of Amphinomos, a man who shows more sensitivity than his fellows, do they end their selfish feasting by pouring a libation to the gods.

Such recklessness, in Zeus' book, wins sorrow and the suitors' slaughter by Odysseus is their just desert. It was the recklessness of Aigisthos in ignoring the gods' warning about marrying King Agamemnon's wife that brought about his death. It was the recklessness of Odysseus' men in slaughtering and eating the cattle of Helios the sun god that was the cause not only of their death but also of the disasters and delays that Odysseus himself had to endure before finally returning home from Troy. Men's recklessness and the justified punishment that ensues is a powerful theme of both *Iliad* and *Odyssey*.

Some men seemed prepared to take things into their own hands, with fateful results. The suitors think it shameful that the gods should thwart their plot to ambush

Penelope's son Telemachos, to remove him from the scene, and now arrogantly decide they must make their own plans for his destruction, as the gods are not much help.

At Troy, the Achaians had built a defensive ditch and wall to provide protection for their beached ships against the Trojan enemy, but this work had been undertaken 'in despite of the immortal gods' and without due sacrifices; as a consequence, 'it was not to stand firm for a long time' [*Iliad* 12:9–10].

Through all the years of his troubled wanderings, Odysseus seems to have been prepared to rely on his own wits and natural cunning to deal with the disasters and challenges he encountered rather than call on his patroness Athene, though she later reveals that she was with him all the time. Frequently he ponders and makes his own decisions, apparently in the belief that he is free to act in any way that seems best to him. Odysseus appears unaware that benevolent gods are never far away, especially his sponsor Athene, helping him against his great vengeful foe, the sea god Poseidon. And yet, when on his return to Ithaka he meets Athene face to face, he lies to her that he had recognized her presence throughout his wanderings.

Athene, who admires the ever-wily Odysseus' deviousness, is herself unrivalled in trickery and deception, as Hektor discovers to his cost. As we have already seen, in his final combat with Achilleus, Hektor believes he is accompanied by his trusted brother Deïphobos; but unknown to him, the 'brother' is Athene in disguise. She vanishes at the critical moment, leaving Hektor to his fate, as he laments, 'At last the gods have summoned me deathward … it was Athene cheating me' [*Iliad* 22:297–9].

So, it seems, men cannot rely on the gods to act always in a straightforward way, as they cheat and deceive. When Achilleus fears he will drown with ignominy in the turbulent river Skamandros, and not die a hero's death beneath the battlements of Troy as his goddess mother Thetis had prophesied, he believes she has deceived him with her lies.

Even if men were able to trust the gods, there remains the question how they were to know what the gods' will is for them, that is, what is the right course of action to take? Seeking the gods' purpose through prayer was clearly a priority. The gods played their part by sending signs and omens: for example, birds passing to the right gave messages of encouragement; those flying to the left definitely spelt bad news. Foolish men ignored the omens. The wise old warrior Halitherses sounds a warning to the suitors assembled in Odysseus' home at Ithaka, interpreting the sight of two eagles as an omen sent by Zeus, warning of Odysseus' return, with the inevitable death and destruction of all the suitors. The cynical suitor Eurymachos, however, makes the fatal error of dismissing the old man's interpretation: 'The sky is full of birds, as they fly around — do not tell me this has some meaning. No, take it from me — Odysseus is dead. He will not be coming back.' [*Odyssey* 2:181–4]

Hektor also ridicules the idea of putting one's trust in birds: 'I care nothing for these, I think nothing of them' [*Iliad* 12:238]. He believes he can rely on the support of Zeus. In the end, he is mistaken. Although Zeus acknowledges the faithfulness of Hektor in honouring him with sacrifices, he finally assents to his death. It is fated now that Troy's greatest hero has met his end and is to go down to the underworld, where Hades is lord of the dead.

* * *

Such, then, was the world depicted by Homer, a mythic world the workings of which could largely be explained by an interventionist family of gods. Those gods may have lived far away on Mount Olympos; but they were forever coming down from the mountain to play an active role, for good or ill, in the lives of both Greeks and Trojans. Men and women did well to remember that their lives were in the gods' hands. Things might be expected to go well, and even prosperity enjoyed, when due regard was given to the immortals, and honour shown through right practices. But disaster was likely to follow when mortals neglected sacrifice, denied hospitality to strangers, paid no heed to omens, or recklessly took things into their own hands.

How different from this was the world of the Hebrew patriarchs, as they understood and experienced it? What do the books of Moses have to say about an interventionist God, and to what extent was this world an historical one? Or may the events chronicled there have some other meaning? Let us return now to the story of the Israelite exodus.

Chapter Fourteen

Out of Slavery into History

Like the world of Homer's *Iliad* and *Odyssey*, where the affairs of men and women could be explained in terms of divine will and purpose, the world described by the biblical authors was also a world controlled by many gods, gods to be feared and placated — Ba'al, Astarte, Dagon, Moloch, Marduk, Chemosh, El the Bull-god, El Shaddai, and more besides. The gods of Egypt, too, would doubtless have been familiar to the Hebrews during their generations of slavery there: Amun the great god, Osiris god of the underworld and the symbol of resurrection, his falcon-headed son Horus the sky god, and the other deities worshipped in the Egyptians' temples.

The Hebrew Bible tells how a god named El Shaddai — known from Ugaritic sources to have been a Canaanite deity — revealed himself as the Almighty One to a nomad named Abram or Abraham. Throughout the stories about the generations that followed, the god of Abraham was ever-present as the god who not only watched over his people, but also made very plain what he required of them. The Bible's stories are told in terms of this god's purposes, his instructions, his support and provision for those who obeyed, and his displeasure with and punishment of those who did not. Like Homer's world, the biblical world is explained by divine interventions.

It seems clear, however, that even with their new awareness of El Shaddai as their tribal god, the nomadic Abraham-Isaac-Jacob clans could not yet conceive of him as the only true god. Images or idols of local gods were retained within their families. This can be found in the *Genesis* story of Jacob's moonlight flit with Rachel, when, unknown to him, she has stolen the household gods of her father Laban, thus incurring his wrath and hostile pursuit of the fleeing couple [*Genesis* 31:13ff]. When later God the Most High comes to Jacob Israel at the town of Shechem in Canaan, telling him to strike camp and move on to Bethel and settle there, Jacob calls to his people to get rid of the idols of their foreign gods, before setting out on their journey [*Genesis* 35:1ff].

Eventually, according to the exodus narrative, the god El Shaddai reveals himself to Moses as Yahweh, declaring that this is now the name by which he is to be known for all time. Number one in the list of ten commandments which Yahweh later gave to Moses on the holy mountain was unequivocal: 'You must have no other god besides me' [*Exodus* 20:3]. Emphatically *must*. No option. No discussion.

We have already recounted the biblical exodus narrative, concerning events which may have occurred at some time perhaps in the mid-thirteenth century BCE. It tells how the people of Israel, freed from slavery in Egypt, journeyed to a land which they believed had been promised by the god of their ancestor Abraham. During the Israelites' forty years of wandering in the desert, their leader Moses met with Yahweh face to face on a mountain, perhaps Sinai, perhaps Horeb; and according to the Hebrew Bible, it was through this divine encounter that a covenant was established between Israel and their god.

This theology of being God's elect was written back into the Jews' earlier 'history' and even pre-history. In the story of the flood, for example, God established a covenant with Noah and his descendants. Later, he appeared to the Hebrew Abraham, renewing the promise of an everlasting covenant. At that time, God instituted male circumcision as a sign of his promise to Abraham, a rite which Jews retain as a physical symbol of the covenant.

God's promise of a perpetual homeland was confirmed to Abraham's son Isaac and in turn to Isaac's son, Jacob Israel; and so within their tradition the Jews embedded God's covenant with the patriarchs as a precursor to the covenant of Sinai.

The exodus narrative, Thomas L Thompson has suggested, tells the story 'about a god who was without either a home or a people. He chose a people who similarly were without either a home or a god' [Thompson 1999]. So this was an early beginning to the transformation of Abraham's descendants, through adversity and suffering, into a nation whom God could entrust with his laws. Their god had set this people free from human bondage, but he was now about to bind them to himself. They were always to remember the night when Yahweh brought them out of slavery in Egypt, as he instituted the statute of the Passover, a solemn festival to be observed at the appointed time from year to year, throughout all generations.

The celebration of Passover, *Pesach,* has been a holy festival in Judaism to this day. Wherever the Jews were dispersed after the Romans' destruction of the temple in Jerusalem in 70 CE, they faithfully remembered year after year their god's commandments and the events of the exodus from Egypt.

Just three months into the Israelites' desert journey, according to the exodus narrative, Moses was called by Yahweh, who entrusted him with a momentous promise to pass on to the Israelites: if they undertook to listen to this one true god and keep his covenant, then they would become his special possession, a kingdom of priests and a holy nation.

God was now ratifying his covenant for all time: if this people would undertake to obey his law, God would give them the land he had promised them. But God's contract contained more demanding clauses than that: the Israelites had not been chosen just for special favours, to be protected by God and to have it easy, walking unopposed and unhindered into a land flowing with milk and honey. They

were chosen to be a kingdom of priests and a holy nation.
And that involved responsibilities.

The fulfilment of that destiny is thought by Jews to be
the purpose of God's calling Israel to be 'a light to the
nations'. In *A Jewish Theology*, Rabbi Louis Jacobs makes
clear that being God's chosen people has nothing to do
with exclusivity. This is not a matter of

> a tribal god protecting his people, responding to their
> attempts to buy his favour ... The doctrine is not of a Her-
> renvolk whom others must serve but on the contrary of a
> folk dedicated to the service of others. [Jacobs 1973]

To be a kingdom of priests among the other nations of
the earth required the Jews to play an atoning role. Being
set apart, called out from other nations to accomplish
God's purposes, was the highest privilege but also
involved the greatest responsibility.

The complex and detailed law which the exodus narrative describes as being dictated by God to Moses spelt out
the cost of disobedience:

> if you fail to keep all these commandments ... if you break
> my covenant ... I shall bring upon you sudden terror ... I
> shall set my face against you, and you will be routed by
> your enemies. [*Leviticus* 26:14–17]

When Moses had finished relaying God's words to the
people of Israel, they answered with one voice: 'Whatever
the Lord has said we shall do'. They had not only been chosen by God. They had also chosen God.

However, as we have already seen, Israel's commitment
was to be short-lived and God's very first commandment
was about to be broken. Moses was away, making one of
his frequent visits to God on the holy mountain, and was
longer than expected in returning. The Israelites became
restless and made a golden calf as their new god. When he
eventually returned, the enraged Moses interceded on the
unfaithful people's behalf. God was persuaded not to
destroy the Israelites in his fury, but nonetheless punished
the idolatrous people for making the bull-calf.

Here the writer of *Exodus* sets out a reminder that
Israel's belief in the one true God, and faithfulness to him,

was central to the covenant. Disregard of the obligation to worship the one true God had a terrible price. There were perils in idolatry.

The first new generation of settlers in the promised land, following the death of Joshua and his contemporaries, 'did not acknowledge the Lord and did not know what he had done for Israel' [*Judges* 2:10]. Already, God's commandment seems to have been forgotten: succeeding generations had neglected to tell their sons and daughters that the Almighty God had brought them out of the land of Egypt, freeing them from the land of slavery. The Israelites began to worship Ba'al and Astarte, the gods of the Canaanite peoples among whom they lived, and their unfaithfulness angered Yahweh. As he had promised he would do, he

> made them the prey of bands of raiders and plunderers; he sold them into the power of their enemies around them, so that they could no longer stand against them. [*Judges* 2:14]

To several generations of Israelites in later years, God's prophets continuously reiterated the warning against idolatry, as the chosen people went 'whoring after strange gods'. It was the uncompromising theme of Hosea, one of the last prophets before the northern kingdom was destroyed by the Assyrians: 'for like an unchaste woman this land is guilty of unfaithfulness to the Lord'. But Hosea also brought a promise from a God who, while vengeful against the wayward, was forgiving to those who returned to him:

> When Israel was a youth, I loved him;
> out of Egypt I called my son;
> but the more I called, the further they went from me;
> they must needs sacrifice to the baalim
> and burn offerings to images. [*Hosea* 11:1–2]

However, destruction and suffering would result from their waywardness, unless they accepted God's invitation:

> Return, Israel, to the Lord your God …
> I shall heal my people's apostasy:
> I shall love them freely,
> for my anger is turned away from them. [*Hosea* 14:1 and 4]

The prophets' message was clear: if the people chose other gods and so broke the covenant that they had with the one true God, the inevitable consequence would be suffering; but if they turned away from their idolatry and kept faith with God, they would prosper.

However, the prophets' unambiguous call went unheeded. The stories are told how generation after generation of monarchs both in the northern kingdom of Israel and in the southern kingdom of Judah 'did what was wrong in the eyes of the Lord'. Not all were idolatrous, however; but while a few kings are said to have done 'what was right in the eyes of the Lord', they were half-hearted in their devotion and took no steps to rid the land of the idols and shrines to the false gods, and the people continued to sacrifice and burn offerings there. One, King Ahab, 'did more to provoke the anger of the Lord the God of Israel than all the kings of Israel before him' [*1 Kings* 16:33].

Yahweh continued patiently to speak through his prophets: 'Give up your evil ways; keep my commandments'. But the people paid no heed, and went from bad to worse. 'Following worthless idols they became worthless themselves ... Thus it was that the Lord was incensed against Israel and banished them from his presence' [*2 Kings* 17:15 and 18]. It was then that Israel was over-run by Shalmaneser's hordes, and the people were deported from their homeland to exile in Assyria.

In the southern kingdom of Judah, one or two reforming kings were noteworthy for returning their people to the worship of Yahweh. King Hezekiah smashed the shrines, cut down the sacred groves, and destroyed the bronze serpent said to have been made by Moses hundreds of years before, to which the Israelites had been burning sacrifices. Hezekiah's son Manasseh, however, returned to idolatrous practices, and thereby earned God's condemnation. God's judgment was that because Manasseh had done these abominable things and outdone his predecessors in wickedness, disaster would fall on Jerusalem, and all that remained of God's people would be handed over to their enemies.

Some generations were to come and go before God's sentence was carried out. Judah's king Josiah, perhaps the most righteous king since his forefather David, ordered the damaged temple in Jerusalem to be repaired; and while the work was under way, a long-lost scroll of the law of Moses was found. Josiah then set about root and branch religious reform. The scroll was read to the people and they pledged themselves to the covenant. At Josiah's command, the whole nation was cleansed of idols and shrines, Ba'al's altars were overthrown and all the abominations and profane practices surrounding the worship of Astarte and Moloch were abolished. Josiah got rid of the necromancers and called for a national Passover to be observed. 'No king before him had turned to the Lord as he did, with all his heart and soul and strength, following the whole law of Moses; nor did any king like him appear again' [2 *Kings* 23:25].

God's wrath against Judah did not abate, however. Josiah was followed by a number of idolatrous kings, and the Babylonians under Nebuchadnezzar overthrew Jerusalem and the people of Judah were taken into exile.

* * *

The two kingdoms had ceased to exist, with the people carried away into captivity and that is where we left them at the end of chapter twelve. But it was also suggested there that this was not to be the end, but a beginning. The biblical account states that the people of the northern kingdom of Israel were destined never to return to their homeland, and Samaria was now settled by other displaced and idolatrous peoples. Those deported from the southern kingdom of Judah, on the other hand, were not to be in Babylon for ever.

The Bible's book of *Kings* tells that at the time of Nebuchadnezzar's siege of Jerusalem, in 597 BCE, the leaders of Judah were transported to Babylon. The prophet

Jeremiah wrote to them from Jerusalem, to impart a reassuring promise that he had received from God:

> When a full seventy years have passed over Babylon, I shall take up your cause and make good my promise to bring you back to this place ... If you invoke me and come and pray to me, I shall listen to you ... and restore you to the place from which I carried you into exile. [*Jeremiah* 29:10–14]

In 586 BCE, virtually the whole people were deported to Babylon, and a Hebrew song tells of their homesickness:

> By the rivers of Babylon we sat down and wept
> as we remembered Zion ...
> for there those who had carried us captive
> asked us to sing them a song ...
> How could we sing the Lord's song
> in a foreign land? [*Psalms* 137:1–4]

However, Jeremiah had long been speaking of a new covenant between God and his people, and of a time when they would be restored to their homeland. The words 'I am the Lord your God who brought you out of Egypt' occur frequently in the Hebrew Bible, perhaps more than a hundred times. Now, however, Jeremiah was looking forward to a time when, instead of speaking of deliverance from Egypt, men would speak of 'the Lord who brought the descendants of the Israelites back ... from all the lands to which he had dispersed them' [*Jeremiah* 23:7–8]. Did this mean that there was to be a second exodus? Or was this in fact to be the first *historical* exodus?

In 539 BCE, Babylon was conquered by the Persians and a new era was about to begin for God's people. By an edict of the Persian king Cyrus in 538, the exiled peoples were given leave to return from Babylon to their various homelands, if they chose to do so. Quite probably, though, there would have been uncertainty among the Jewish exiles about whether they wanted to make that long and arduous journey to Jerusalem.

Understandably, many may have questioned why they should exchange the new freedom that they had been granted within the civilised comfort of Babylon for an

unknown desolation across many hundreds of miles of
desert to the west. Most of the people living in exile had
never seen Jerusalem anyway. But it seems that over a
period of time, perhaps even a century and a half, people
began to return to the land that was traditionally the land
of their ancestors, now part of the Persian empire. It is
thought that Jerusalem's derelict temple was rebuilt at
some point late in the sixth century BCE and the city's
ruined walls repaired in the fifth century. It seemed that
the people of Israel had at last come home.

* * *

All of this has been recounted here as though it is history.
Some of it is, some of it may be. But the purpose of this discussion is not so much concerned with attempting to separate historical fact from legend (probably an impossible
task) but more with looking at the mythic character of
these biblical narratives — myth, as has been emphasised
more than once, in the sense of explaining today in terms
of once-upon-a-time, especially with reference to the gods'
dealings with mankind.

In that sense, the stories of the patriarchs, of the Israelite
slaves in Egypt and their liberation, their settlement in the
promised land, the tales of great heroes during the time of
the judges, and the doings of the kings of the golden age of
the united monarchy and of the two kingdoms that followed — all of these may with more justification be read as
myth than as history. As we concluded earlier, myth will
almost certainly be based on legendary tradition, the legends themselves incorporating to one extent or another
elements of what we today would call historical truth —
actual events, actual people. But, to use a phrase from an
earlier chapter, 'it wasn't quite like that'.

It has already been pointed out that there is precious little independent and verifiable evidence for the historicity
of the events described in these narratives and the people
who took part in them, any more than there is in the
Homeric epics or in the Arthurian legends, for that matter.

Details of attacks on Judah are to be found in the Assyrian annals of Sennacherib, and the annals of Shalmaneser mention kings of Israel by name. Within the Babylonian chronicles of Nebuchadnezzar there are details about the fall of Judah which resemble the biblical narratives. This may constitute corroboration; but of the ages before the exile, little or nothing is known.

Much current biblical scholarship concludes (or at best, accepts provisionally) that sources for the pre-exile story of Israel exist nowhere other than in the Bible itself. Archaeology from the Hellenistic period and the Dead Sea scrolls, for example, authenticate post-exilic settlements in Palestine; but of the period of the two kingdoms there seems to be little or no historical evidence. It is known that there were settlements both in the north and the south of Palestine; but no independent evidence has yet been found of the land being united under one monarch. It is questioned whether there ever was a great capital at Jerusalem, in an unsurpassed golden age of Israel, under a succession of hero kings — Saul, David, Solomon. That is the view put forward by Thomas L Thompson in *The Bible in History*: 'Finding an archaeological Jerusalem fit for David ... is proving just as difficult and more embarrassing than it was to find an archaeologically suitable Ai or Jericho for a Joshua' [Thompson 1999] .

There were without doubt many nomadic movements and migrations of populations during the ages ascribed to the patriarchs. The great Mycenaean drought during the late Bronze Age, and the attendant famines, may lie behind the legends of *Genesis*. It is probable that during that period of drought and famine a number of starving clans and tribes would have left arid Canaan and made for Egypt, a fertile land thanks to the Nile's regular annual flooding, where there was corn in plenty. Equally, some tribes may have stayed behind in Canaan, just as others may have remained in Egypt and not returned home. Thus, the *Genesis* account of one people journeying to Egypt, being enslaved there, leaving the country *en masse* (however that came about) and becoming a nation once they were back in their original country, may well be an over-simplification — or a metaphorical rendering, indeed — of a far more complex series of events.

Similarly, centuries later, it is very probable that there were many instances of people being carried into exile from Palestine, and such movements would not have been limited to those two or three written about in the Bible's book of *Kings*. Deportation and resettlement of defeated peoples was already a well-established and common politico-military strategy adopted by conquering empires at the time of the fall of the two kingdoms, and continued to be. It is very likely, therefore, that there was much coming and going of groups and tribes, some remaining in the country to which they were exiled, others returning home, while some were displaced by people from other lands. So again, the account of a whole nation going into exile and then returning as a body may be an over-simplification of what actually happened.

A question already asked about the Israelites' period of slavery in Egypt is, Why is there no narrative record of it? It is interesting now to observe that in the case of the later Assyrian and Babylonian exiles, unlike the exodus narratives, we have authentic names and dates that impart a very real sense of history, but still no biblical narrative of the exile itself. It could be claimed that the book of *Esther* in part fills this gap; but the Jerusalem Bible's introduction to *Esther* points out that 'These stories treat history and geography with a good deal of freedom ... Moreover, at the time indicated by the narrative, the queen of Persia and consort of Xerxes was Amestris; history leaves no room for ... [Queen] Esther' [*Jerusalem Bible* 1966].

Within Judaism, there appears to be little concern about 'proving' the historicity of these events. For religious Jews, there are three unquestioned certainties: the existence of God, the gift of his sacred *Torah,* and their role as his chosen people. It is accepted that at some time, God the Most High made an everlasting covenant with this people and gave them his *Torah*, the divine law by which his people are to live. For Orthodox Jews the *Torah* is holy writ, received by Moses on Sinai direct from the Most High; and across the centuries rabbinic *midrash*, interpretation, has made the *mitzvot*, commandments or obligations, equally applicable to succeeding generations. Reform Jews also value the *Torah* as God's law; but they accept that Judaism is bound to change and develop, as their religion adapts to a changing world, and they feel that the Bible too may be open to question and subject to revision.

That more liberal view of the Bible is not unique to Reform Jews. In 1957, a book was published which was soon to cause a theological storm. In *We Have Reason to Believe*, conservative rabbi Louis Jacobs wrote that 'the Jew ... must be free to investigate the classical sources of Judaism with as much objectivity as he can command [...] The result of such investigation ... and an unbiased approach to the texts yields a picture of the Bible and the Talmud as works produced by human beings, bearing all the marks of human literary production, influenced in style, language and ideas by the cultural background of their day' [Jacobs 1965].

A widely-held view is that the Pentateuch if not the whole Hebrew Bible – this 'human literary production', with its underlying ideas and cultural background – is the culmination of a major post-exilic editing of ancient songs, poems, legends, and chronicles. These traditions, both oral and written, dated back over many centuries and were drawn from diverse peoples in Palestine and Mesopotamia. After the Babylonian exile, the documents and narratives were brought together and edited, possibly by a man named Ezra, although such a vast literary undertaking must have occupied more than one man and taken many years of work.

Ezra is believed to have left exile in Babylon and come to Jerusalem possibly in the mid-fifth century BCE or the very beginning of the fourth, during the reign of one of the Persian kings named Artaxerxes (it is unclear which one). Ezra's task was to re-establish, or even establish for the first time, religious faith and practice among the returning Jewish community. It may be that Ezra, with perhaps a band of fellow scholars, collected, collated and edited a huge array of traditions about the 'past' of a mythic Israel, including the 'books of Moses', which had long been in existence in various forms. Through this huge literary enterprise, the new 'bible' became the basis of life for a new-born Israel, the law by which the people were to live, just as the temple became the focus of their worship. Thus a new nation was brought into being—not re-born but new-born.

If this is indeed the origin of a new, post-exilic Israel, it may be that neither *one* exodus nor *one* exile can be insisted upon as an historical event. But what can be said is that the biblical stories, primarily that of the exodus and the covenant, form a sacred narrative which is explanatory, explaining how out of mythic origins a people gained an identity and a purpose.

It was into this historical Israel that Jesus, the man from Galilee, was one day to be born.

Chapter Fifteen

The Man From Galilee

> Jesus was born at Bethlehem in Judæa during the reign of
> Herod. After his birth astrologers from the east arrived in
> Jerusalem, asking, 'Where is the new-born king of the
> Jews? We observed the rising of his star, and we have
> come to pay him homage' [*Matthew* 2:1–2].

So begins one of the birth narratives in the Christian New
Testament, and it brings us back to one of the questions
asked at the outset, the question — or quest — of the historical Jesus. Implications of that question will occupy the
remaining chapters of this book.

What is the background to this story, which begins with
little preamble and appears to assume the reader's knowledge? Who was Herod, and why was there a king in
Judæa, which was now part of a Roman province? Since
Herod was on the throne, what did the astrologers mean
by a 'new-born king of the Jews'? Was this Jewish baby
Yeshu'a born to be king? What had been happening, anyway, during the hundreds of years between the Jews'
return from Babylonian exile in the sixth century BCE and
these new events?

To try to answer these questions, we need to turn to the
deutero-canonical books of the Apocrypha, as well as to
what is known about Greek and Roman history of this
period. Most importantly, it is necessary to keep in mind
the Jewish people's age-long expectation of the coming of
their Messiah.

The Land of Promise to which the exiles returned from Babylon remained a part of the Persian empire until 331 BCE, when it fell to Alexander the Great and his Macedonians. Following Alexander's death in 324 BCE, Judæa became a province of the Ptolemies, the Greeks of Egypt. Like the Persians and Macedonians before them, the Ptolemies tolerated their subject peoples' religions; and although Greek culture was introduced throughout the land, the Jews were left in peace, free to practise their religious life. However, when the Syrian Greeks, the Seleucids, conquered Ptolemaic Palestine in 200 BCE, everything changed.

Centuries earlier, in the years before the exile, the biblical texts tell how prophets had reminded the people of a promise made by their God long before, to David, the greatest of their kings:

> Your family and your kingdom will be established for ever in my sight; your throne will endure for all time.
> [2 *Samuel* 7:16]

The prophets looked forward to a new era, when the Anointed One, God's vice-regent and a king in the ever-lasting royal lineage of David, would re-establish the great golden age, an age of lasting peace and freedom, security and prosperity, justice and godliness. Perhaps when the eighth century prophet Isaiah foresaw the advent of a new David, he was praying for the literal intervention of a king or a warrior-prince who would save the people from the invading Assyrians. But, as the biblical narratives make clear, that was not to be.

The prophetic vision survived the Babylonian exile, however, and Israel's expectation of a saving *Mashiah* did not fade. A number of different messianic concepts developed, and in the last two centuries BCE, as many as three Messiahs, or three Messiah-roles, were envisaged. The Dead Sea scrolls speak of the coming of a King-Messiah, who would defeat the Jewish people's enemies. He would then defer to the authority of a Priest-Messiah, who would teach the people righteousness but not before he had been subjected to humiliation and suffering. The forerunner of the Priest-Messiah would be an Elijah-figure, the Prophet-Messiah.

One of the Dead Sea scrolls, dating from the first century BCE, and commonly referred to as the 'Resurrection fragment', pictures the End of Days, when

> [the hea]vens and the earth will listen to His Messiah …
> He who liberates the captives, restores sight to the blind
> … He will heal the wounded, and revive the dead and
> bring good news to the poor. [Vermes 2004]

The Jewish people could not have looked more eagerly for a redeeming Messiah, to liberate them from an idolatrous tyrant, than during the Seleucid occupation. In the mid-second century BCE, the Seleucid king Antiochus Epiphanes consolidated the Hellenisation begun by the Ptolemies; and the enthusiasm shown by some Jewish leaders for this foreign 'modernisation' met with condemnation by traditionally religious people, who believed that profane disregard for God's laws was the most serious matter.

In 169 BCE, Antiochus plundered Jerusalem's temple and removed its treasures to his capital, Antioch. Worse followed. He dedicated the Jewish temple to Zeus, the pagan Greek god, and encouraged profane sexual practices throughout the temple precincts. The Jews, forced to relinquish their ancient traditions, could no longer live their lives according to their God's laws, and were even forbidden to admit to being a Jew. They were made to eat pork and the entrails of sacrificed animals, and to participate in festive celebrations for the Greek god Dionysus. Those who refused to conform were put to death.

Armed insurrection resulted, led not by a mystical Messiah but by the three sons of Mattathias the Hasmonean, leader of the *Hasidim*, the Pious Ones. Under the command of Judah the Maccabee and his brothers Jonathan and Simon, tens of thousands of Jewish warriors took up arms against the Syrian Greeks. Judah was killed in battle, but eventually the Jewish army prevailed, and removed their Seleucid overlords.

An hereditary Hasmonean dynasty was established under Simon, to reign until the true prophet appeared. By the beginning of the first century BCE, however, the relentlessly-expanding Roman empire was becoming an indomitable presence in the Middle East. In 63 BCE, Pompey took Jerusalem and the Hasmonean dynasty was abolished. But within two decades or so, the Romans came under Parthian threat from the east; and, in need of an ally in Judæa who could be trusted to keep the lid on any potential uprisings there, Rome re-established the Hasmonean dynasty under a puppet king, Herod.

It was into this world that Jesus was born, and it was into this world, according to the nativity story, that the astrologers came, bearing gifts.

* * *

Sources for the Jesus narrative are limited to four short books, referred to as the gospels, at the beginning of the Christian Bible's second part, the New Testament. Further background is provided by fewer than twenty much less familiar and non-canonical 'gospels', which have survived in fragmentary form.

First, let us look at the origins of the four canonical gospels and think about their purpose; and then come to the question, what, if anything, do they tell us about an historical Jesus?

It is probable that the gospels were written several decades after the crucifixion of Jesus by the Romans, which may have taken place within a few years of 30 CE. No original manuscripts of the gospels or, as far as is known, any direct copies of original manuscripts have survived. New Testament versions of the gospels are translations of copies of copies, manuscripts dating from no earlier than the fourth century CE. Dates of the gospels' composition, the order in which they were written, and exactly who their authors were, continue to be subjects for scholarly debate.

The first three books, those attributed to Matthew, Mark and Luke, are referred to as the *synoptic* gospels, as they appear to look at events very much from the same standpoint (in fact, that is a huge over-simplification, one requiring a whole book to itself). By and large, the content of the synoptic texts can be arranged side by side in three columns, since on the whole they tell the same stories, record the same teaching, and use the same language to do so. However, to some extent, they follow events in different sequences, and some authors include material which is unique to their own account, while some gospels omit material which appears in others.

The fourth gospel, John's, is thought to have been written much later than the others, possibly in the closing years of the first century CE. John's language and style are quite different from those of the synoptics, and some scholars argue that the differences suggest that he was unaware of the other three gospels. John, possibly one of Jesus' apostles, but more likely a man known as John the Elder, seems to have been influenced by the teaching and thinking of the Qumran community, whose scriptures are included in the Dead Sea scrolls, with an emphasis on the imminence of the End of Days and the expectation of the *parousia*, the divine Coming.

The general consensus is that the earliest of the gospels was Mark's, written perhaps at some point between 65 and 70 CE. The date of composition may have been a little later, if Mark's reference to the Romans' destruction of the temple in Jerusalem was something that had already happened—in 70 CE—rather than a prophecy attributed to Jesus, and an event still in the future. It is suggested that Mark recorded the memories of the apostle Simon Peter, and he may have been a young man who had moved somewhere on the fringes of Jesus' inner circle.

Independently of each other, Matthew and Luke drew on Mark's text and in effect copied much of it. In addition, both used another source, now lost but referred to as Q (the initial of *Quelle*, the German word for source), providing material which does not appear in Mark. Matthew and

Luke also include material unique to their respective gospels.

The author of *Matthew* is traditionally thought to have been the tax-collector apostle, and that may be true. Luke, the only non-Jewish author of a New Testament book, is said to have been the Greek doctor who travelled with Paul on his journeys. There is no certainty that any of the gospel writers knew each other.

The gospel narrative consists largely of Jesus' teaching and healing, as well as stories about miraculous events. Something like a third of Jesus' teaching contained in the gospels was in the form of parables, simple genre stories and similes, employing everyday images to ensure that his message was memorable. Matthew's gospel states that 'In all his teaching to the crowds Jesus spoke in parables; indeed he never spoke to them except in parables' [*Matthew* 13:34].

Between them, the four gospels include some forty-five miraculous events, mostly stories of healing, but others concerned with happenings which mirror the prophecy of the Qumran *Messianic Apocalypse*: 'the Lord will accomplish glorious things which have never been' [Vermes 2004] — for example, Jesus is said to have fed five thousand people with just five loaves and two fish, and to have walked on the water of the Sea of Galilee to go out to meet his disciples, who were out on the lake in their fishing boats. More significantly in this context, the gospels tell of Jesus restoring at least three dead people to life: his own friend Lazarus, the daughter of a synagogue official, and the son of a widow at Nain.

The concept of resurrection from the dead was by this time already familiar, although not universally accepted. The Sadducees, a priestly party, denied the idea, whereas their *Hasidim* enemies, the Pharisees, were more inclined towards apocalyptic views, including a belief in spirits, angels and, significantly, resurrection. Resurrection was intrinsic to the developing messianic teachings. During the Babylonian exile, the prophet Daniel declared that at the End of Days, many who had died and were buried in the earth would be woken, and arise to everlasting life. In the apocryphal *Book of the Maccabees*, a Jew being tortured by Syrians defiantly cries out his belief that God, the king of the universe, will raise him to a new, everlastingly life.

On one of his customary Sabbath visits to the synagogue, Jesus stood up to read. Handed the scroll of the prophet Isaiah, he selected this passage:

> The spirit of the Lord is upon me
> Because he has anointed me;
> he has sent me to announce good news to the poor,
> to proclaim release for prisoners
> and recovery of sight for the blind;
> to let the broken victims go free,
> to proclaim the year of the Lord's favour.
> [*Luke* 4:18–19]

The same words appear in the Qumran 'Resurrection fragment', with the addition of the revival of the dead, and were clearly associated with the coming Messiah. When Jesus finished reading from the scroll, he added 'Today in your hearing this text has come true'. The congregation was outraged and ejected him from the synagogue and from the town, indeed would have killed him. For Jesus to appropriate the words 'the Lord … has anointed me' was something approaching blasphemy, claiming to be the Messiah, the Anointed One, the King.

It is quite possible, if not most likely, that when the gospels' authors came to compile their works, they wrote back into their texts concepts which more closely reflected their later beliefs than words which had actually been spoken by Jesus. It is difficult to determine to what extent Jesus believed himself to be the Messiah, although the gospels portray perfectly clearly his single-minded purpose in proclaiming the presence of the 'Kingdom of God', signalled by the miraculous events which accompanied his itinerant mission.

There was a current belief that the great prophet Elijah — one of the two men in the Hebrew Bible not to have died, but to have been 'taken by God' — would return before the End of Days, and Jesus named John the Baptist as 'the destined Elijah', the Messiah's forerunner. Herod Antipas had had John beheaded; and when he heard of Jesus and his miracles, he was afraid that this was John raised from the dead. There appears to have been a general atmosphere of expectation that the End of Days was at hand.

For their part, it seems to be clear that the gospel writers had no doubt: Jesus was the *Mashiah*. The Hebrew word, transliterated in the Greek-language gospel texts as *Messias*, appears in only two gospel episodes; and in both places the author, John, explains that the word has the same meaning as the Greek *Christos*, the Anointed One, a title which appears frequently in the gospels. For the gospel writers, Jesus was The Christos, the one anointed as king.

So far, the word gospel has been used here as little more than a synonym for a book, but it is important to be clear about the meaning of the word itself. The familiar modern phrase 'it's the gospel truth' is employed to add weight to the assertion that something is absolutely true, whereas 'don't take that as gospel' is used to caution that something may not be true. That common usage is misleading, however. Truth is not essentially the meaning of gospel: the Old English word *godspel* means simply good (*god*) news (*spel*).

The gospels, then, were intended by their authors to impart good news: the good news that the Messiah, so long awaited, had come at last. Their aim was to portray the preaching and the works of Jesus the Christos in a way that matched the prophecy of Isaiah and others—the unknown author of the Qumran 'Resurrection fragment', for example—representing Jesus as God's 'Messiah, who liberates the captives, restores sight to the blind, heals the wounded, revives the dead and brings good news to the poor'.

From this, it is clear that the gospels' authors were not merely writing biographies or even history, had they understood the word. They give no description of Jesus' physical appearance, for example. They have practically nothing to say about the years between his birth and his baptism as an adult by John the Baptist. The one exception is Luke: in a unique passage, he describes an episode when the twelve year old Jesus went missing during his family's annual Passover visit to Jerusalem. When his anxious parents found him at last, Jesus was in the temple, deep in discussion with the religious teachers, who were amazed at the boy's intelligence.

The non-canonical gospels, by contrast, contain many fascinating stories about the young Jesus: he moulds sparrows in clay and they fly away, he brings a dead child back to life, he stretches a wooden beam until it is long enough for a job that his carpenter father Joseph is doing in his workshop.

Only two of the four canonical gospels include Jesus' nativity, and they tell it differently: Luke's story involves the manger, the angels and the shepherds, detail which some suggest he may have gathered from Jesus' mother, Mary. Matthew's account, on the other hand, while limited to the astrologers' visit, is full of symbolism. As in so many stories of princely births (that of the infant Arthur is an example), we read of mysterious or magical visitors bringing gifts for the new-born baby. In Matthew's story, the astrologers offer gold, frankincense and myrrh, symbols of the three-fold messianic expectation of prophet, priest, and king. The author of Matthew's gospel would have been familiar with the many references in Hebrew scriptures to the one who would come and save Israel; and he goes to great lengths to include in his account ways in which Jesus' words and actions fulfilled those ancient prophecies — having him born in David's city Bethlehem, for example, even though he was more likely born in Nazareth. The story of the astrologers' homage, borrowed from the prophet Isaiah, can be seen as evidence of Matthew's belief in Jesus as the Messiah.

Both Matthew and Luke include a genealogy to authenticate the pedigree and peerless ancestry of Jesus, but again their accounts differ from each other. Matthew shows Jesus' descent from Abraham, the father of the Jewish people, and from David, the heroic king of the nation's golden age. He is at pains to point out that, by his reckoning, there were fourteen generations between Abraham and David, fourteen between David and the Babylonian exile, and fourteen between the exile and Jesus. It would be interesting to know why Matthew chose the Babylonian exile as a marker and not the Egyptian exodus. Luke also traces Jesus' family tree to David and Abraham, but rather more ambitiously lists his ancestors all the way back to the first man, Adam. However, from the time of David to Joseph, Jesus' father, the genealogies compiled by Matthew and Luke have only two names in common.

The climax of the gospel narratives is the trial and execution of Jesus. Once more, the sequences and detail vary between the gospels, but they agree that Jesus was brought before the high priest and the council on charges of blasphemy. Under questioning, he appears to have assumed various messianic titles, and so was judged worthy of death. Jesus was then taken before the Roman procurator, Pontius Pilatus, whose authority was needed before the death penalty could be carried out. After a brief interrogation of Jesus, Pilatus did his best to find ways of releasing him; but he quickly changed his mind when a taunting crowd began chanting 'If you let this man go, you are not Caesar's friend!' and 'The only king we have is Caesar!'. Jesus was crucified and Pilatus defiantly had a sign placed on the cross: *Jesus of Nazareth, King of the Jews*.

For the writers of the gospels, however, that was not to be the end of the story. On the third day after the crucifixion, they say, women came to where Jesus had been buried, in a tomb provided by a rich man from Arimathæa named Joseph, but found the tomb empty. Again, the accounts vary: in *Matthew*, there is an earthquake, and two women see an angel roll away the rock that had sealed the tomb; *Mark* and *Luke* say three women visit the tomb, while *John* tells of only one, and all three writers state that the rock was already rolled away.

Then, three of the four gospel writers say that a risen Jesus appeared to his followers on a number of occasions.

None of the narratives seems to have a clear-cut ending, however: *Matthew* closes with Jesus saying to his disciples 'I will be with you always, to the end of time'. *Luke* tells how Jesus led his friends out to Bethany 'and in the act of blessing he parted from them'. *John* leaves Jesus talking with Peter and the others over breakfast.

Interestingly, the most ancient manuscripts of the first gospel to be written, *Mark*, have a quite different ending, suggesting that there may have been a somewhat different story to be told. In reporting the women's discovery of an empty tomb, the narrative comes to an abrupt end: 'They said nothing to anyone, for they were afraid' [*Mark* 16:8].

* * *

The gospels were not written as histories, then, and their meaning is not to be found in any historical content, but in their mythic nature — myth in the meaning of a sacred narrative which explains how or why things are as they are. The books may record what Jesus said and did, but it is the meaning of what he said and did that is significant. The gospel writers believed him to be the Messiah, and represented his proclamation of the arrival of the Kingdom of God and the 'signs' that he performed as authentication of that belief.

Given that the gospels were not written as biographies, and as they cannot be regarded as histories, is there anywhere we can go for the independent evidence which would be required to label the narratives or any part of them as historical? Unfortunately, the answer has to be something very close to no.

Evidence from outside the gospel sources is so sketchy that it could probably be written on the back of a small envelope, with room to spare. The sources are limited to the handful of Romans referred to in the introduction, men who were writing at the very end of the first century or in the first year or two of the second, as well as some Jewish authorities dated a little later.

The Roman historian Gaius Suetonius recorded a disturbance among Jews in Rome, resulting in their being expelled from the city by the emperor Claudius. It seems that the disturbance was caused by a certain Chrestos or perhaps Christian preachers, attempting to persuade the Jews that Jesus was the Christ.

A little later, Gaius Plinius Secundus (Pliny), governor of a Roman province in Asia Minor and a contemporary of Suetonius, wrote to the emperor Trajan, seeking advice about troublesome Christians, who were disloyal to the empire. Increasing in numbers and influence, the Christians and their worship of The Christos were adversely affecting local devotion to Rome's gods. Pliny judged their religion to be a degraded superstition.

Cornelius Tacitus, another Roman historian, recorded the emperor Nero using the Christians as scapegoats for the fires which devastated Rome, and subjecting them to cruel and hideous deaths. Tacitus also stated that the Christians were followers of Christus, executed in the reign of Tiberius, by order of the procurator Pontius Pilatus.

The Jewish Roman historian Flavius Josephus referred to Jesus as one of a number of nationalist troublemakers, mentioning him in connection with the execution of his brother, James. Josephus also stated that the followers of the dead 'miracle worker' believed that he was alive again.

Early Jewish rabbinic writings also refer to Yeshu'a of Nazareth, who practised sorcery and was hanged as a false teacher who led Israel astray.

Some question the validity of Josephus' reports, claiming that there is a possibility that they are later Christian insertions. Be that as it may, while these few non-biblical records, at best neutral and at worst hostile, make scant reference to Jesus himself, they leave little doubt that the influence of his followers had spread through the Roman empire by the second half of the first century CE.

It is true to say that the gospels themselves include a number of pointers to history but in effect they do no more than set the stories in an historical context. Luke's nativity narrative begins with a census decreed by the Roman emperor Augustus (30 BCE to 14 CE) and carried out while Quirinius was governor of Syria. His dates are uncertain; but it is thought that if there was a census (and that too is uncertain) it may be dated between 8 and 6 BCE. According to the gospels, Jesus was born in the reign of Herod 'The Great'. Matthew's nativity story tells how, on hearing from the astrologers that a king had been born, Herod gave orders that all boys aged two years and under were to be killed. This implies that Jesus may have been born at some point during the two previous years. Jesus was saved from the massacre of the innocents: an angel came to his father Joseph in a dream, and told him to take the child and his mother to Egypt and wait there until Herod died and it was safe to return. Herod died in 4 BCE. The birth of Jesus may therefore be dated no later than 6 BCE and possibly a year or two earlier. It may not have gone unnoticed, by the way, that the story of the infant Jesus being taken into exile until it was safe to return home, when those who would have killed him had themselves died, bears a passing resemblance to the story of Moses.

Luke places his story of John the Baptist in the fifteenth year of Tiberius — emperor from 14 to 37 CE — and it is in this year, 29 CE, that the adult Jesus enters the gospel story, as he comes to be baptized by John in the River Jordan. If Jesus was born between 8 and 6 BCE he would by then have been about thirty-five or thirty-seven years old. The length of Jesus' public career is difficult to define from the gospel narratives: the synoptics' timescale may indicate only one year, whereas John's suggests three. The crucifixion of Jesus by the Romans, ordered by Pontius Pilatus — who was procurator from 26 to 36 CE — may therefore have taken place between 30 and 32 CE, when Jesus was aged anything up to forty. This Jesus, in his early middle-age, contrasts with the traditional image of him as a young man. It also matches a gospel incident when some of Jesus' critics, thinking he claimed to have seen Abraham, exclaimed, 'You are not yet fifty years old. How can you have seen Abraham?' [*John* 8:57].

All of this, though, is no more than small-time sleuthing. It cannot (as yet) be authenticated as history, and it does not come any nearer to providing historical evidence for the resurrection of Jesus, the man from Galilee. It is not doubted here that Jesus lived, and was crucified by the Romans. After his death, however, his followers, who believed Jesus to have been The Christ, attributed to him the characteristics of God's Messiah, ideas with which they were familiar both from their Hebrew scriptures and from then current messianic beliefs. In their minds, historical events and myth blended with each other, as stories about Jesus developed and circulated. Eventually the gospel writers collected these oral traditions; and as they wrote their books to express their belief in Jesus the Christ, they incorporated messianic concepts and language in what was for them a wholly natural and honest way.

However, that was very far from the end of the story.

Chapter Sixteen

Rome's New God

An historical Jesus may prove difficult to find, but there can be little reason to doubt that the man from Galilee did in fact live during the first few decades of our era, was a radical itinerant teacher, was thought by some of his Jewish contemporaries to be their Messiah, and was crucified by the Romans. Beyond this, however, no independent, verifiable historical evidence has yet come to light for other episodes contained in the gospel narrative.

It can be assumed that within a short time after his death, stories began to be told about wondrous deeds and events associated with Jesus of Nazareth, the most remarkable of them being that he had in some way been raised from the dead. A few decades later, a number of these stories were collected and written down, and they have been preserved in the four short books known as the gospels, which open the Christian Bible's New Testament.

The gospel narrative continues in the New Testament's fifth book, *Acts of the Apostles*, probably written in the last few years of the first century CE. By that time, many stories had long been circulating about the apostles, the small band of men who had been closest to Jesus, stories about their exorcising what were believed to be demonic spirits, healing sick people, and even bringing the dead back to life. In effect, the book of *Acts* does not have a great deal to say about *the* apostles, or all of the apostles. It may be more accurate to translate the book's Greek title as *Acts of Apostolic Men*, since it is only Peter and John who feature to any extent in the early chapters. In fact, the story which dominates the book is that of a man named Paul, who had not been one of the apostles or disciples of Jesus.

There are a number of reasons for believing that the author of *Acts* was Luke the gospel writer. *Acts* begins by saying that the author's first book was an account of all that Jesus did, which suggests that it was a gospel. Both *Luke* and *Acts* are dedicated to Theophilos, customarily thought to be a friend of Luke's. It is possible, though, to suggest that this opening greeting is a Greek pun addressed to 'One who loves God' (*philotheos*). Another clue to Luke's authorship of *Acts* is the use of the pronoun 'we', which appears in a number of episodes in the book; and Paul states in one of his letters that he is accompanied by his friend Luke, the doctor. There is continuity between the end of *Luke* and the beginning of *Acts* — somewhat disjointed, admittedly, but continuity none the less.

The first chapter of *Acts* tells how the assembled apostles, bursting with messianic expectation, ask the resurrected Jesus whether he is about to re-establish a kingdom in Israel. His answer is that it is not for them to know the detail of God's plans. The story then goes on to say that in some way Jesus 'was lifted up before their very eyes, and a cloud took him from their sight' [*Acts* 1:9]. As the apostles gaze into the sky, two men dressed in white appear and tell them that Jesus has been taken up to heaven, but will return in the same way.

At this distance in time, and with only the New Testament as a source, it is not possible to know what actually happened after the crucifixion. The gospel narrative is unclear. When Jesus was arrested, his disciples are said to have deserted him and run away, while Peter, who had hung back to see what would happen, denied all knowledge of Jesus. Almost certainly disillusioned, confused and frightened, they seem to have returned to their homes in the north, and resumed their fishing on the Sea of Galilee. Gradually, inevitably and increasingly, possibly over a number of months, they began to think back to their time with Jesus, and shared fond memories of their amazing experiences with this man whom they had adored.

Through the iterative process of story-telling familiar to them within their tradition, the links between their images of Jesus and the messianic expectation began to build. Possibly a part of that imagining was the idea, quite feasible in their minds, that God had raised Jesus into his presence.

In any event, the early chapters of *Acts* tell how the apostles, newly inspired by the spirit of Jesus, returned to Jerusalem. Peter had found a new courage, and with others of the disciples spent his days teaching both in the temple and in private houses, preaching the good news of Jesus the Messiah. The number of believers swelled into thousands. More than once, Peter and John were imprisoned. The priestly party, the Sadducees, were especially incensed by the disciples' zealous preaching about 'resurrection', a concept and belief which were contrary to their own doctrines.

According to *Acts*, the religious establishment began intense persecution of this new, rapidly-spreading heretical Jewish sect. One man who was particularly active in harrying believers in the new 'Way' was an ardent Pharisee named Saul, who went from house to house in Jerusalem, uttering murderous threats and arresting anyone identified as a member. With the high priest's authorisation to extend the prosecution of these heretics and purge synagogues in other cities, where clearly there were already adherents to the new beliefs, Saul set out for Damascus.

While still on the road to Damascus, the story in *Acts* continues, Saul had a blinding vision of the risen Jesus, who asked Saul why he was persecuting him. The voice told the blinded Saul to complete his journey to Damascus; there he would be met by a man named Ananias, who had already received his instructions from God. Saul did as he was told, his sight was restored, and he was baptized. Saul — or Paul, as the new man was renamed — who had been the most committed persecutor of the Way, now became its most ardent exponent and ambassador.

The theme of the book of *Acts* is the spread of belief in Jesus as the Christos in the middle years of the first century. In about 39 CE, Paul began a series of extensive missionary journeys, which over the coming twenty years took him throughout the lands of the eastern Mediterranean, visiting the Roman provinces in present-day Syria, Cyprus, Turkey, Greece and eventually Rome itself.

In strictly historical terms, little is known about Paul; but, as in the gospels, a few extra-biblical dates place some episodes in an historical context. While he was in the Greek province of Achaia, for example, the Jews attempted to arraign Paul before the Roman proconsul, Gallio, who is known to have been in office in 52 CE. Some years later, back in Judæa, Paul was arrested and taken before Antoninus Felix, who was proconsul there from 52 to 59 or 60 CE. Paul remained in prison, although Felix was hoping for a bribe, so that he could release him. Porcius Festus succeeded Felix as proconsul in 59 or 60 CE; but, as *Acts* observes, Felix wanted to curry favour with the Jews and so left Paul where he was.

According to the *Acts* account, Paul was eventually taken to Rome for trial by imperial tribunal, although, as Festus had observed, he could have been set free, had he not exercised his right as a Roman citizen and made an appeal to the emperor. It is possible that after two years in prison in Rome, Paul was released; and there is a tradition that he made a journey to Spain. However, the fires which caused such extensive damage in Rome in 64 CE were blamed on Christians, and it is thought possible that Paul was caught up in the persecution which followed, imprisoned once more, and finally executed.

During his journeys throughout the Roman empire, Paul would have written letters of encouragement to the companies of believers as well as to individuals in each of the cities he visited. Thirteen such letters, attributed to Paul, are included in the biblical canon of the New Testament, although it is not certain that Paul was the author of them all. It is thought that the first of these preserved epistles may have been the letter to the assembly in the Greek city of Thessalonika, written about 50 CE; and the last, to

Paul's young friend Timothy at Ephesus, written perhaps
a year or two before his death in 67 CE or thereabouts.

None of this is by any means certain, however. For
example, another contender for the title of the first Pauline
letter is the one written to believers in the province of
Galatia. There is no agreement, though, about *which*
Galatians the letter was addressed to; some scholars hold
that they were believers living in the south of the Roman
province, while others make a case for a region much further to the north. The *Acts* account of this part of Paul's
journeying is ambiguous.

In every town and city which Paul visited, he met with
the Jews in their synagogues, and the message he brought
was of Jesus the Christos, a crucified but resurrected Messiah. Although his message was intended first for the Jews,
it was not long before Paul and the other apostles came to
the realisation that the message should be taken to the
Gentiles too.

A number of factors facilitated Paul's long journeys and
the rapid growth of what was to become a new religion. In
the three centuries or more since the time of Alexander the
Great, Judaism had been spreading throughout the Mediterranean lands; and by Paul's time, synagogues had long
been established over much of what was now the Roman
empire. Judaism's monotheism and moral beliefs had
increasing appeal at a time when the worship of the Greek
and Roman gods was beginning to be practised less fer-
vently than it had been for centuries. New ideas from the
east had not merely novelty value, but were attractive both
philosophically and intellectually. As he travelled in the
Roman empire, Paul had no national borders to cross, the
roads were good, and his language, Greek, was the
empire's *lingua franca*.

The first converts, and the apostles themselves, of
course, were Jews, and many or most retained their Jewish
faith, continuing to follow the Jewish law and observe
Jewish practices. Paul himself was a Pharisee who had
studied under the eminent doctor of the law, Gamaliel the
Elder. Paul's writings demonstrate a keen legal mind, evi-

denced not least by the density of some of his language and the complexity of his arguments.

Then, as many Gentile 'pagans' began to be converted to the Way, a dispute arose over whether or not the new believers should also convert to Judaism. The traditionalists demanded that they should. Feelings ran high. The apostles assembled in Jerusalem and after long debate determined that it would not be right to impose undue restrictions on Gentiles when they converted. It had now become an article of faith that belief in Jesus the Christos, and in the doctrine of his atonement for mankind's sin through his sacrificial death, freed the believer from any requirement to follow the Jewish law.

A new and distinct religion was now beginning to emerge from Judaism, the religion that was to become Christianity.

*   *   *

Following the story of Jesus' ascension at the beginning of *Acts*, the narrative continues with the apostles gathered in Jerusalem, constantly at prayer, with a number of women including Mary the mother of Jesus, and his brothers. The book of *Acts* records that this growing community, the *ekklesia*, 'met constantly to hear the apostles teach and to share the common life, to break bread and to pray [and] the believers agreed to hold everything in common: they began to sell their property and possessions and distribute to everyone according to his need' [*Acts* 2:42–5].

It does seem premature to see this Jewish community as the early church, or to describe the sect as primitive Christianity. It is worth noting that the word Christianity is not used in the New Testament at all, and the word Christian appears only three times, all three dating many years after these early events. *Acts* tells how in later years the label 'Christian' was not chosen by the believers themselves, but was given to them by others, possibly in a derisive sense [*Acts* 11:26]. One of Paul's persecutors spat out the word Christian with contempt [*Acts* 26:28]. Later still, the word Christian is used almost in passing, in a letter attributed to Peter [*1 Peter* 4:16].

In those early days, the members of this new *ekklesia* or gathered community were Jews, who were looking for the imminent arrival or return of their Messiah. It was about Jesus the Messiah that the emboldened Peter spoke to the authorities, when he declared, 'There is no salvation through anyone else; in all the world no other name has been granted to mankind by which we can be saved' [*Acts* 4:12]. Peter's words expressed an essentially Jewish expectation of a saving Messiah. It was only very much later that these words were taken out of this context and used in Christian evangelical fervour, appropriated as a 'proof text' to underpin Christianity's claim to be the exclusive path to salvation.

The gathered community of believers met daily at the temple and shared meals in their homes. There are many indications in the opening chapters of *Acts* that these people eagerly expected an early return of the Jesus whom they believed to have risen from the tomb and ascended to heaven. Before Jesus left them, the apostles had clearly come to believe that now was the time for him to establish his messianic kingdom, as a natural response to his words to them before his death, concerning the End of Days. The ascension story tells how they had been assured that Jesus would return in the same way as he had left them. They now believed that his return was about to usher in the longed-for Messianic Age, and Peter's early preaching made clear that he believed these to be the last days.

Central to the teaching of Jesus had been the imminence or indeed the presence on earth of what he called the Kingdom of Heaven or the Kingdom of God. If, as appears to be true, he taught and accepted that the Messianic Age was at hand – whether or not he believed himself to be the Messiah – it seems to make no sense to suppose that he was setting out to form a new religion or to found a 'church' or any other formal or structured organisation. He and his disciples were Jews, observing Jewish law and practice; and their expectation would have been to continue to live within that ancient tradition, after the Messiah's redemption of the Jewish people, and indeed of all mankind.

At one point in the gospel narrative, Jesus is said to have given his disciple Simon the nickname *Petros* — a modern equivalent might be 'Rocky' — and on this 'Rock', Jesus said, was to be built the *ekklesia*, a Greek word for an assembly or a company of people called together for a common purpose. This one gospel text [*Matthew* 16:18] appears to suggest that Jesus had in mind that Simon Peter would become the first leader of the *ekklesia*. It is possible, though, that this story of *Petros* is an example of the way in which later concepts were written back into the text, retrospectively authenticating subsequent developments in belief and dogma.

According to the account in *Acts*, however, Peter's leadership role quickly passed to Paul; and from the literary evidence at least, which in effect is all that we have, it appears unrealistic to suggest that Peter became the leader of a 'church'. *Acts* has little to say of any significant authority being accorded to Peter. Paul barely referred to him in his letters, and when he did, it is in rather derogatory terms. He spoke of Peter as one of those 'reputed to be something, not that their importance matters to me' [*Galatians* 2:6]; and at one point, they were in public dispute, when Paul 'opposed [Peter] to his face, because he was clearly in the wrong' and confronted him 'in front of the whole congregation' [*Galatians* 2:11 and 14].

These early believers in The Way met in each other's homes, with neither special buildings for their assembly nor formal organisational structure. It was not until very much later that any 'ecclesiastical' meaning was given to *ekklesia*, with the institutional attributes associated with the word church today. Cathedrals and church buildings, hierarchies and clergy, creeds and liturgy, synods and schisms, doctrinal and denominational differences — all of these lay in a far distant future.

That is not to say that differences and divisions did not make themselves felt at an early stage of the development of this new movement. As Paul journeyed between the cit-

ies and provinces of the Roman empire, he found that
departures were already being made from the orthodoxy
of his teaching. In Corinth, for example, he found believers
who said there was no resurrection of the dead. Others
were beginning to form factions, identifying themselves as
followers of this teacher or of that, and giving themselves
divisive denominational labels [1 *Corinthians* 1:11ff].

It was to be the best part of three hundred years before
the leaders of the new religion codified their beliefs, with a
need to protect orthodoxy against heresy. In 325 CE, a
church council defined the essentials of Paul's religion,
with its worship of an incarnate God and a crucified and
resurrected Christos, in what became known as the Nicene
Creed. To this day, that creed is recited every week
throughout Christendom, affirming the belief that Jesus
came down from heaven and became man, was crucified,
and buried, but on the third day rose again.

It is assumed that for his teaching and writing, Paul
drew on what he was able to learn from the apostles and
from traditions about Jesus which were already developing. Since the gospels were not written until after Paul's
death, he obviously had no recourse to them, but would
have had to rely on oral sources similar to those drawn
upon later by the gospels' authors.

A reading of the book of *Acts* and of Paul's letters indicates that he did not write or speak about Jesus' life prior to
the events of the evening before his trial and execution. He
says nothing about the content of Jesus' teaching, does not
refer to the sick being healed, nor does he mention any
miracles. The one reference which *Acts* does make to Paul
quoting words of Jesus is interesting in itself. In one of his
speeches, Paul reminded his listeners that Jesus had said
that there was more happiness to be had in giving than in
receiving [*Acts* 20:35]; but these words, if Jesus did indeed
say them, did not find their way into any of the gospels
when they came to be written. This one simple example
illustrates the difficulty of validating the words of Jesus
recorded in any of these narratives.

That there were common sources for Paul and the gospel writers to draw upon seems to be clear, however. In one of his letters, Paul quoted Jesus, as he gave instructions about the observance of what was beginning to be called 'the Lord's Supper'. Paul wanted it to be clear to his readers that 'the tradition that I handed on to you came to me from the Lord himself' [1 *Corinthians* 11:23]. He then continued with a detailed description of what Jesus said and did at the Passover meal, the last supper which Jesus shared with his disciples on the night he was arrested, but at which Paul had not been present. The text of Paul's letter closely resembles parts of the synoptic gospel narratives, which were written much later, and clearly there is a question about where this material originated.

It is difficult to know what Paul meant by his claim that the 'tradition' had come to him 'from the Lord himself'. In a verse not included in all manuscripts of the gospel story of the last supper, Jesus invited his disciples to meet from time to time after his death, to share a meal and so keep his memory alive. There seems to be little reason to suggest that this invitation, if it was made, was extended to anyone beyond the twelve at that last supper. It was Paul, on the other hand, who later chose to formalise the *eucharistos* (thanksgiving) meal, instituting it as an essential part of the new faith, as a memorial to the crucified Jesus. Paul's instruction applied to every member of all the communities of believers with which he had contact. He made it a requirement that the regular sharing of bread and wine become a part of their religious practice, to commemorate the death of Jesus, until the day of his expected and possibly imminent return. Preparation and readiness for the second coming of Jesus was at the heart of Paul's teaching.

From this ritual stipulated by Paul grew the practice which was to become one of the two sacraments that have remained at the very heart of Christianity, the eucharist or holy communion. The other ritualised practice was baptism.

In his letters, Paul referred over and again to a requirement for converts to be baptized, to demonstrate the start of a new life and to mark entry to membership of the *ekklesia*. At the start of his public ministry Jesus had been baptized by John the Baptist. It seems to be clear from the gospel narrative, however, that Jesus did not baptize others himself, although his disciples did so. There is little in the gospels to suggest that Jesus made baptism an essential requirement of anyone, including his own disciples.

The celebration of the eucharist or holy communion continues to be the most sacred rite in the great majority of Christian denominations. Similarly, baptism is practised almost universally, although its interpretation and the form it takes vary widely. The Religious Society of Friends (Quakers) is an example of the few Christian bodies that observe neither holy communion nor baptism, believing that their religious experience does not depend on outward sacraments.

Letters written by Paul to seven of the cities that he visited during his travels, and which have been preserved in the New Testament, make clear his role in founding and shaping the Christian religion. He established and set down rules and guidelines for the local *ekklesia* and its members, telling them how they should incorporate these rites into their religious life, and how to order both their individual and their corporate affairs. But above all, Paul's letters argued the case for his new beliefs and it was from his theology that Christianity developed.

As a result of Paul's preaching and writing, the emphasis of the Christian gospel had now changed. It was no longer a continuation of the message *of* Jesus of Nazareth, the radical proclamation of the coming of God's kingdom on earth, with its announcement of 'good news to the poor, release for prisoners, recovery of sight for the blind.' It had become a message *about* Jesus, a crucified and resurrected redeemer. The focus of Paul's religion was no longer on the Sermon on the Mount, but on a cross on a hill.

*   *   *

For two or three centuries, Christians experienced everything between tolerance and persecution. In 312 CE, however, there occurred what was perhaps the most
significant turning point in the evolution of the Christian
religion: indeed it could be argued that these events
secured the future of western civilisation.

On the evening before a battle at the Milvian Bridge, the
Roman emperor Constantine is said to have had a vision of
Jesus' cross, on which he saw emblazoned the assuring
message *In this sign you will conquer*. Constantine not only
won the battle that ensued, but also, in accepting that his
victory was divinely ordained, converted to Christianity.
The motivation and quality of that conversion may be
questioned, perhaps. Not for the last time in history, a
ruler had come to believe that he had been chosen by
heaven and endued with a divine right to rule (and even to
wage wars), and that his faith validated his actions. Be that
as it may, the fact remains that Constantine declared
Christianity the official religion of the Roman empire, an
event which not only ensured the rapid spread of Christianity, but also laid the foundation for its survival.

The new religion outlived imperial Rome, which came
to an end in 476 CE, in the west at least, and even survived
the centuries of the so-called Dark Ages which followed.
The faith was kept alive by the monasteries, but Paul's religion was now set to pass from the people to the princes. By
the end of the first millennium, powerful rulers who had
been building castles had begun to build cathedrals and
churches. Christianity had become, and was to remain,
enshrined within a patriarchal, authoritarian and censori-
ous church organisation, an organisation of privilege and
political power.

By the middle of the sixteenth century, though, this
Roman church was under attack. A Protestant reformation
was sweeping through Europe. The reformers attacked
what they saw as the wealth and corruption of the church
of Rome, its superstition and dogma, its abuses and
unwarranted political power and influence. The reformers
challenged papal doctrine and presented new and radical

teaching which, they believed, would return the Christian faith to its gospel roots.

The Reformation reached Britain. For personal and political reasons, Henry VIII initiated reforms which led to a split with Rome and the establishment of the Church of England under his supremacy. Henry's belief in a king's divine right to rule persisted in Britain and the country's history can in large measure be set within a religious frame, although it may more justifiably be seen as a picture of politics than one of personal piety. In 1535 the Act of Supremacy placed the king constitutionally at the head of the Church of England, where the monarch remains to this day. Kings and queens were variously Protestant and Roman Catholic, until the 1701 Act of Settlement finally established a Protestant succession.

The political, philosophical and scientific influences of the eighteenth century Enlightenment, or Age of Reason, are said to have heralded the beginning of release from ignorance and superstition; and there may be some reason to believe that as a result, the Christian faith in England began to decline. By the early years of the 1800s, however, church attendance was on the increase again, partly as a result of recent evangelical revival.

That seemingly most religious era of all, the Victorian age, was about to dawn.

Chapter Seventeen

Honest Doubt or Double Standards?

So far, the focus of the discussion has been on ways in which the past has been crafted by story-tellers, and how their stories' meaning and value may lie more in their mythic quality than in any strictly historical content, which may itself be in question. It has also been argued that myth helps to make sense of today by presenting stories from days that used to be.

If there is a possibility that sacred narrative and myth contained within the traditions and writings out of which the Christian religion grew have meaning for men and women in the twenty-first century, it may be as well to take a view of the current state of Christianity in Britain, and how it came to be the way it is.

First, then, we will dip into the history of the Victorian era, to catch glimpses of religion during that period. That will clear the way for the penultimate chapter, in which some options will be proposed for our modern days; and finally, some tentative conclusions reached.

Even today we live in the shadow of Victorian religion. Visit any British city or town, or almost any village for that matter, and you quickly see just how religious the second half of the nineteenth century must have been. Or so it may appear, if the abundance of Victorian churches and chapels still very much in evidence can be taken as a reliable indicator. The Coketown of Dickens' *Hard Times* was typical of its day, with all the new church building that 'the members of eighteen religious persuasions had done'.

Whether or not the tally was indeed eighteen, those multiple 'persuasions' represented the many denominations into which Christianity had divided over the centuries, variants of the one religion that had been based on Paul's teaching and later codified in the creeds. Not that the dissenting nonconformist chapels wanted any truck either with creeds or with a 'Catholick and Apostolick Church'; but they would have been able, had they been asked, to assent to most of the creed's stated beliefs.

During this period, Britain's churches – especially the nonconformist denominations – saw very substantial growth, although the figures still represent a minority of the total population. In *Religion in Victorian Britain*, Gerald Parsons has provided some impressive and useful data. Between 1800 and 1850, Methodist membership increased from 93,793 to 489,286, while the Congregationalists' numbers grew from 35,000 to 165,000, and the Baptists' from 27,403 to 140,277. During the years of Victoria's reign, 1837 to 1901, the Church of England built more than 5,500 new churches, and in the same period, the Scottish churches built more than 1,800. The nonconformists were equally busy – 1,500 new chapels were put up by the Congregationalists alone. At the same time, the numbers of clergy increased dramatically: the Anglicans added eleven thousand parish clergy, the Scottish churches added 1,700, and Methodist and Wesleyan ministers increased by the same number [Parsons 1988a, 1988b].

There is a possibility, however, that these remarkable figures do not so much measure religious health and vigour, or the depth of personal piety within the nation, as indicate division and conflict within the churches, and reflect other current social values and political influences. The Church of England, for example, was deeply divided between the Anglo-Catholic 'high' church, the Evangelical 'low' church, and the liberal 'broad' church. For all their differences, though, Evangelicals and broad churchmen found common cause against Anglo-Catholic rituals (at that time partly illegal) and what they considered to be the 'popery' of the high church. A different but equally unlikely alliance was that between high churchmen and Evangelicals, united against the perceived near-heresy of broad church theology. Meanwhile, members of the disenfranchised and disadvantaged nonconformist denominations fought establishment privilege and power in an attempt to be free from social and religious disablements.

It was not all internal strife and conflict, however. Although their religious practices and denominational doctrinal differences set them apart from each other, the churches almost universally shared a seemingly unshakable belief in the Bible as the word of God, holy writ which was both historically and factually true. Furthermore, all denominations were united in their hostility to the rationalist intellectuals who were seen to be undermining the churches' authority and doctrine. They also shared a desire to secure the allegiance of an apparently apathetic working class, considered to be a potential threat to social stability — for which read, a threat to a privileged and comfortable *status quo*. Even so, Rev Sabine Baring-Gould, author of the popular hymn 'Onward! Christian soldiers', seemed to have been unaware of any irony when in 1865 he wrote 'We are not divided, All one body we — One in hope and doctrine, One in charity'.

As the churches busied themselves with their separate and competing building programmes, many other changes were taking place in mid-Victorian Britain which were to add impetus to the churches' expansionist activities: among them, the so-called papal aggression, and the first-ever census of religion.

In 1850, the Pope restored the Roman Catholic hierarchy in England, where there had been no Catholic bishops since the seventeenth century, and appointed Nicholas Wiseman as Archbishop of Westminster. Protestant reaction was immediate and vigorous. The establishment's mouthpiece, *The Times*, thundered against what it considered an unwelcome and intrusive development with a 'No Popery!' leader. Protestant mobs damaged Catholic property, and effigies of the Pope were burnt on bonfires. In a letter to *The Times*, the Prime Minister asserted that the

Pope's aggression against England's Protestantism was insolent and insidious, and that what he saw as a pretension of supremacy over the realm of England was inconsistent with the Queen's supremacy. The implication was that Roman Catholics' loyalty to the Crown could not be relied upon, since their supreme allegiance was to a foreign power, the Vatican. This was not seen primarily as a religious question, then, but one of national security.

Continuing anti-Catholic feeling was coupled with anti-Irish prejudice. In the summer of 1852, the *Manchester Guardian* regretted that it had to record 'disgraceful riots ... arising out of the perpetual feuds between the Irish catholics and the lower class of English factory hands'– aggravated, the newspaper added, by the Tory government's 'popularity-hunting attack upon Roman catholic ceremonials'.

In the first half of the nineteenth century, the Roman Catholic population of England, Wales and Scotland had increased exponentially from something rather more than one hundred thousand to very nearly a million, mainly through Irish immigration. These impoverished masses settled in the new, sprawling industrial cities, living in crowded, filthy slums. In what were in effect ghettoes, Roman Catholic priests and missioners were able to reach, influence and relieve the suffering of their working class parishioners — something which Protestant clergy (those who had tried, at least) had never been able to do, now aspired to do, but in effect remained unable to do. The successes of the newly-energised Roman Catholicism presented direct challenges to Britain's Protestant churches.

This perceived new threat, coupled with resentment of implied political interference from abroad, and fear of possible unrest among a disaffected working class, lay behind the second stimulus to the churches' building programme.

For mid-Victorians, the French Revolution was comparatively recent history. Throughout the thirty or so years after the Napoleonic wars ended in 1815, waves of revolution rolled through Europe. Victorian Britain dreaded a similar fate, initiated (as elsewhere) by impoverished and underprivileged proletarian masses. The feared revolutionary unrest would be led, respectable Victorians imagined, by members of the vast underclass of labouring men. And it was a widely-held belief among the religious establishment and the emerging and increasingly influential church-going middle classes that a threat to social stability lay in the apostasy of the working classes.

When, therefore, the findings of the first-ever census of religion in England and Wales were made public, the scale of this imagined threat became shockingly clear. The census, carried out on Sunday 30 March 1851, the day before the ten-yearly national census, revealed that half the population was not in church on that day. The census commissioner commented that the middle classes were distinguished by their strictness of attendance to religious services; and that for the upper classes, regular church-attendance was now ranked amongst the recognized proprieties of life. However, he added that the same could not be said of the labouring classes; and it was readily observable that an insignificant proportion of a church's congregation was composed of artisans.

In addition to recommending that more churches be built, to provide additional accommodation for the absentee worshippers, the commissioner's report suggested improvement to the appalling slum conditions in which the labouring classes were forced to live. However, this argument was not put forward primarily for humanitarian reasons, but in the belief that alleviated poverty might make these people mindful of their religious obligations, thus reducing the threat of social unrest. It was the report writer's conclusion that the extent to which a nation was orderly and free was in proportion to the degree that religious practice was acknowledged and observed.

The methodology of the 1851 census of religion derived from the belief that people's outward conduct provides a better guide to their religious state than can be gained by merely vague profession of belief. That concept was, and is, open to question. Another commentator at the time, aware of the argument that church attendance might equally be taken as an indicator of hypocrisy, pointed out that the classes which habitually attended church frequently did so from other than religious motives. To speak of widespread apostasy among the working classes, or of their being actively opposed to religion, was simply nonsense.

The question of what people in Victorian Britain did in fact believe, compared with what they practised — the latter could, of course, be observed — is likely to remain unanswered. What is much more clearly evidenced is that Victorian Britain became an era of religious *doubt*.

Doubt and agnosticism were occasioned by an increasing number of scientific discoveries and theories, and the writings of philosophers and secularist and rationalist thinkers, all of which were seen at best to question and at worst to undermine Christian belief and shake the biblical foundations of faith. Charles Darwin's *Origin of Species*, published in 1859, may be the most obvious example, although he declared 'I had no intention to write atheistically ... my views are not at all necessarily atheistical'. There were many other influences, though. Britain had its own home-grown intellectuals — Thomas Huxley, George Eliot, John Stuart Mill, Thomas Carlyle, Leslie Stephen — but there was also powerful influence from the continent: Hegel, Schopenhauer, Kierkegaard, Nietzsche, Marx. Their published writing proliferated, disseminating ideas and beliefs wholly at variance with the Christian orthodoxy of the day.

The prevailing spirit, neither of unquestioning faith nor of atheistic rejection of belief, but of uncertainty, was exemplified in Tennyson's poem *In Memoriam*, published in 1850, the very year in which that solidly establishment figure was appointed poet laureate. T.S. Eliot was later to observe that it was not the depth of its faith but the intensity of its *doubt* that made *In Memoriam* a religious poem. Tennyson's doubt was not vague agnosticism, however, but (he claimed) an *honest* doubt, although he did not reject the creeds altogether:

> There lives more faith in honest doubt,
> Believe me, than in half the creeds.

Perhaps it was more honest to admit 'I cannot be certain …' than to recite habitually, and possibly without thought, 'I believe …'

Tennyson's *In Memoriam* is deeply concerned about immortality and a search for confidence in the church's teaching about life after death; but the poet felt that there could be no certainty:

> Behold a man raised up by Christ!
> The rest remaineth unreveal'd;
> He told it not; or something seal'd
> The lips of the Evangelist.

The evangelist to whom Tennyson refers was the author of the Bible's *Gospel according to John*, who told the story of Jesus restoring his dead friend Lazarus to life. As he relates that story, the gospel writer ascribes to Jesus the words 'I am the resurrection and the life'. In the painting *The Doubt* by Henry Bowler, a contemporary of Tennyson, those same words can be seen engraved on the tombstone on which a young woman leans. She contemplates the grave of John Faithful and ponders the biblical question in the painting's subtitle: 'Can these dry bones live?' The adjoining tombstone bears the one word *Resurgam … I shall rise again*. But there is room for doubt.

The question of 'honest doubt' was about to become an issue, not only for lay people, but more significantly for the clergy. In 1860, six broad church Anglican clergymen and one layman published *Essays and Reviews*, in which their liberal theology challenged a whole range of Christian orthodoxy. One essay, with direct reference to the then current German biblical scholarship, argued for the application of scientific and literary criticism to the Bible. Another questioned the 'miraculous' content of biblical texts. Other essays challenged the *Genesis* creation narratives, in light of the new science of geology, and proposed multiple authorship for the five 'books of Moses'.

One of the most scandalous suggestions in *Essays and Reviews* was made by Benjamin Jowett, who believed that the Bible should be 'interpreted like any other book'. Jowett was perfectly clear that 'There are many respects in which Scripture is unlike any other book' but those differences, he suggested, would 'appear in the results of such an interpretation'. Jowett seems to have been generations before his time in his anticipation of semantics and hermeneutics, and what would become revolutionary literary theory in the twentieth century. But he already appeared to understand that the meaning of a text is not fixed or capable of only one interpretation, but is for readers to 'create' for themselves. By following the rules of literary criticism, Jowett contended, 'the Bible will still remain unlike any other book [but] It will be a Spirit, not a letter.'

Essays and Reviews caused uproar and outrage, although in the event the book was to go through thirteen editions during the next five years. In 1864, two of the authors were charged with heresy and found guilty, but on appeal the church court's judgment was overturned.

A second heresy trial followed in 1866. Bishop John Colenso, another theologian who argued that the authorship of the Bible's first five books could not be attributed wholly to Moses, believed that much of the numerical detail in the Pentateuchal narratives simply did not add up. Colenso earned the wrath of his archbishop, was invited to resign, refused, and was deposed and tried for heresy. Although he was found guilty, the verdict was later overturned.

Such controversy was not solely the domain of the established church. In 1856, Samuel Davidson, a lecturer at a Congregational theological college, also published a book questioning the Mosaic authorship of the Pentateuch; but more contentiously, his argument against the literal truth of the whole Bible held that its 'infallibility' applied only in a religious and moral sense. The college committee voted for Davidson's suspension while they examined the book's contents; but he pre-empted their verdict, chose to resign, and took up a secular teaching post.

Scotland was not to be left out. W Robertson Smith, professor of Hebrew at the Free Church college in Aberdeen, contributed a number of articles to the ninth edition of *Encyclopaedia Britannica*, notably a feature on Hebrew language and literature. Familiar with the work of German biblical scholars (he had studied in Germany), Smith also argued for the Pentateuch's multiple authorship; but worse, he proposed a complete re-think of the order in which the Bible's books were traditionally believed to have been compiled and collected. The new *Britannica* appeared in 1875, and Smith immediately fell foul of the leadership of the Free Church of Scotland. After five years of prolonged confrontation with his critics, Smith was dismissed from his post by the church's General Assembly.

For the clergy, such controversies had already given rise to the issue of 'honest doubt'. Not surprisingly, it was questioned whether an Anglican or any other clergyman could with integrity hold his ordained appointment within the church and at the same time subscribe to the views being expressed in publications such as *Essays and Reviews*. In 1861, the Bishop of Oxford declared his belief in the incompatibility of the opinions of the essayists and authentic Christianity. At the same time, a letter from a number of bishops to the Archbishop of Canterbury expressed alarm at 'the spread of rationalistic and semi-infidel doctrines among the beneficed clergy of the realm' — not least because these 'speculations would rob our countrymen, more especially the poor and unlearned, of their only sure stay and comfort for time and for eternity'. The archbishop replied that he could not understand how the essayists or any clergyman could hold the opinions expressed in *Essays and Reviews* and at the same time subscribe honestly to the formularies of the Church of England.

The probability is that to the man and woman in the pew, many of the issues proposed and discussed by the authors of *Essays and Reviews* and by men like Colenso, Davidson and Robertson Smith, were unfamiliar and largely remained so, and the 'poor and unlearned' were blissfully unaware of the ways in which the foundations were being shaken. However, for an unknown number of clergymen — and this applied equally to nonconformist ministers — the ethical dilemma was real and they had to consider their position: could they agree with the 'new theology' at a personal level, and at the same time continue with any honesty to preach and teach in the ways that the church expected of them?

Even at the end of the century, the question was still being asked. Lay people, those who were even aware of the dilemma, were free to continue to believe the contents of the creed to be literally true and historically factual, or else to declare quite openly that they understood them as myth or metaphor. That was not a course so readily available to the clergy.

As the twentieth century dawned, the Victorian age was drawing to its close, and religion had become far less central to British society. Within the Church of England, the old rivalries and conflicts between conservative Evangelicals and liberal broad church were less in evidence. Anglo-Catholic ritual had been legitimised. Nonconformists, freed by legislation from their long-standing social disabilities, had become respectable and prosperous, as their opulent if not ostentatious churches and chapels bear witness. Among the Congregationalists, there were by now a number of ministers who accepted the kind of liberal theology which fifty years earlier had landed Samuel Davidson in hot water.

Over all, however, Britain's Christian denominations remained conservative and evangelical, partly as a result of four popular missions conducted between 1873 and 1892 by two American evangelists, Dwight Moody and Ira Sankey. The churches' preaching was dogmatic, based on a literal belief in the Bible as God's revealed word. They proclaimed a supernatural and interventionist God, with an emphasis on sin, a call for repentance, and equal certainty about blessedness for the 'saved' and hell and eternal punishment for those who did not see the light. Church attendance continued to decline as a proportion of a rapidly-growing population — rather less than twenty-one million in 1851, but thirty-seven million by 1901 — and remained largely middle class. Only the Roman Catholic church could lay claim to genuinely working class congregations.

Victorian religion reached far into the twentieth century. In the early 1940s, Sunday school children (I was one of them) were still singing hymns from a book published decades before, at the time of the Moody and Sankey missions:

> Jesus loves me! This I know,
> For the Bible tells me so:
> Little ones to Him belong;
> They are weak, but He is strong.

The hymn concluded with these lines:

> If I love Him, when I die
> He will take me home on high.

Already, probably aged no more than five, we were being influenced to 'believe' that on the unquestioned authority of the Bible, we could know that we were loved by an invisible (but apparently alive) Jesus, that we were dependent on him, and that, conditional upon our reciprocating his love, we would join him 'on high' when we died — not necessarily a thought uppermost in five-year-old minds.

Another hymn which we sang (and which others may recall) assured us that

> There's a Friend for little children
>   Above the bright blue sky,
> A Friend that never changes,
>   Whose love will never die.

The hymn promised a number of other things 'above the bright blue sky', which would presumably appeal to little children: a rest from every trouble, a home where all are happy, a crown of brightest glory, a song that will not weary, and a harp of sweetest music. Whether or not that hymn is still in present-day hymnals, I do not know; but it was certainly to be found in hymn books well into the seventh decade of the twentieth century, and perhaps even later than that.

As Victorian evangelicalism continued to dominate Christian religion in twentieth century Britain, the issues that had surrounded 'honest doubt' in the mid-nineteenth century had not gone away. Throughout the first half of the nineteen hundreds, theological scholarship continued to advance ideas that presented challenges to orthodoxy, and by mid-century no clergyman worth his salt would have been unaware of the work of theologians such as Karl Barth, Dietrich Bonhoeffer, Rudolf Bultmann and Paul Tillich, and the implications of their thinking and writing.

Lay people, on the other hand, even educated lay people, may have remained unaware of these developments, had it not been for a paperback book which burst upon the scene in 1963 amid much publicity, and promptly sold a million copies worldwide. In *Honest to God*, John Robinson, Bishop of Woolwich, summarised in popular form these four theologians' thinking, in what was to become known as the 'Death of God' controversy (borrowing Nietzsche's words, 'God is dead!'). *Honest to God* explored 'religionless Christianity', argued very cogently against the traditional belief in a 'God out there', and presented instead the concept of a 'God within', as 'the ground of our being'. The book placed great emphasis not only on the myth within the biblical narratives, but also on the need to interpret the myth: the way in which the universe is now understood (so far, at least) is wholly different from any notions which people had two thousand years ago or more. An obvious example is that the biblical concepts of 'above' and 'below' have long been obsolete.

In making these ideas widely accessible to lay people who may otherwise have remained unaware of them, *Honest to God* uncovered what the Cambridge theologian Don Cupitt has more recently described as the

> well-known and freely-admitted fact that church leaders nowadays have two faiths. There is the common ecclesiastical faith to which they are institutionally committed by their office, and which they must unhesitatingly

> defend in public; and there is the personal faith to which
> they have been led by their own study and thinking.
> Every church leader who is theologically educated is
> aware of the gap between the two, and of the devices that
> must be used to conceal it. [Cupitt 2004]

Cupitt added that the prophet Elijah might well ask today,
'How long will you go limping with two different opinions?'

We cannot know, of course, how many ordained men
and women are caught, or have any sense of being caught,
in this dilemma. What we may be sure of, however, is that
few if any are unaware of the disparity between what can
no longer be termed 'new theology' and the conservative
orthodoxy that they continue to present, and are expected
to present, in their churches. During their studies at theological college, ordinands will to one extent or another
have become familiar with liberal theology — which is not
to suggest that it should be mandatory for them to accept it
or agree with it — and therefore cannot be unaware of the
gap between pulpit and pew, let alone the gulf between pulpit and pavement. Quite apart from any ethical question,
there does appear to be a matter of intellectual honesty.

This book began with a reference to a Baptist minister
and an Anglican vicar who used the phrase 'the historical
evidence for the resurrection'. Significantly, neither man
offered his listeners any information to substantiate his
claim, but left the statement hanging in the air, as an
apparently authoritative statement of fact. However, these
speakers would have known from their own studies that
there *is* no historical evidence, as we have already seen. In
making the claims which they did, they were being less
than helpful to their listeners, who (it may be reasonably
assumed) would on the whole have accepted and believed
what they were hearing, simply because the speakers,
authority figures, had studied at theological college and
they had not. Thus, myth is dressed up as history, and in
effect untruth is spread and perpetuated.

I have argued that we live in the shadow of Victorian
religion and that its influence is with us still, with a literal

belief in a supernatural creator God 'out there', an emphasis on a divinely-inspired, infallible God-given Bible, a belief in Jesus as an historically incarnate God-man, and in his redemptive death and physical resurrection. It seems remarkable that after generations of theological advance and a vast array of international biblical scholarship, coupled with once inconceivable and exponential expansion of our knowledge of the world and universe in which we live, such literal beliefs continue to be presented as fact.

To have lost sight of the value of myth seems to be both retrogressive and regrettable, and to have confused myth with history — indeed, actively to present myth as though it were history — is questionable both intellectually and in terms of integrity.

In 2005, the interdenominational Evangelical Alliance adopted a new version of its published basis of belief. This twenty-first century 'update' of a mid-nineteenth century original re-affirms a belief in the personal and visible second coming of Jesus, who will return to fulfil God's purposes — although the new version appears to have watered down the pre-2005 statement of belief that on the judgment day, all people will be raised; and while those who are redeemed will enter into eternal life, the lost will go to eternal condemnation. Some three thousand five hundred churches are affiliated to the Evangelical Alliance; and while several hundred of these are to be found, as might be expected, among the emergent 'new frontier' and Pentecostal churches, far and away the greatest proportion of the affiliated churches are Anglican and Baptist — in other words, not on the fringes but in the mainstream of institutional Christianity in Britain.

The time has long since passed when such outdated evangelical dogma should be challenged with vigour. In the nineteenth century, the Victorians developed alternative ways of thinking and talking about religion, history and myth. There are alternatives available to twenty-first century men and women, too, and in the next chapter, we will consider some of those options.

Chapter Eighteen

Human, All-Too-Human

In questioning what grounds there may be for believing that there is historical truth in some of the stories which are told, my argument has been that the stories' meaning and value may be said to lie in their mythic quality rather than in their possibly historical content. The discussion was initiated by claims made for the historical evidence for the resurrection of Jesus. These claims are mistaken, I have argued, not simply because of the absence of reliable, independent evidence for this as an historical event, but more significantly because a greater value for the story is to be found in its mythic or metaphorical meaning.

In this penultimate chapter, I want to press this argument further, and suggest possible meanings for the myth in the twenty-first century, before coming to a tentative conclusion, which in effect is not an ending at all, but a beginning.

Myth should not be dismissed, I believe, as though it has been made obsolete by our scientific age, something which modern men and women have outgrown. What I have in mind is the Jungian concept that if men and women cease to value myth, they are in danger of losing an essential inner quality. It is as myth (or as a metaphor, if you will) that the resurrection — to use the example at the centre of this discussion — provides a powerful model of the potential for transcendent values in the twenty-first century.

The process is a challenging one, requiring a radical reappraisal of the meaning of religion and of Christianity.

It is intended both for those who call themselves Christian, whatever meaning they give to the word, and whether they position themselves inside or outside any of the churches; and for those who so far and for whatever reason have found no place in their lives for institutional religion, but who none the less are open to ideas about what might be labelled 'the spiritual'.

On the evidence which follows, there appears to be good reason to suggest that Britons may remain intrinsically religious. But, as ever, a question has to be asked: What do we mean by religious?

In 2001, Britain's national census included a voluntary question: What is your religion? Each individual in every household was invited to tick one of a number of boxes: there was a box for each of the six principal religions, one for 'Other religions', and another for 'No religion'. Analysis of the census results showed that nearly seventy-two percent of people ticked the box marked 'Christian'. The five other main religions between them accounted for a little over five percent of the population, and nearly twenty-three percent either chose 'No religion' or gave no answer [Office for National Statistics 2001].

It is the first group and the last that are of prime interest here: but before moving on, it would be interesting to theorise about two questions: On what basis did those who ticked a box against any of the other five major religions do so? And how precisely would they be able to define the beliefs or practices most essential to their religion, were they asked? Answers to the first question would probably include birth, family, community, ethnic origin, national tradition, conversion or conviction. Answers to the second might well range from comprehensively correct to rudimentary.

How well would those who ticked the 'Christian' box fare, if asked the same questions? Possibly the answers would be little different from those given by adherents to the other religions. One thing appears certain, however: church attendance is unlikely to feature very high in the majority's definition of essential practice.

Statistics for church attendance in twenty-first century 'Christian' Britain which come even vaguely close to accuracy are notoriously difficult to find. The mid-Victorians were shocked when the 1851 census revealed that only half the population attended church. Today, it is suggested that perhaps five or maybe seven percent of the UK population attend church at all regularly, although the numbers are higher at Easter and at Christmas. That may be as good a guess as any. Whatever the proportion is, it is a small minority, and it continues to decline.

The point at issue here is this: there is clearly a huge disparity in the numbers, between nearly three quarters of the population who label themselves Christian and the small percentage who attend church. There seems therefore to be a critical question: What did 'Christian' mean to those who ticked the box?

Unfortunately for our discussion, the census analysis does not provide answers to questions such as, Did those who ticked the 'Christian' box do so because they knew that they were not Jewish or Hindu, for example? Did they identify themselves as Christian because they live in a 'Christian' country or a 'Christian' society and not in, say, a Muslim or a Buddhist one? How would they have answered if there had been no boxes to tick, but the question had been presented simply as an open one, What is your religion?

And what of those who chose either to state that they have no religion or to give no answer? They constitute a significant proportion of the total population — nearer to a quarter than a fifth — two out of three choosing the 'No religion' option, and the other giving no reply. We know nothing of the latter: but the former may include many who have no specific religious affiliation rather than no religion, or who, for one reason or another, have rejected organised religion or have no interest in its formal observance. They may have thrown out baby with the bath water, but that does not necessarily make them irreligious or without religion, of course.

True atheism, I suspect, is comparatively rare: that is to say, relatively few people maintain a thought-through conviction that there is no god of any kind, or that there is *nothing* either outside or within themselves that can be addressed as 'other'. That is perhaps rather nicely illustrated by the man who called a BBC phone-in programme and declared 'Thank God I'm an atheist!'

It is interesting in this context to recall Voltaire, who suggested that if God did not exist, it would be necessary to invent him. One might expect that out-and-out rejection of religion would result in a growth in rational humanism, but it is not clear that that is happening. It is possible, of course, that to some extent a substitute for traditional religious belief is to be found in cultic organisations or in New Age practices.

On the other hand, agnosticism — not being sure — can be said to be much more in evidence. Consider still-popular Christmas carol services, for example: carols may be no more than a sentimental facet of traditional seasonal celebrations, but their undeniably supernatural content seems not to have been rejected entirely. And the so-called rites of passage — hatches, matches and dispatches — have by no means yet lost their religious, that is to say church-related, associations.

It may be relevant at this point to revisit briefly the meaning of belief, or at least to have a working understanding of what may be meant by the word. In an earlier chapter it was suggested that belief can be taken to mean accepting that something is true, as a matter of opinion or conviction; but in this sense, belief is differentiated from knowledge by its absence of verifiable evidence. The *belief that* water freezes at zero Centigrade, or the *belief that* the Statue of Liberty can be seen on a visit to New York, clearly constitutes an acceptance that a statement is true or that something exists.

That level or quality of belief can be contrasted with a *belief in* freedom of speech (let us say). This kind of belief goes much deeper. It is a conviction, something that the believers-in are prepared to stand up for and defend, and a belief-in to which they may even wish to convert others. They are likely to continue holding that belief until something more powerful and persuasive comes along and changes their mind. There is clearly a difference, too, between the belief that Jesus lived in Galilee in the first decades of the present era — an intellectual belief-that — and a belief in him as the incarnate son of God who returned from the dead — unquestionably a religious belief-in. What may be open to question, though, is whether some (many?) Christians' belief-in may be not so much a thought-through conviction, as an assenting response to what is expected of those wishing to belong, a readiness to sign up to their particular religious community's 'rule book' for membership.

So, back to that seventy-two percent of people who call themselves Christian, and the not insignificant minority who state that they have no religion. What is it that the former believe in? And what belief have the latter rejected, or have no place for in their lives? It would very significantly aid this discussion, were we to know the answers to those questions.

It could be argued that there is more than one Christianity, given the wide variety of organisational structures, ritual practices (or absence of them), and denominational emphases and doctrines, let alone schism, dispute and division, which are evident in the churches. However, at the centre of this multi-stranded Christianity lie four beliefs *essential to orthodoxy* (a vital emphasis): God's perfect creation; the fall of Adam and Eve, to whose sin all mankind is heir; hence the incarnation of God's son Jesus and his redeeming death and resurrection; and the final judgment following the resurrection of the dead. Of these the one irreducible belief (from the orthodox standpoint) is that of an incarnate God, a God who became fully man and yet remained fully God.

In the previous chapter, it was suggested that Britain's churches remain predominantly conservative and evangelical, upholding the fundamental beliefs expressed in the creed, whether or not they are credal denominations. It may be understandable that modern, secular men and women respond 'But that I can't believe', when presented with a six-day creation, a God 'out there' (or 'up there'), angels, the virgin birth of a God-man, miracles performed by him, or his return from the dead and ascension to 'heaven'. Yet an ABC poll in 2004 suggested that in the USA at least (where, proportionally, church attendance is at a very high level), an overwhelming number of evangelical Protestants believe in the literal truth of the Bible. According to the American survey, eighty-seven per cent accept as fact the biblical account of the creation, ninety-one per cent believe that Moses and the Israelites crossed the Red Sea on dry land as described in *Exodus*, and eight-seven per cent have a belief in the literal truth of the biblical story of Noah's ark [*Washington Times*]. If such a survey were made of British church members today, the findings may not be dissimilar.

Across the USA, conservatives' active promotion of creationism, the belief that a supernatural God created the universe literally in six days and made Eve out of Adam's rib, has caused educational controversy. In recent times, schools in a number of states attempted to teach creationism as a fact, in place of evolution as a theory. This contravened a supreme court ruling in 1987, that it was unlawful to ensure 'that creationism was taught if anything at all was taught' and that the exclusive teaching of creationism 'did not have a secular purpose and that it did not advance academic freedom'. Subsequent attempts were made to introduce the concept of 'intelligent design' into school science lessons, but a federal judge ruled that this violated the American constitution. 'Intelligent design' is merely creationism in disguise. Similar controversy is making itself felt in Britain, where there is secular concern about evangelical organisations' involvement in state education, with their goal of introducing fundamentalist agenda.

It needs to be remembered that the conservative evangelical interpretation of the faith is not the only one. Whereas evangelicals claim the Bible *to be* 'The Word of

God', those who take a liberal standpoint would say that the Bible *contains* the word of God. Like their Victorian forebears, Colenso, Robertson Smith, Davidson and Jowett, liberal Christians today regard the Bible as a collection of books with a human origin, requiring critical reading like any other literature. That is not to say that the Bible is thought to be 'like' other literature, however great that literature may be. To one extent or another, liberals also consider much of the biblical narrative to be imagery or myth, not taking literally such stories as the creation, Noah's ark, the Red Sea crossing, or even the gospel miracle narratives. So far, so good.

Unfortunately, one of the problems with this kind of pick-and-mix thinking is that, in contrast with the cut-and-dried statements of the creed — if taken literally — one cannot be clear what is to be believed. It is difficult to know what 'shape' such a Christianity has. It is reminiscent of the parable of the six blind men of Indostan, who try to describe an elephant by feeling it: the man who bumps against the animal's side thinks an elephant resembles a wall, whereas the man who feels a leg believes the elephant to be like a tree; others feel a tusk, an ear, the trunk or the tail, and conclude that the elephant resembles a spear, a fan, a snake or a rope. In attempting to define this creature, each of the blind men was partly in the right, but in effect all were in large measure mistaken.

Radical voices are to be heard, some in high places, which seek to shake the foundations. In 1998, John Shelby Spong, at that time Episcopal Bishop of Newark, New Jersey, wrote:

> The frame of reference in which Christianity was originally cast is gone. The message of Christ was proclaimed inside first-century thinking, making assumptions that people cannot make today ... How can one continue to proclaim such pre-modern and psychologically destructive concepts in our post-modern world? [Spong 1998]

A century and a half after Colenso, Robertson Smith and Davidson, church leaders and priests are still being deprived of their living as a result of going public with their radicalism. It may be difficult to believe, but as recently as 2002, Andrew Furlong, at that time the Anglican dean of Clonmacnoise in Ireland, was brought to trial for heresy. While unequivocally acknowledging his belief in God, he does not subscribe to a faith claim that God entered human history and became a man. His bishop asked him to resign from his post, because of his inability to accept the concept of Jesus as God incarnate, or the doctrine of his death atoning for mankind's sins.

In his book, *Tried for Heresy*, Andrew Furlong quotes from a number of the many letters of support he had received, one from a recently-retired Anglican priest, who wrote, 'Most of my clergy acquaintances, many senior in their dioceses, hold views similar to yours (and mine) but manage to keep them well concealed, so as not to rock the boat and risk their status and their security' [cited in Furlong 2003]. Clearly, the Victorian 'honest doubt' dilemma has neither gone away nor been resolved.

A radical way of re-defining Christianity — and I am borrowing the term already in use, Christian humanism — is to see religion as a human creation, and God as a human concept, with no place for the supernatural. This approach is being taken and advocated by a growing number of writers, theologians and (encouragingly) clergy, as well as many lay people. The Sea of Faith Network, for example, promotes 'the validity of creative, human-centred religion', and yet retains the affirmation of

> the continuing importance of religious thought and practice as expressions of awe and wonder and as celebrations of spiritual and social values.

Predictably, this does not go down very well with the religious establishment. One such proponent of this new way of thinking is Anthony Freeman. His bishop removed him from his post as priest-in-charge of an Anglican parish in Sussex, following the publication of his book in 1993, *God In Us: A Case for Christian Humanism*. In it, Anthony Freeman describes what he calls a conversion experience which 'released [him] to find a new meaning in the word God'. He explains:

> Only when I had accepted that 'I do not believe in God'
> (my old God) was I free to discover how with integrity I
> could still say 'I believe in God' (understood in a new
> way). [Freeman 1993]

Asked 'Do you believe in God?' Anthony Freeman
answers, 'Yes, I do believe in God, and one of the things I
believe about God is that he does not exist.'

This most radical way of re-defining religion and belief
presents twenty-first century men and women with a
wholly reformed Christianity which they may recognize
and accept as more relevant and appropriate to their lives.
Now may be the time of a new Reformation. Christian
humanism seems to hold out a new way of being to many
who may have ticked that 'Christian' box in the census,
men and women who have grown up in a Christian culture but who, for whatever reason, have not felt able to
make a place in their lives for a faith as traditionally
defined.

What is being questioned here is whether the increasingly improbable conservative evangelical position is any
longer tenable, as it continues to defend the literal existence of a supernatural God, with all the trappings of a
faith which are left-overs from a pre-scientific and pre-
critical age — and even attempts, as we have seen, to shore
up its position by claiming historical evidence for 'events'
which may be more rationally defined as myth.

It is argued, too, that the liberal view, which is content to
rationalise or explain away some of the conservatives' articles of faith, does not go far enough. Rather than recogniz-
ing and wholeheartedly embracing the concept of myth,
the liberal position becomes ineffective through this
reduction of core beliefs.

Voltaire's suggestion that if God did not exist, we would
have to invent him, may be what mankind did in fact do.
Traditionally, the God 'out there' was posited as an eternal, supernatural being, omnipotent, omniscient, omni-
present, but made known in the only way available to us,
through our language. The thirteenth century mystic
Meister Eckhart understood this: 'When we speak of

divine matters, we have to stammer, because we are forced
to express our experiences in words' [Fox 1983]. Paradoxi-
cally, a limitless and infinite God has been limited by finite
human vocabulary. For countless generations, words
without number have been (continue to be) used to create
images of God and to give expression to his nature, even
though, by definition, God is unknowable and therefore
impossible to describe:

> Immortal, invisible, God only wise,
> In light inaccessible, hid from our eyes,
> Most blessed, most glorious, the Ancient of Days,
> Almighty, victorious, Thy great Name we praise.

Even if there were an invisible God, inaccessible and hid
from our eyes, it would not be rational to claim knowledge
of his existence, simply because he would be literally
beyond our comprehension. We could not know whether
his existence was a fact or not; it could only be an article of
faith, or belief-in, for those who chose to accept and maintain it.

It seems to be true, then, that any way in which men and
women may attempt to give expression to God, and any
way in which they may claim to experience him, can only
be through human understanding and in human terms.
The Bible, for example, is believed by many to be God's
revelation to mankind; but since it was without question
written by men — however inspired they may be thought
to have been, or believed themselves to be — it is not possible to know whether it is divine revelation. Christian
humanism holds to the view that God, as a supernatural
being, is a human concept, and a religion which maintains
supernatural beliefs is a human creation.

We have already noted the need to reject long-outdated
concepts of a three-tiered universe and the pre-Coperni-
can 'above' and 'below' language which was natural not
only to the biblical authors but also to those who compiled
the creeds. It should not be possible in the twenty-first century to continue subscribing to a belief-in which takes literally a first century world view. That world also accepted
the idea of an interventionist God, who, like Homer's

Olympian gods, 'came down' and played an active role in the lives of mortals, for good or ill. Like the great god Zeus, who, in his dealings with men and women, 'moves now in evil, again in good fortune', this interventionist God rewarded those who obeyed his laws and punished the wayward and the unfaithful.

Long-obsolete supernatural language includes belief in life after death and in a God who on some future judgment day will raise all people, either to eternal life or to eternal condemnation. Christian humanism questions the concept of an after-life, preferring to place the emphasis on *this* as our life, the here-and-now. It is not possible to know of any other. William Blake's lines, written in 1818, seemed to indicate his belief that eternity is *now*:

> Thou also dwelst in eternity.
> Thou art a Man, God is no more,
> Thine own Humanity learn to Adore.

Not only is Man already living eternal life, but, in Blake's view, God is no more than human, and men and women need to learn to value their humanity, or 'adore' it in place of worshipping a divinity.

It may be that this gives meaning to the myth of the resurrection, the myth of a man who once was dead but is alive again, which can be taken as a metaphor for making a new beginning, creating a better life, a better world. The optimist, it is said, proclaims that we live in the best of all possible worlds, and the pessimist fears that this is true. It would be a remarkable optimist, on the other hand, who believes that our world is as good as it can be; and it would be a remarkable pessimist who did not believe that something can be done about it.

The man from Galilee, Jesus of Nazareth, went round proclaiming the good news of the kingdom: news of healing and freedom and new life, what today we might call social justice, equality, peace and reconciliation. Like motherhood and apple pie, it is unlikely that anyone is going to be against these things. But 'doing good' and doing the right things seems to be more easily said than done. The common experience is doubtless the one about which Paul wrote in one of his letters: 'The good which I want to do, I fail to do; but what I do is the wrong which is against my will' [*Romans* 7:19].

At this point, though, Christian humanism would have to part company with Paul, as he claims in the same letter, 'It is no longer I who perform the action, but sin that dwells in me.' To shift the blame to a 'sinful' nature, or even a personified 'tempter', appears to be no more defensible than it was for Agamemnon to blame Zeus for his actions: 'I am not responsible but Zeus is ... what could I do?' It is the child who says 'It wasn't my fault!' Adults have to take responsibility for their own actions; there is no one else to blame but ourselves.

It may be that, like Mark Twain's obituary, the report of God's death was an exaggeration, or was at least premature. Christian humanism suggests that what needs to die is our old, supernatural (superstitious?) image of God. It is not a new idea. Meister Eckhart prayed for God to rid him of God, ridding him of the inadequate and limiting images which he had created in his own mind. It was when Anthony Freeman let go of his old images that he found he had been 'released ... to find a new meaning in the word God'. That God is no longer a God 'out there' but, in Freeman's words, 'the sum of all my values and ideals in life' — the God-within [Freeman 1993].

The religion described by Christian humanists as man-made, 'the ground of our being', is experienced as the sum of the highest values and ideals to which we can *aspire* — no doubt including those that Paul said were demonstrated by people who live in the spirit of their God: love, joy, peace, patience, kindness, goodness, fidelity, gentleness and self-control. The God-within becomes the focus not simply for idealism but more significantly for actively seeking *to become all that one is capable of becoming*.

To aspire to that continuous process of becoming, and to be aware of and committed to concerns and causes outside oneself, are characteristic of those whom the humanistic psychologist Abraham Maslow called self-actualizing people. Such people 'manage somehow simultaneously to love the world as it is and to try to improve it' and 'hope that people and nature and society could be improved.' [Maslow 1976]. But Maslow did not leave things there; he visualised a stage beyond self-actualization, which he defined as transcendence. For 'transcenders', the world and everything in it is seen and understood in terms of spiritual values, and such people are at home with what we have been calling the mythic. According to Maslow, 'They can sacralize everything at will; ie perceive it under the aspect of eternity'. Above all, transcenders are 'holistic about the world ... Mankind is one and the cosmos is one.' It is perhaps what Matthew Fox sees as 'humanity's potential to act divinely both in ways of compassion and of beauty-making and sharing' [Fox 1983].

This sense of one-ness and the ability to perceive life as eternity are implicit in a phrase much-loved by Quakers, taken from one of George Fox's letters, which speaks of seeking 'that of God' in everyone. This engenders an optimistic view of humankind and the potential for good that lies within every individual: which is not to say that we should naïvely deny our own dark corners or be blind to the ghastly things that we see all around us. John Donne was perhaps four hundred years ahead of his time when he wrote 'No man is an island, entire of itself ... any man's death diminishes me, because I am involved in mankind'.

Within Einstein's view of possible universes was the concept of entanglement, which physicists were later to call nonseparability. Nonseparability suggests that as matter exploded outwards from the infinitely small pin-point of the big bang, it did not divide for all eternity into billions upon billions of separate particles, but retained its oneness and has done so ever since that creation-moment. Everything remains a part of everything else. In some literally matter-of-fact way, quantum mechanics appears to show (and it is a mystery I am content to accept) that we are all a part of an infinite whole, living within an inseparable unity. Each of us is a part of the other.

* * *

In all of this, then, there are suggestions for meanings to be found in the resurrection, an interpretation of the myth. The man from Galilee presented a model for mankind; and Christianity's metaphorical assertion that 'Jesus lives!' may encourage men and women today to aspire to live out the teaching of his Sermon on the Mount.

This has to be heard as a universal message, though, freely and unconditionally accessible to all men and women, and not narrowed down into exclusive and excluding dogma. There was a suggestion in chapter sixteen that Peter's first century words have since been misappropriated – 'There is no salvation through anyone else; in all the world no other name has been granted to mankind by which we can be saved' – resulting in Christianity's assumption that it can validly present itself as the unique path to 'salvation', to the exclusion of all other faiths. It seems unlikely that the reconciliation of the family of mankind lies that way. The call is to build bridges, not barriers.

The resurrection can not to be proved to have taken place as a literal event at a specific point in an historical past, although many will choose to continue believing it did, and some may continue to make claims for historical evidence. But the resurrection does serve as an image for a here-and-now breaking through from the finite into the infinite.

Thus it is possible to see eternity as a quality of the life in which all men and women, of all faiths and none, are bound inseparably together, each responsible for the good of the other. A perfect world may remain an ideal, and religion may represent a path toward it rather than itself form a destination. But when all has been said, religion remains (to borrow Nietzsche's words) 'human, all-too-human'.

Chapter Nineteen

A New Beginning

We began with questions about historicity: How can we *know* that the events in the stories that are told did in fact take place, or that the people about whom the stories are told did in fact exist? Gradually, though, the discussion began to leave history behind, until in the end its concern was with myth and metaphor. One answer to the question — What grounds might there be for believing the content of biblical narratives to be more historical than the Greek ones? — may be that this is the wrong question. Whether reading *Iliad*, Pentateuch, or gospel narratives, one is entering myth, not history. The point has been made that the value of myth lies not in its truth as fact, but in its truth as meaning.

It seems to me that there is a place for both history and myth: left-brained rational thinking, which insists on the evidence and records the facts; and right-brained creativity, which cherishes the mysterious and dreams of possibilities. It may be true that our modern materialist and scientific world tends to value the former at the expense of the latter; but I have proposed that to lose the age-old facility for myth-making would deprive us of a vital part of our humanity.

On the other hand, the two should not be confused, or one mistaken for the other. It is fascinating to conjecture which parts of the stories of the Trojan war may be fact and which parts glorious fiction: to question to what extent the biblical exodus narrative is history and to what extent it has a mythic meaning for the origins of a people and for their ancient religion and culture: or to get our minds

around the realisation that we have little more historical
evidence for the life of Jesus than we have for the life of
King Arthur. What is unhelpful, though, if not dishonest,
is to present unanswered questions in the guise of historical fact, and to use dubious history as a technique of persuasion.

The ancient stories that are told, and which (it has been
argued) are more myth than history, still have a place in
our modern world, and not merely as literary heritage
(which they none the less are). Their mythic truths are a
part of the eternity in which we and our neighbours dwell,
transcending the here-and-now and affording glimpses of
mankind's potential. Their metaphorical language prof-
fers truths about our interdependence and reliance one
upon another, and offers clues about possible new worlds.

At this point, perhaps, we have joined the *Via
Transformativa*, the way that leads to compassion and
social justice. The transformation begins with renewal, the
metaphorical resurrection of the individual, with the free
offer of peace of mind and deliverance from whatever it is
that is best left behind. But it leads on to an agenda which
reaches far beyond personal redemption, to a concern for
one's neighbour, and for a planet that could be green once
more. That will make demands on each individual in his or
her corner of the vineyard.

The old vocabulary may require revision, a return perhaps to its origins: an outworn, other-worldly 'holiness'
should make way for words which share its Old English
roots — wholeness, healing, health, and (a modern deriva-
tive) holism. Perhaps this kind of wholeness is what we
mean when we say 'God'.

Personal piety should be displaced by meanings which
the Romans gave to their word *pietas*: conscientiousness,
dutifulness to neighbours and country, loyalty, mercy,
justice. That is a big enough programme to be going on
with.

Each man and woman has to determine where to go
from here, and what (if anything) to do about all this.
There is a gospel text which reads, 'when the Spirit of truth

comes, he will guide you into all the truth' [*John* 16:13].
H.A. Williams has said of this verse, 'Nowhere in the New
Testament do we find words more terrifying than these'
[Williams 1965], because the challenge is to step out into
the unknown, in faith. Being prepared to be guided 'into
all the truth' could be a little on the risky side.

Honest searching may bring us back to a place where we
have been before but did not recognise at the time, or
reveal truths that we knew all along but did not know that
we knew. At this point, however, we discover that this is
not an end at all. We may have come home, but we have
not come home to stay. Now there is a journey to make, a
quest to pursue – 'For here we have no lasting city, but we
are seekers after the city which is to come' [*A Letter to
Hebrews* 13:14]. As we set out, we may catch something of
the Old Testament prophet's vision, a vision of re-birth
and renewal:

> See, I am creating new heavens and a new earth!
> The past will no more be remembered nor will it ever
> come to mind. [*Isaiah* 65:17]

Acknowledgements

The author and publisher thank the following for their permission to quote from copyright material:

Blackwell Publishing Limited: *The Young Hemingway* by Michael Reynolds

Constable and Robinson: *The True Wilderness* by H.A. Williams

Darton, Longman and Todd: *The Jerusalem Bible*; and *A Jewish Theology* by Louis Jacobs

Faber and Faber, London, and W.W. Norton, New York: *Beowolf*, translated by Seamus Heaney

Anthony Freeman: for extracts from his book *God In Us: A Case for Christian Humanism*

Guardian Newspapers Limited: 'Why We Are Irrelevant' by The Rt Rev John S Spong

A.M. Heath: *The Bible in History* by Thomas L. Thompson (Copyright © Thomas L. Thompson 2000)

David Higham Associates: Eric Hobsbawm, writing in *The Guardian*

The Controller of HMSO: Figures from the 2001 national census, Crown copyright

Macmillan Publishers Limited: *Unreliable Memoirs* by Clive James (USA: Peters Fraser & Dunlop)

O Books: *Tried For Heresy* by Andrew Furlong

The Open University: 'On reading Homer without knowing any Greek' by P.N. Furbank; 'The Homeric Gods: Poetry, Belief and Authority' by Chris Emlyn-Jones; 'From Dissenters to Free Churchmen: The Transitions of Victorian Nonconformity' and 'Victorian Religion, Paradox and Variety' by Gerald Parsons

Oxford University Press: *Narrative in the Hebrew Bible* by D.M. Gunn and D.N. Fewell; 'The Limits of Knowledge' by Nicholas Rescher, in *The Oxford Companion to Philosophy*; and (with Cambridge University Press): *The Revised English Bible* (biblical quotations throughout are from this translation)

Penguin Books Limited: *Geoffrey of Monmouth: The History of the Kings of England*, translated by Lewis Thorpe; *Homer: The Odyssey*, translated by E.V. Rieu; and *The Complete Dead Sea Scrolls in English*, translated by Geza Vermes

The Society of Authors (as literary representative of the poets' estates): 'A Shropshire Lad' by A.E. Housman; and 'The Seekers' by John Masefield

University of Chicago Press: *The Iliad of Homer* translated by Richmond Lattimore

University of Toronto Press: *The God Within* by E.L. Fackenheim

Vallentine Mitchell: *We Have Reason to Believe* by Rabbi Louis Jacobs

Bibliography

Bonhoeffer, Dietrich, 1953, *Letters and Papers from Prison*, London: SCM Press

Cupitt, Don, 2004, 'God Language in *Honest to God* and God Language Now' in *Honest to God: Forty Years On*, (ed) Colin Slee, London: SCM Press

Emlyn-Jones, Chris, 1992, 'The Homeric Gods: Poetry, Belief and Authority' in *Homer: Readings and Images*, (eds) Chris Emlyn-Jones, Lorna Hardwick and John Purkis, London: Duckworth/ The Open University

Fackenheim, E.L., 1996, *The God Within: Kant, Schelling and Historicity*, (ed) John Burbidge, Toronto: University of Toronto Press

Fox, Matthew (trs and ed), 1983, *Meditations with Meister Eckhart*, Santa Fe: Bear and Company

Freeman, Anthony, 1993, *God in Us: A Case for Christian Humanism*, London: SCM Press. 2001, 2nd edition with a new foreword by Bishop John Shelby Spong, Exeter: Imprint Academic

Furbank, P.N., 1992, 'On reading Homer without knowing any Greek' in *Homer: Readings and Images*, (eds) Chris Emlyn-Jones, Lorna Hardwick and John Purkis, London: Duckworth/ The Open University

Furlong, Andrew, 2003, *Tried for Heresy*, Winchester: O Books

Gunn, D.M. and Fewell, D.N., 1993, *Narrative in the Hebrew Bible*, Oxford: Oxford University Press

Heaney, Seamus (trs), 1999, *Beowolf*, London: Faber and Faber

Hobsbawm, Eric, 2003, London: *The Guardian* 1 November

Housman, A.E., 1989, *Collected Poems and Selected Prose*, (ed) Christopher Ricks, London: Penguin Books

Jacobs, Louis, 1965, *We Have Reason to Believe*, 3rd edn., London: Vallentine Mitchell
   1973, *A Jewish Theology*, London: Darton, Longman and Todd

James, Clive, 1980, *Unreliable Memoirs*, London: Macmillan

Jerusalem Bible, The, 1966, London: Darton, Longman and Todd

Lattimore, Richmond (trs), 1951, *The Iliad of Homer*, Chicago: University of Chicago Press
   1965, *The Odyssey of Homer*, New York: HarperCollins

Masefield, John, 1923, *The Collected Poems*, London: William Heinemann

Maslow, Abraham H, 1976, *The Farther Reaches of Human Nature*, New York: Penguin Group (USA)

Office for National Statistics website: http://www.statistics. gov.uk/ (Crown copyright)

Orwell, George, 1968/1946, 'Looking Back at the Spanish Civil War' in *Collected Essays and Journalism 1940-43*, London: Secker & Warburg

Parsons, Gerald, 1988a, 'Victorian Religion, Paradox and Variety' in *Religion in Victorian Britain*, volume 1, *Traditions*, (ed) Gerald Parsons, Manchester: Manchester University Press/The Open University

1988b, 'From Dissenters to Free Churchmen: The Transitions of Victorian Nonconformity' in *Religion in Victorian Britain*, volume 1, *Traditions*, (ed) Gerald Parsons, Manchester: Manchester University Press/The Open University

Rescher, Nicholas, 1995, 'The Limits of Knowledge' in *The Oxford Companion to Philosophy*, (ed) Ted Honderich, Oxford: Oxford University Press

Revised English Bible, The, 1989, Cambridge: Cambridge University Press

Reynolds, Michael, 1986, *The Young Hemingway*, Oxford: Basil Blackwell

Rieu, E.V. (trs), 1946, *Homer: The Odyssey*, Harmondsworth, UK: Penguin Books

Schofield, J.N., 1964, *Introducing Old Testament Theology*, London: SCM Press

Spong, John Shelby, 1998, 'Why We Are Irrelevant', London: *The Guardian* 18 July

Thompson, Thomas L., 1999, *The Bible in History*, London: Jonathan Cape

Thorpe, Lewis (trs), 1966, *Geoffrey of Monmouth: The History of the Kings of England*, Harmondsworth, UK: Penguin Books

Vermes, Geza (trs), 2004, *The Complete Dead Sea Scrolls in English*, revised edition, London: Penguin Books

Washington Times, 2004, Washington DC, USA, 16 February

Williams, H.A., 1965, *The True Wilderness*, London: Constable

Index